Construction Site Planning and Development

Construction Site Planning and Development

CHARLES A. HERUBIN, P.E.

Professor of Civil Engineering Technology
Hudson Valley Community College

A Reston Book
Prentice Hall
Englewood Cliffs, New Jersey 07632

Library of Congress Cataloging-in-Publication Data

Herubin, Charles A. (date)
  Construction site planning and development.

  Includes index.
  1. Building sites—Planning.   2. Civil engineering.
I. Title.
TH375.H47   1988   690   87–14484
ISBN 0-13-168964-9

Cover design: 20/20 Services, Inc.

© 1988 by Prentice-Hall, Inc.
A Division of Simon & Schuster
Englewood Cliffs, New Jersey 07632

Printed in the United States of America

10   9   8   7   6   5   4   3   2   1

ISBN 0-13-168964-9

Prentice-Hall International (UK) Limited, *London*
Prentice-Hall of Australia Pty. Limited, *Sydney*
Prentice-Hall Canada Inc., *Toronto*
Prentice-Hall Hispanoamericana, S.A., *Mexico*
Prentice-Hall of India Private Limited, *New Delhi*
Prentice-Hall of Japan, Inc., *Tokyo*
Simon & Schuster Asia Pte. Ltd., *Singapore*
Editora Prentice-Hall do Brasil, Ltda., *Rio de Janeiro*

Contents

CHAPTER 1

Site Investigation

Preface

This book is intended to help the reader prepare to work in a technical capacity in the heavy construction industry, particularly in subdivision development.

It deals with the development of subdivisions from preliminary investigation through the construction of the public works. Zoning and subdivision regulations and their purpose of protecting the public are explained. Routine construction is covered and enough design information is given for an appreciation of why the construction methods are the way they are.

A person who completes a course covering the contents of this book should be able to work as a technician for a development company and avoid asking "dumb questions," while learning more about the business. In addition, that person should be able to answer questions to which some others in the organization do not have answers.

This may seem to be a modest claim. However, to be that well prepared in this field is not a modest accomplishment and this book has the information needed.

Charles A. Herubin, P.E.

Development of a *site* (plot of ground) takes many forms. Any change made to improve the land is called *development*. This book deals with improvements made to the land in preparation for the construction of buildings, specifically homes.

A *developer* is a person or organization that buys land, makes improvements to it and, if all goes well, sells the improved land at a profit (more than was paid to buy and develop it).

The developer must investigate the site thoroughly before deciding whether or not to develop it. Information that is easily accessible is obtained first. As each additional step of investigation indicates that development is feasible, the expenditure of more effort and more money is justified until it is finally determined whether development will be profitable or not.

A logical sequence includes:

- Checking zoning regulations
- Map study
- Checking on proposed government development
- Checking municipality design standards
- Field walk
- Subsurface investigation
- Property survey
- Topographic mapping

Zoning

A first step is to determine if the intended development is legal. Town, village, and city governments often have zoning laws that divide their entire land area into zones and provide rules governing the lot size, type, and size of structures that may be built and the use that may be made of the land or structures in each zone. Excerpts from zoning laws are contained in Appendix A.

The developer must be certain the desired development is allowed. A brief check of the law shows what kinds of development are allowed, what kinds are not allowed, and what kinds are allowed under certain conditions with the issuance of a special permit called a *variance*. However, the conditions of the zoning law might make the development unprofitable. For example, minimum allowable lot size for each house may be so large that not enough houses can be built to make a profit.

Sometimes, even though the intended development is not allowed automatically, a variance allowing it can be obtained from the zoning board of appeals, provided certain conditions are met to make the development unobjectionable. If the developer wants a variance, a hearing is held, the developer's proposed development is explained, special conditions are agreed upon, and the board grants a variance to permit the proposed development or refuses to grant it. The special conditions of the variance may increase the cost of development enough to make it unprofitable.

Map Study

Two aspects must be investigated when determining the feasibility of development. One is the suitability of the property itself for development and the other includes the features of the surrounding area that make this property one that the developer will be able to sell. Both must be investigated through the use of maps.

The area must be studied on a *topographic map* (which indicates ground shape by contour lines) to determine whether it has suitable features for the desired development. Slope of the ground, waterways, and nearby development can be seen on a map. Locations of such things as highways, railroad tracks, schools, shopping centers, recreation facilities, and nearby industries are important in determining whether or not there is a market for the type of development planned.

A U.S. Geological Survey map is very helpful for preliminary investigation and most of the United States has been mapped by the USGS. Scales are either 1 inch equals 2000 feet or 1 inch equals 1 mile and contour intervals are 10 feet or 20 feet. A section of a U.S. Geological Survey map is shown in Figure 1.1.

Some of the land may be unusable for various reasons. Bodies of water including swamps, and slopes too steep for development can be recognized on a map. Bedrock near the surface and flood plains usually must be seen in the field to be identified.

Developable area is determined by deducting unusable areas (water bodies and steep slopes) from the total area. Approximately 15 percent of the usable land is needed for public streets, depending on

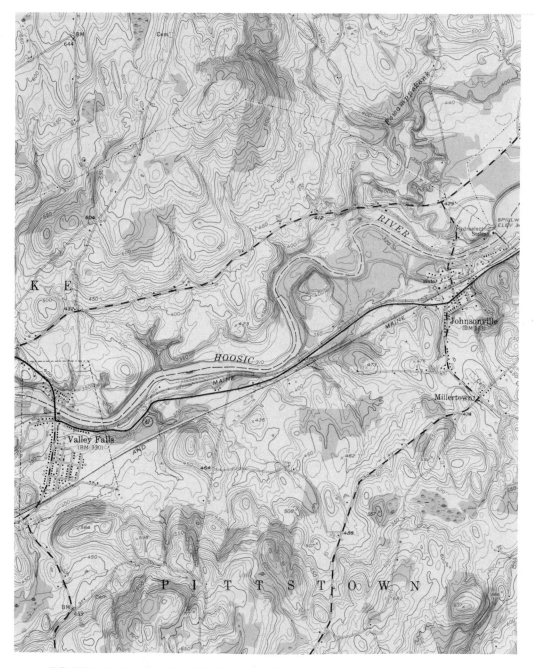

FIGURE 1.1 Portion of a U.S. Geological Survey Map (Often Called a Quadrangle Map).

street width required by local regulations and lot size required by the zoning law (smaller lots result in higher percentages for streets). The rest of the area is divided into lots.

The developer estimates the number of lots that will be available for sale using the lot size required by zoning law. Average lot size is 5 to 15 percent larger than minimum allowable size. Income expected from the sale of lots is weighed against the costs of developing the site.

Steep slopes can result in very attractive home sites and an imaginative developer may make more profit on steep terrain than on flatter land even though lots must be larger and site work is more expensive. It can be done only if there is a market for expensive homes. Development of very flat land can be more expensive than development of a hilly surface. This is explained in succeeding chapters.

Wetlands (swamps, ponds, bogs, marshes) deserve additional comment. They are undesirable for most development. Past practice often was to fill them with earth and develop the new land over them. In many states, this is no longer allowed because wetlands are so valuable. An application must be made for permission to fill wetlands and permission is seldom given.

The benefits of wetlands left in their natural state include:

1. They provide habitat necessary during some or all life stages of many species of wildlife.
2. They retain storm water runoff, preventing flooding in downstream waterways.
3. They control stream pollution by reducing many pollutants.
4. They collect silt that would otherwise be carried in streams to the detriment of stream life.
5. They hold rainwater so that it percolates into the ground, recharging the ground water.

The municipality may have an *official map* showing locations and sizes of streets, highways, parks, and drainage ways. These cannot be seen on the ground until they are developed and can be located only on the official map until then. Streets, highways, parks, or drainage ways within or near the land under consideration will affect its development for better or for worse.

Additional maps may show proposed facilities even though land for them is not yet owned by the municipality. Schools, water and sewage facilities, sanitary landfills, and incinerators, as well as the facilities shown on the official map, are types of proposed development that could be included and are of interest to the developer.

Government plans for the future location of facilities that are not yet shown on a map could also be of interest to the developer and should be sought out if possible. Government design standards and policies should also be checked.

For example, one town might require street pavement of a much more expensive type than an adjacent town or the state might require a very expensive intersection where a development street joins a state highway. An increase in development costs means the price of lots and buildings must be increased in order to make a profit. The developer must decide whether or not there is a market from which a profit can be made.

Field Investigation

Although much can be learned from a map, a field visit must be made to verify what was seen on the map and to obtain more details. A site might be rejected on the basis of map information alone, but should not be deemed acceptable without further investigation. Some of the information that can be obtained from a field walk is illustrated in Figure 1.2.

Figure 1.2 indicates some subsurface information that cannot be obtained without excavating. Usually, a few holes dug with a small backhoe at key locations provide sufficient information. However, no excavation can be made without the landowner's permission. Therefore, preliminary evaluation of subsurface conditions must be based on surface evidence. Subsurface information needed for subsurface sewage disposal is discussed in detail in Chapter 10.

Purchasing the Property

If it appears that a profit can be made, a price is agreed on with the owner of the land. Often, the exact acreage is not known and a price per acre is agreed on.

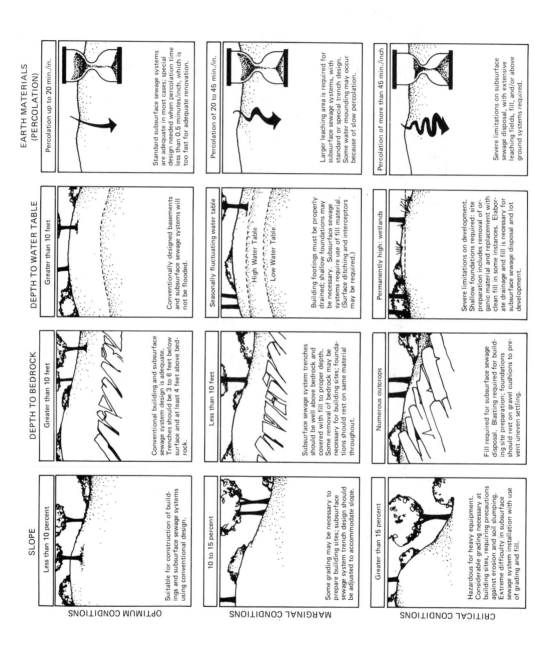

FIGURE 1.2   Conditions to Be Evaluated Before Purchasing Property for Development.

8

The value to the developer depends on certain conditions such as finding a satisfactory water supply and soil suitable for sewage disposal or obtaining municipal agreement to provide services, e.g., sewage disposal, storm drainage, water supply, or street maintenance. In addition, some or all of the following types of permits may be needed to develop the land:

1. Health department permit indicating that plans for public water supply are adequate to protect the public health.
2. Department of natural resources permit indicating that plans for sewage disposal, bridges over small streams, and storm water management during and after construction are satisfactory.
3. Local municipality zoning permit indicating that the proposed development meets requirements of the zoning law.
4. Public works department or highway department permit indicating that streets and drives do not interfere with traffic safety or efficient travel on public rights of way.
5. Development on the watershed of a public water supply reservoir requires a permit from the appropriate authority indicating that the development will not endanger the water supply. Development over a public water supply underground aquifer also may require such a permit.
6. A permit from a nearby municipality with public sewers, storm drains, or waterlines, indicating willingness to extend such services to the subdivision or to add subdivision utilities to theirs.
7. Various appointed commissions or boards issue permits indicating conformance with their regulations governing such things as appearance, shade trees, or historic and archaeological significance.

Usually, an agreement called a *purchase option* is made between owner and developer and the developer makes a deposit to be held by the owner while further investigation takes place. The developer must excavate to check soil conditions and the owner might not permit this until a deposit has been paid. Naturally, the developer does as much investigating as possible without making a deposit and does not deposit money unless it appears very likely that development will be profitable.

If the developer buys the property, the deposit is part of the purchase price. If the developer does not buy the property, the owner keeps the deposit as payment for keeping the property off the market and for allowing excavation on the property.

Property Survey

A land surveyor is hired to prepare a property map or *plat* and set markers in the field to indicate property boundaries. A land surveyor must have a knowledge of the legal rules of evidence as well as a knowledge of the procedures used by all surveyors. Land surveyors are licensed by the states. Evidence must be obtained from the field, courthouse deed records, and wherever else it may be found to indicate where the actual property boundaries are. Usually, a deed with a property description is on file in the courthouse.

After the surveyor weighs the evidence and decides where property lines are, markers (usually steel pins or iron pipes) are set at all corners and changes of direction on the boundary, and a map and legal description of the property boundary are prepared. The area of the property is calculated by the surveyor and shown on the plat. This is the area that is paid for if a per acre price was set. A plat is shown in Figure 1.3.

The surveyor must discover all public rights of way and easements and map and describe them, and may have to stake them out. A *public right of way* is an area designated by a governmental body for the use of the general public. It is established to allow people to pass through. Streets and highways are public rights of way. If no improvements are yet constructed, the developer might not know a right of way is there until shown by the surveyor.

An *easement* is the granting of the right to specific persons or to the general public to enter one's property or a specified part of one's property for general usage or for some particular purpose. This often includes the giving up of some right by the owner (in addition to the right to keep people off the property).

An easement is granted in return for something of value and granting it lessens the value of the property. The easement continues in effect for a specific time or forever, whether ownership changes or not. Easement agreements are often on file in the courthouse. Evidence may be found on the site; for example, power lines crossing the property indicate that the power company has an agreement allowing employees to enter the property to maintain the lines and prohibiting any development by the owner that would hamper their maintenance work.

A map is needed that shows the ground shape in greater detail than shown on a U.S. Geological Survey map. A typical map used for subdivision design has a contour interval of 1, 2, or 5 feet. Additional

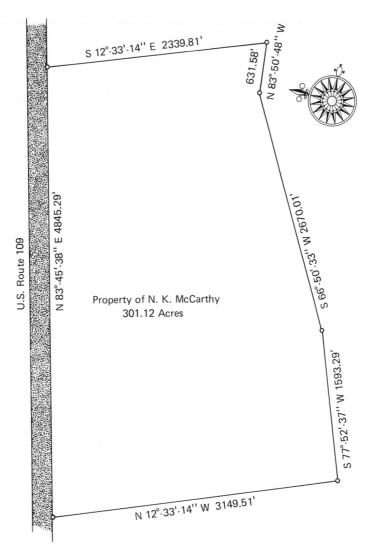

FIGURE 1.3 Typical Plat.

information discussed earlier in this chapter is also shown on the map to help the designer.

Contour lines and other information are needed adjacent to the property to be developed. Streets and other facilities built on one property will eventually be extended to other properties and conditions there should be taken into consideration during design.

Although a land surveyor's license is not required for gathering topographic information and mapping it, the land surveyor usually prepares the topographic map.

A lawyer must determine that the present owner has the legal right to sell the property to the developer. At times, legal ownership is not clear. It would not be wise to purchase property unless the owner has a *clear title,* meaning that there are no other legal claims to ownership of the property or any part of it.

REVIEW QUESTIONS

1.1. Define a plat.

1.2. Define a topographic map.

1.3. Define an easement.

1.4. Explain why it is important to check the zoning law as one of the first steps in planning a development.

1.5. Name types of development nearby that would affect the demand for lots in a proposed residential development and describe the possible ways it would be affected.

1.6. List ways in which each of the four types of municipal property shown on an official map will affect private development if (a) within the property to be developed or (b) near the property.

1.7. What information in addition to contour lines is helpful on a map that is to be used for subdivision design? Why?

CHAPTER 2

Subdivision Regulations

The words *subdivision* and *development* are used interchangeably by the general public to refer to a group of buildings showing some evidence that they were planned to be built together. However, the term *subdivision* refers to the act of dividing one parcel of land into more than one whether development follows or not. The term thus means division. The purpose of subdivision is to sell the new lots to individual owners.

The term *development* means improvement to the land. In this book, *development* refers to improvements for the benefit of the public or *public works,* most of which are in streets. Development is required to make the subdivision suitable for residents. Paved streets, sanitary sewers, storm drains, and waterlines are needed. The new owners cannot be expected to build these things. Therefore, the subdivider/developer is required to perform extensive development before lots can be sold and houses built.

Purpose

The typical finished development consists of land subdivided into privately owned lots with a house on each lot and into publicly owned streets containing pavement and service utilities. When development is completed, the municipality, meaning the taxpaying general public, takes over the ownership and maintenance of the public streets and all facilities constructed therein. The municipal government controls the quality of the facilities the public will be taking over by adopting subdivision regulations and appointing a planning board to administer them.

Subdivision regulations describe procedures a subdivider must follow to present plans for subdivision and development to the planning board for its review. They include a timetable of required submissions, lists of information to be presented at each submission, and also general requirements for the size, slope, and layout of streets, lots, drainage facilities, and recreation areas. The subdivider must design the subdivision within these general guidelines.

Subdivision regulations also require adherence to the municipality's design and construction standards. These standards are used by the municipality, its consulting engineers, and its construction contractors to design and build public works for the municipality. They are not a part of the subdivision regulations. Excerpts from typical subdivision regulations and design and construction standards are contained in Appendix B.

Standards are adopted to protect the municipality from inheriting poorly designed or poorly built facilities. Subdivision regulations also protect home buyers from purchasing poorly developed lots. They also protect future residents by requiring that streets be designed for safety and convenience, that space for recreation be left undeveloped, that future maintenance of utilities be considered, and, in short, that good and efficient use be made of the land.

Good design and construction mean that service, repairs, and maintenance expenses will be reasonable and that homeowners will be pleased with the results and, therefore, willing to pay fair taxes. Subdivision regulations help to ensure that the cost for future services that must be supplied by the municipality can be covered by tax returns from the developed area and, therefore, they protect the general public from increased taxes to support a development that cannot support itself.

Streets

Subdivision regulations control street patterns, in order to achieve safety and convenience, by specifying such things as street right of way width, pavement width, maximum and minimum length of blocks, abruptness of horizontal and vertical curves, maximum and minimum slopes, and maximum length of dead-end streets.

Traffic arterials and residential streets have different purposes and should have different design criteria. The purpose of the major arteries is to carry heavy traffic swiftly, efficiently, and safely over long distances with as few intersections as feasible.

The purpose of the residential or neighborhood streets is to carry light traffic safely over short distances where there is necessarily much interference from pedestrians and traffic at intersections. Speed and efficient routing are not of importance. In fact, residential street traffic routes should be somewhat circuitous to discourage through traffic.

Streets that carry traffic from residential streets to arterial or major thoroughfares fall into an intermediate category and are often called *collector streets*. Generally, three types of streets—major, collector, and minor—are recognized by the regulations and design criteria are provided for each.

It is difficult to foresee where major and collector streets are needed before development takes place. The developer cannot determine locations because they depend on many things outside the development. Because the major and collector streets require wider and stronger pavement and better drainage than minor streets and are, therefore, more expensive, the developer would rather not build any.

If the municipality has a master transportation plan, the locations of future major streets and, possibly, collector streets are set forth. The locations may be fairly accurate or very general.

Subdivision regulations require that the municipality's proposed street locations be used. If there are none, major and collector street locations are coordinated as subdivisions are developed so that continuous streets are formed when subdivision development is completed. The coordination is supervised by a municipal official such as the public works director or traffic engineer.

Procedures

Procedures are set up so that the subdivider is able to design to suit his or her preferences, subject to review by the municipality to assure compliance with the subdivision regulations and the municipality's design standards. Because of the influence development may have on the general welfare, the general public is able to view the plans and discuss them with municipal officials and the subdivider at meetings open to the public. The planning board is expected to take comments from the general public into account when approving or disapproving the subdivision.

A typical schedule of submissions, public hearings, and approvals is shown in Figure 2.1. Time limits are listed for the subdivider so that the planning board is not held to its decisions for a period of time so long that changing conditions might make those decisions inadvisable. Time limits are listed for planning board action so the subdivider is not delayed unduly in trying to make a living.

An early conference at which a sketch plan is submitted is required

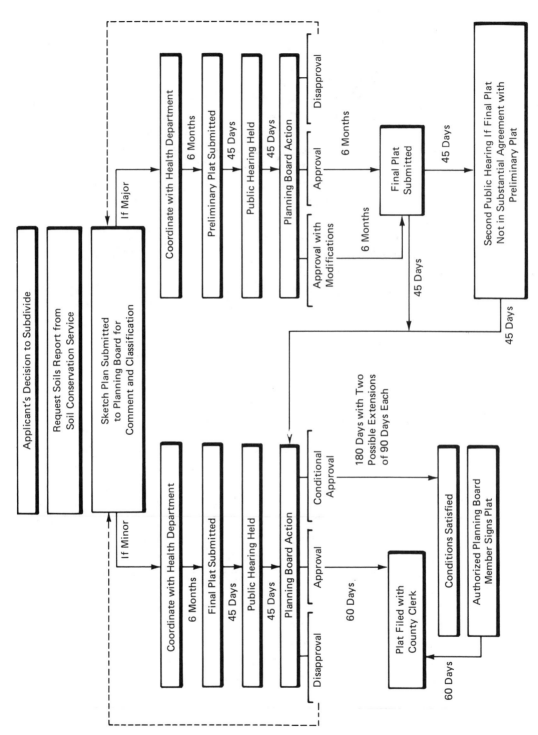

FIGURE 2.1 Subdivision Review Schedule.

18

by the regulations outlined in Figure 2.1. It is useful for the planning board to decide at this time whether the subdivision is *major,* requiring a detailed review, or *minor,* requiring a limited review. The reason for designating a subdivision as minor is to avoid bureaucratic red tape. The municipality must control development that will affect the general public. However, a complete review is costly and time consuming and is not always needed.

If the subdivision includes any new street or utility that could become a municipal responsibility, it requires a detailed review and should be designated a major subdivision. If there is no new street, water supply and sewage disposal are on private property, no storm drainage facilities are to be built, and storm water will not drain from public property onto private property, a limited review is sufficient and the subdivision should be designated as minor.

It is advantageous to the subdivider to confer early with the planning board before the property has been purchased and before much money has been spent investigating the property. Such a conference may or may not be required by the regulations. The planning board may have useful information the subdivider is unaware of, especially if this municipality is new territory for the subdivider. Additional informal meetings may be held but are not required. Two meetings, a preliminary submission and a final submission, are required.

Preliminary Submission

A formal submission of the street and lot layout together with results of subsurface soil and water exploration, location of nearby development affecting the subdivision, and preliminary construction information are presented to the planning board and a hearing is held for the general public, planning board, and subdivider to discuss the subdivision. The information submitted is made available to the general public before the hearing for a length of time specified in the regulations.

How much detailed information the subdivider must present depends on the municipality's regulations. The purpose of the preliminary submission is to allow the planning board to review and offer comments, and to alert the general public that development will take place and give them a chance to voice objections or give advice so that changes can be made before the subdivider has had the expense of preparing final plans. The planning board decides to approve or disapprove the preliminary submission after the public hearing.

Final Submission

A second formal submission includes a finished plat showing final lots and streets; finished construction plans, profiles, and details; and approvals and permits referred to in Chapter 1. Public access is allowed to the information submitted and a public hearing is held before the planning board decides whether to approve or disapprove the subdivision. The planning board must give final approval to the plat before lots may be sold or houses built.

It is difficult to require the subdivider to obtain permits after some of the lots have been sold. The planning board review provides a good means of checking that all other permits have been obtained before the subdivision is approved by the planning board.

Construction Control

Subdivision construction is different from the usual construction in which an owner hires a builder to build something for him or her and also hires an engineer to look after his or her interests and arbitrate differences between owner and builder. Subdivision development is done by the owner or by a builder hired by the owner but it is built for the municipality. The owner may hire an engineer to look after his or her interests. The municipality that will eventually own, maintain, operate, and repair all the public works must look after its interests before and during construction to protect itself in the future. Subdivision regulations provide a way of doing this.

Provisions are made before the plat is approved to assure that the subdivision development will be completed according to the municipality's standards. There are two ways for this to be done. One way is for development to be completed to the satisfaction of the responsible municipal official (usually the municipal engineer) after the planning board determines that plat and construction drawings are satisfactory but before their approval is granted. In this case, security to complete construction is not needed except for an amount to cover possible repairs needed during the warranty period. A typical amount is 10 percent of construction costs held for one year. If the developer cannot complete construction, the municipality has no responsibility because the unfinished work is on the developer's private property. Lots cannot be sold so no one's money is involved but the developer's; and homes cannot be built so there are no residents depending on the completion of the facilities.

The other method is for security to be deposited with the municipality by the subdivider before approval is granted. The security may be a performance bond, letter of credit, or cash. The purpose of the security deposit is to enable the municipality to complete development at no cost to the municipality if the subdivider becomes bankrupt or for any other reason does not complete the development in time to serve residents. Therefore, the amount of the security must be sufficient to accomplish this.

A *performance bond* is a written guarantee by a company with large assets to pay the cost of completing any construction that the developer fails to complete by the completion date. The developer pays a fee to the bonding company for this guarantee and the municipality accepts the pledge of the bonding company because it has much more money than the developer.

A *letter of credit* is a letter from a bank specifying an amount of money that the municipality can obtain from other banks and charge to the issuing bank. The bank will not issue such a letter for a subdivider unless it has the means to obtain that amount of money from the subdivider.

Once security is posted and the planning board approves the plat, it is filed in the county courthouse. Now lots can be sold and houses can be built while development is being completed. Houses are not permitted to be occupied until necessary development is completed. The municipality controls this by not allowing people to live in the houses until an occupancy permit is issued by the municipality.

As phases of development are completed, the amount of security is reduced so that it covers the remaining development plus a percentage (commonly 10 percent) of the cost of completed work held to cover possible repairs. When development is completed, the percentage held for repairs is kept for a specified period of time and spent for repairs, if necessary. Usually, the developer would rather make the repairs than have the municipality pay the developer's money to another builder to do it.

It is a good policy not to place the final course of pavement until the houses are completed. This prevents damage to the pavement surface from construction traffic, which is the roughest traffic the street will ever have. It also allows time to observe the behavior of the pavement base under heavy usage. Poor subgrade material may be discovered this way and dug up and replaced at the developer's expense before the finished surface is applied. The municipality retains enough security to cover the cost of finishing the pavement until it is finished and then holds a percentage for the specified time after in case repairs are needed. Security should be required for the final course even if other construction was completed before planning board approval.

The handling of the security deposit and construction inspection are performed by municipal employees. The planning board's responsibility ends with approval of the plat and construction drawings.

REVIEW QUESTIONS

2.1. Discuss the value of subdivision regulations to all parties concerned.

2.2. Discuss the differences between major, collector, and minor streets.

2.3. Why are there public hearings?

2.4. Describe a performance bond.

2.5. Describe a letter of credit.

2.6. Describe the sequence of events when the developer uses a performance bond or letter of credit as a guarantee that development will be completed.

2.7. What is the difference between a minor and a major subdivision according to Appendix B?

2.8. After what specific action may subdivision lots be sold?

CHAPTER 3

Street and Lot Layout

Streets and lots are designed together as two elements of one pattern. Lots are the subdivider's stock in trade. The more lots there are to sell, the more profit can be made. However, if lots are not attractive they may be difficult to sell so that a smaller number of good lots might bring in more money than a greater number of poor lots. Streets are a business expense to the subdivider. Costs of development are roughly proportional to the total length of street.

Pavement and utilities are all roughly the same length as the streets. Storm drains are shorter than streets but their overall length is roughly proportional to the street length. In general, the shortest possible street length is the most economical. In addition, more land taken up by streets leaves less to be sold as lots. It is the responsibility of civil engineers and land surveyors who design subdivisions to design them so that a profit can be made—but, with due regard for public safety and convenience.

Mapping

A U.S. Geological Survey map can be enlarged to a scale of 1 inch equals 100 or 200 feet for preliminary layout. See Figure 1.1 for an example of a USGS map.

The map used for final layout is made from aerial photographs with additional information obtained by field observations. The entire map may be made from the results of a field survey, but this method is generally used only for small areas.

The map should show all information that may influence the location of streets and property lines or construction methods and costs. The information includes boundary lines, contour lines, swamps or other bodies of water, bedrock close to the surface, high water table, trees, easements, and nearby development. This map is used for street and lot layout and also for design of improvements.

The scale and contour interval for final design are designated in the subdivision regulations. A common scale is 1 inch equals 50 feet, although others are used. The contour interval required for good design varies with the ruggedness of the terrain. A contour interval of 1 foot is required for flat land and 5 feet is suitable for hilly land.

Design for Profit

Lot size is controlled by the zoning law. Efficient land use ordinarily demands that lots be of the minimum size allowed or close to it. However, larger lots may sell for much higher prices or sell more quickly at the same price per acre and the subdivider may make a greater or faster profit from them. The shape of the parcel or its topography may dictate that larger lots are necessary. See Figure 3.1 for an explanation.

Lot width may be controlled by zoning law or subdivision regulations. A width of approximately half the length is a good proportion for lots. Lots should be arranged so that natural drainage ways are on lot lines and not through lots.

The side property lines of lots should be perpendicular to the street to prevent future confusion between neighbors over their property lines. On street curves, the side property lines should be radial lines. Corner lots should be larger than interior lots to make room for a building and the required zoning setbacks.

Changing the course of a stream to provide better lots should be avoided. Chances are that the stream has spent centuries finding its present path and is where it wants to be. If rerouted, it may cause a washout trying to return.

Larger lots may be needed adjacent to streams to provide an unobstructed path for high flows, and an easement should be provided to allow municipal employees to clear the stream of debris from time to time. No development that would obstruct water flow should be allowed within the easement.

Every lot must adjoin a street. Streets should follow low land as much as possible to provide good drainage of storm water and sewage from the lots and houses to the street. Streets should be laid out to keep earth moving to a minimum.

For a favorable ratio of street length per lot, each street should be located so that lots are on both sides of it. For instance, if a street parallels a stream or the plat boundary, it should be far enough away to allow for lots between the street and the stream or boundary. Several street and lot arrangements are shown for the same parcel of land in Figure 3.2.

Streets should not be too steep or too flat and neither should lots although it is not so critical for the lots. Both must look attractive or

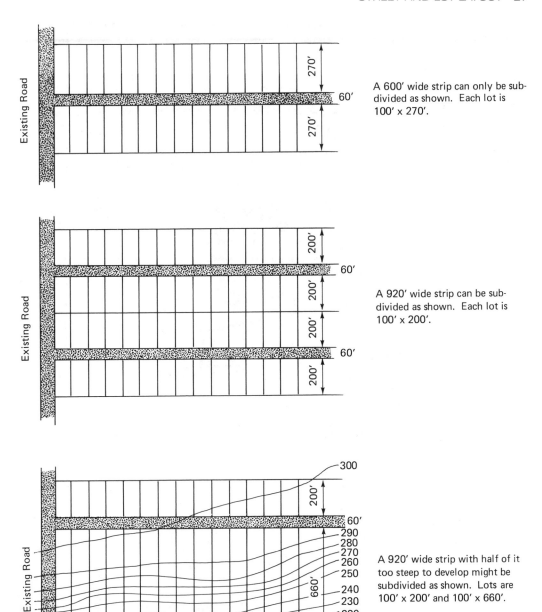

A 600' wide strip can only be sub-divided as shown. Each lot is 100' x 270'.

A 920' wide strip can be sub-divided as shown. Each lot is 100' x 200'.

A 920' wide strip with half of it too steep to develop might be subdivided as shown. Lots are 100' x 200' and 100' x 660'.

For the three examples, minimum lot dimensions are 100' x 200' and required street width is 60'.

FIGURE 3.1 How Parcel Shape and Slope Affect Lot Size and, Therefore, Number of Lots.

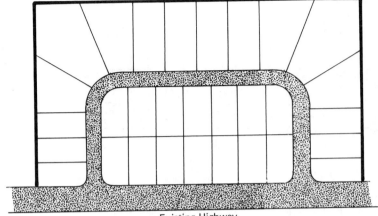

Existing Highway

Rectangular parcel divided into 30 lots 100' x 200' (min. size) with few exceptions.

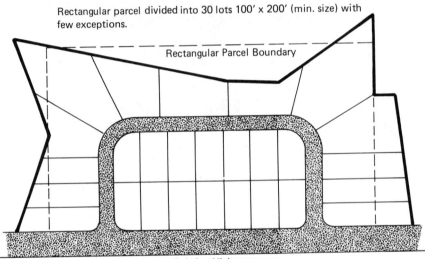

Existing Highway

Parcel of irregular shape approximately same size with same street length and 27 lots, 100' x 200' or larger.

FIGURE 3.1   Continued

the lots will not be sold. Many times, substantial earth moving is necessary to get proper slopes. Excavation volume and fill volume should be made equal or excavation should exceed fill by a small amount. It is much cheaper to dispose of excavated soil than to haul in fill. Usually, excess soil can be spread somewhere on the site.

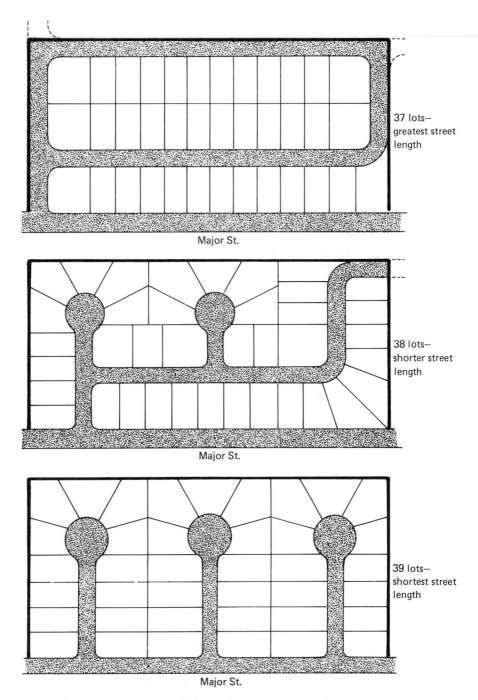

37 lots—
greatest street
length

Major St.

38 lots—
shorter street
length

Major St.

39 lots—
shortest street
length

Major St.

FIGURE 3.2   Three Street and Lot Plans with 75' × 100' Minimum
Lot Size for a 550' × 1090' Parcel on an Existing Street.

Design for Safety

The purpose of residential streets is to provide access to individual lots. For the sake of safety, they should discourage through traffic by not making it too easy to drive through the neighborhood. However, they must provide convenient access for emergency equipment such as fire engines and snow plows.

Dead-end streets can be used to advantage in residential neighborhoods. They eliminate through traffic and provide the very best ratio of street length per lot. However, traffic becomes too heavy if the street is too long. The houses cannot be reached by emergency vehicles if the street is closed for repairs because there is no other way in. For the previous two reasons, the length of dead-end streets is limited by subdivision regulations.

It is common for subdivision regulations to require a circle at the end that is large enough for fire trucks, snow plows, moving vans, etc. to turn around. Such a dead-end street is often called a *cul-de-sac*. A hammerhead shape requiring a three-point turn with backing may be allowed instead. It requires less land and less pavement but is not as convenient.

Tee intersections within the neighborhood can do much to discourage through traffic without hampering emergency equipment. A four-way intersection is more dangerous than a tee unless traffic lights are in use. A driver must look three ways (instead of just two) for oncoming traffic at a four-way intersection and it is not obvious which car has the right of way. However, the four-way intersection looks inviting to each truck driver who is in a hurry to drive through and finds it convenient to assume the right of way. At a tee intersection, it seems natural that the driver on the through street has the right of way.

Tee intersections are also satisfactory at junctions of minor streets with collector or major streets because the shape of the intersection indicates who has the right of way. At intersections where the cost of traffic lights is justified by the heavy traffic, a four-way intersection is more economical because it takes the place of two tees and one set of lights takes the place of two. It also results in fewer points of interference with the through traffic of the major or collector street.

The subdivider usually does not have any way of knowing where collector and major streets will be needed unless the property to be developed is large enough to require its own collector streets and possibly even a major street. A subdivision of fewer than 100 lots (this includes most of them) usually does not need a collector street and often there is no indication of where one should be built to serve future development.

However, the municipality's master traffic plan or official map may require a collector or major street through the proposed subdivision. The subdivider must then design streets and lots around the required street. The subdivision regulations may have provisions for the municipality to pay the extra cost of building the required collector or major street.

The purpose of major and collector streets is to move traffic and there should be no tee intersections in the way. There should be few intersections of any kind because they all interfere with traffic movement. Private driveways should not be allowed on major or collector streets. A large number of driveways cause more interference and are a greater safety hazard than a few intersections.

Two good ways to avoid the connecting of private driveways to major or collector streets are illustrated in Figure 3.3. One requires a parallel minor street with lots fronting on it with rear yards toward the major or collector street. All driveways enter the parallel minor street. The lots are known as *reverse frontage lots.* The other method requires a *marginal access street* which is a narrow street close to and parallel with the through street to collect traffic from the driveways and carry it to the through street at a few points.

Intersections at sharp angles and tee intersections offset so little that they are almost four-way intersections are hazardous on all streets. They are even more hazardous at the higher speeds on major and collector streets.

Street curves must be flatter for higher-speed traffic. The centrifugal force that tends to pull vehicles to the outside of a curve is proportional to the square of the speed and to the sharpness of the curve. Regulations governing street and lot layout taken from typical subdivision regulations are contained in Appendix B.

Streets often must be laid out to be continued into adjacent property in the future. A street of this kind must end at the property boundary with full width available to any subdivider for future continuation when and if the neighboring property is developed. In the meantime, it is a dead-end street with a circle at the end entirely within the subdivided property.

The circle is not needed when and if the street is extended and

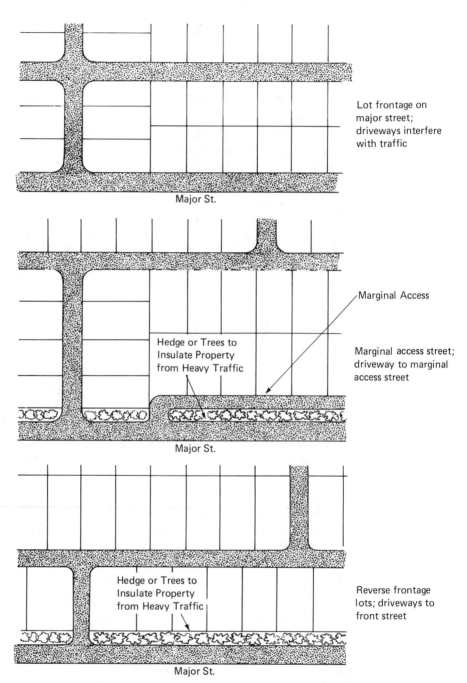

FIGURE 3.3   Ways to Avoid Driveways onto Major Streets.

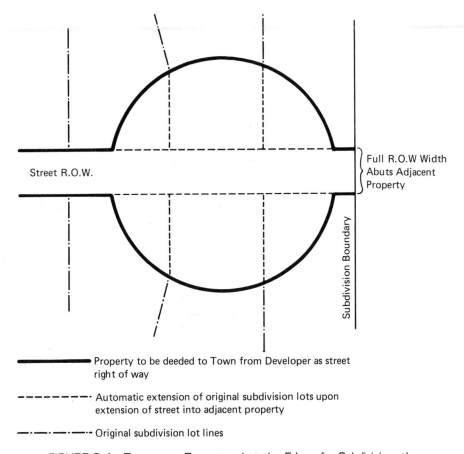

Street R.O.W.

Full R.O.W Width
Abuts Adjacent
Property

Subdivision Boundary

━━━━━━━━► Property to be deeded to Town from Developer as street right of way

— — — — —· Automatic extension of original subdivision lots upon extension of street into adjacent property

—·—·—·—·· Original subdivision lot lines

FIGURE 3.4   Temporary Turnaround at the Edge of a Subdivision; the Street Is Designed to Be Extended into Adjacent Property.

should automatically revert to the adjoining property owners at that time. One way of accomplishing all this on the final plat is shown in Figure 3.4.

Street Patterns

Many old cities have a street pattern of rectangular blocks superimposed on the landscape with little regard for original topography and broken only by major interruptions such as large streams or steep hills. This is called a *rectangular* or *grid pattern*.

Land use appears to be efficient. However, if the natural ground is reshaped to suit the grid, earth-moving costs are high; and if the ground is not reshaped, street and lot slopes and street sight distances are not satisfactory. (See Chapter 11 for a discussion of sight distances.) Construction of sanitary sewers and storm drains is also costly because they must be built at greater depths. Traffic movement is neither safe nor efficient. Every intersection is a four-way intersection with the unsafe features discussed in the preceding section.

A more recent practice is to consider the topography when deciding on street and lot locations. The result is curved streets and many tee intersections. This pattern is referred to as *curvilinear.* Length of street per lot is about the same for curvilinear as for grid patterns. However, lots are more attractive and more variety is available to the buyer.

Less earth moving is required because the streets and lots are placed to suit the existing ground. Sanitary sewers and storm drains need not be so deep because they flow in the direction of the ground slopes and they, therefore, cost less. Traffic movement is safer because when streets are placed to suit the topography, four-way intersections and short sight distances at vertical curves seldom occur.

Street pavement is somewhat more expensive because of the many curves. It is difficult for visitors, delivery services, and emergency callers to locate particular houses because of the confusing curve pattern.

A curvilinear pattern is sometimes superimposed on the landscape with no regard for topography so that there is no economy in earth moving or pipeline construction. There is little advantage to the curvilinear pattern then, because with a little imagination, a grid pattern can also be made safe for traffic by the use of dead-end streets and loops.

The *cluster pattern* consists of clusters of small lots with publicly owned space between them. Each privately owned lot is smaller than specified by the zoning law but the total of privately owned and publicly owned land, not including streets, amounts to at least as much as the total area required by the zoning law for that number of lots. Even so, there may be a few more lots because less land is required for streets. Not all zoning laws and subdivision regulations allow cluster development. See Figure 3.5 for an example of a cluster pattern.

Development costs per lot are lowered for the obvious reason that the length of streets is short for the number of lots; but, also, because the few streets required can be placed in the best possible locations for economy of construction. The size and shape of the spaces between streets is not of great importance so that streets can be placed to the

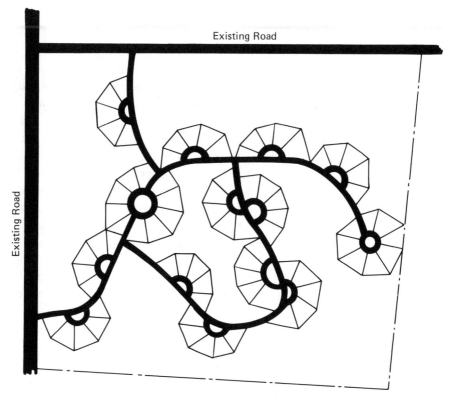

FIGURE 3.5 Typical Cluster Street and Lot Pattern.

best advantage without considering the effect their locations have on the lots. Then the lots can be put in at the best remaining locations. This makes design simpler and, therefore, less costly.

Designing traditional subdivisions requires a juggling process between requirements for good streets and requirements for good lots. The cluster building lots are fitted relatively easily into the large spaces between streets without compromising on street locations. A further benefit is that the lots can readily be laid out so that all houses can be properly oriented with respect to sun, shade, and wind. This is next to impossible with traditional patterns and quite often is not even attempted.

The cluster pattern also results in nearby recreation areas for all. Each resident has a small area to maintain and a large area to use.

The municipality seldom accepts ownership of the public land because of the difficulty of administrative and legal responsibility for the odd-shaped area so near to residences and because the area is a benefit primarily to a small group of citizens—the residents of the subdivision—and the municipality's responsibility is to all its citizens.

The ownership of the public land must usually be assumed by a *neighborhood association* of the property owners. The association administers the property, raises money for improvements, and is legally liable for claims against it as the owner. The terms of the deed to each lot may bind the owners to membership in the association. Membership in the association can result in more unpleasantness than one usually has with one's neighbors. The association has authority to assess each property owner to pay for improvements and much unpleasantness can arise from discussions on what improvements are needed.

The final plat must be drawn to scale with each lot and right-of-way parcel defined by metes and bounds or angles and distances so that there is sufficient information to write a legal description and to set stakes at all corners of each parcel. Although the locations of streets and lot lines are based partially on ground contours, swamps, depth to bedrock, and trees, these are not necessary on the plat. The plat often contains only property boundaries and those bodies of water that form property boundaries.

REVIEW QUESTIONS

3.1. What professionals design subdivisions?

3.2. What scales and contour intervals are used for final layout of subdivisions?

3.3. Explain why a smaller contour interval is needed for design on flat land.

3.4. Discuss the advantages and disadvantages of tee intersections versus four-way intersections.

3.5. Discuss the pros and cons of dead-end streets.

3.6. Sketch the two design methods of avoiding private driveways on major or collector streets.

3.7. Illustrate with sketches how sight distance can be shortened by excavation at a crest or fill at a sag.

3.8. Discuss the advantages and disadvantages of the cluster pattern for the subdivider, residents, and municipality. Include all the cost savings to the subdivider.

3.9. Discuss the advantages and disadvantages of neighborhood associations.

CHAPTER 4

Clearing, Earth Moving, and Miscellaneous Work

This chapter covers the miscellaneous work that is performed in preparation for the actual construction of streets and utilities. Included are tree removal, clearing and grubbing, topsoil stripping and stockpiling, and earth moving and rough grading.

Tree Removal

Tree removal is the first step. Trees must be removed where streets, utility lines, driveways, and buildings will be built and where grade is to be changed. Accurately placed stakes or laths are needed to indicate boundaries of tree removal areas and are placed by a surveyor. Removal of all trees could very well be cheaper when the cost of surveying stake out and the difficulty of performing other construction operations among the trees are considered. However, standing trees are of so much value that this is seldom done.

Trees protect buildings from wind and sun, reducing heating and cooling costs and making yards more pleasant. They reduce storm water runoff and they reduce erosion from water and wind. The right kind of trees in the right place can be very nice just to look at and listen to. An agency of the local government such as the planning board or shade tree commission may even designate trees that cannot be removed and require posting of a bond or letter of credit by the developer to guarantee that they are not damaged.

Equipment must be operated carefully near trees that are to remain. Often, bark is scraped from them or roots are damaged. A good way to protect individual trees or even a clump of trees is with an inexpensive, easily visible fence such as a snow fence, beyond the limits of exposed roots. Small trees might be replaced more cheaply than they can be protected, especially if transplanted from the same site.

Some trees that must be removed may have enough commercial value as lumber or firewood to attract loggers to bid for them. A forester can determine whether this is so. If they are of sufficient worth, the forester can be hired to mark the trees to be removed, prepare contracts and bidding forms, and advise on the awarding of a contract. If the subdivider removes the trees, there is usually a little money to be made by selling firewood.

Trees that are eventually to be removed for construction need not be protected from the ravages of the typical logging operation but all others should be. The logger should be required to post a bond or letter of credit as a guarantee that trees will not be harmed.

Some of the trees outside the removal areas, even though they appear to be valuable for aesthetic reasons, may be near the ends of their lives. These can be identified by an expert and included for harvest while they still have commercial value.

Other trees that appear marketable may be obviously worthless to an expert eye because of rot, shakes (wind-caused separations along the annual rings), or insect damage.

After commercial opportunities and preservation are taken care of, the remaining trees are removed as efficiently as possible. Bulldozers may be used to push the trees over. The bulldozers simply break smaller trees off with the blade. For larger trees, a blade cut is made through the roots behind the tree and the tree is pushed over, roots and all, from the front.

Trees can be taken down more efficiently with tractors equipped with special blades. One type is similar to a bulldozer blade but angled and is equipped with a pointed "stinger" on the lower forward corner of the blade. The blade is used to push down small trees and the stinger is driven into large trees splitting them into smaller ones that can be knocked down with the blade. Another type has a vee snowplow-type blade with a stinger at the point.

Logging equipment is available that can grasp a tree trunk 8 or 10 feet above the ground, shear the tree at the ground surface, and carry it out with limited disturbance to the surrounding trees. Many subdivisions are not large enough to justify the use of specialized equipment and trees are cut down with chain saws. Trees and brush are removed by pushing with a bulldozer or by use of specialized crawler or wheel-mounted equipment that clamps onto a pile of brush or a few trees, hoists its load into the air, and carries it away.

The cheapest way of getting rid of trees and brush that are down is by burning. Oil or gasoline is used to start the fire and oil may be needed to keep it going if the wood is green or wet. Rubber tires may be burned to keep the fire going. Equipment is available to spray oil onto the fire in a continuous blast of air, providing fuel and oxygen to consume the wood.

Fires are prohibited in many municipalities and usually require a permit from any municipality that allows them. Trees and brush are often buried under earth fill. Limbs should be removed and trunks sawed into pieces to prevent air pockets under the fill. They should not be buried under streets or elsewhere where soil settlement caused by their eventual decomposition will be objectionable.

Trees should not be buried near buildings because termites may live in the buried wood and, after they consume it, they go looking for the nearest new home. Mechanical chippers can greatly reduce the bulk of trees and brush and prevent air pockets, thereby reducing the settlement of overlying fill. The chips can be buried, spread wherever they are not objectionable, or used as mulch to help prevent soil erosion during and after construction.

Grubbing and Topsoil Removal

The work of *grubbing* includes removal of stumps, roots, and debris of any kind, not including trees and brush. This woody material must be removed from areas that will be paved. It is also removed from areas to be filled unless the fill is to be greater than about 6 feet. Decomposition results in settlement unless the fill is high enough for the small amount of settlement to be lost in the fill. If grubbing is not needed, stumps are cut low or removed by chipping with stump removal equipment and roots are left.

Removed stumps and roots cannot be burned unless stacked and dried through one summer at least and so are usually buried under earth fill. Stumps should be placed right side up, side by side in one layer to prevent air pockets under the fill. The precautions for burying trees also apply to burying stumps and roots.

Topsoil is bulldozed into stockpiles from areas that will be paved, cut, or filled or that will be torn up so much by construction traffic that the topsoil would be lost. Topsoil is a poor foundation because of its organic content and because it is highly compressible. However, it is valuable for growing plants. It is needed on cuts, fills, and disturbed areas for reseeding and, if there is more than needed, it can be sold.

Earth Moving and Grading

Earth moving and grading consist of removing earth from areas that are higher than desired and adding and compacting earth in areas that are lower than desired. Earth may be removed from the site or brought in to the site; but, ideally the earth is rearranged without hauling any soil onto or off the site.

Existing and proposed contour lines are shown on the construction plans (see Figure 4.1). The proposed contour lines are laid out to provide satisfactory topography with excavation and fill made equal if at all possible.

The term *earth moving* is usually used to refer to rearranging the ground surface substantially as in deep cuts or high embankments. The term *grading* refers to smaller adjustments such as shaping a front yard to a more satisfactory slope or filling in a shallow depression. Many subdivisions do not require work worthy of being called earth moving but grading is always required.

The first stage is called *rough grading*. It consists of filling and excavating streets and easements approximately to their final shape. Lots are also graded if they need extensive work. If not, they are graded when houses are built. Lots often are finished close to their original elevation especially if trees remain on them. *Fine grading* takes place at the time of pavement construction and is covered in Chapter 11.

Care must be taken when grading near trees. Most trees will not survive if the soil over their roots is raised or lowered by more than a few inches. It is often best not to disturb soil at all within the overhang of the branches of any trees that are to be saved.

Retaining walls are sometimes built to hold ground around trees at its original level when nearby ground is raised or lowered. The walls are built to prevent soil from being deposited over the roots when the

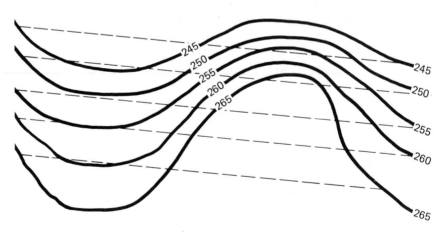

Valley on left and ridge on right (━━━) are to be graded to form a uniform slope (— —)

FIGURE 4.1 Required Earth Moving Shown by Existing and Proposed Contour Lines.

surrounding ground is raised or to prevent soil from being eroded away from the roots when the surrounding ground is lowered. A specialist such as a landscape architect should design any complex earthwork project involving trees.

It is usually advantageous to finish all rough grading at one time before the next step, pipe laying, begins. Usually, the most efficient way to perform a one-time operation on any construction project is to move equipment onto the site, complete the operation with as little interference as possible, and move the equipment to another job. The rough grading operation is one that often is done this way. An exception is that a pipeline to be located under a high fill might be installed before the fill is built to avoid trench excavation through the fill.

It may be necessary to remove some bedrock. It is broken up by blasting or ripping and the debris is then hauled away. The expectation that a substantial amount of blasting is needed would be reason enough not to develop the land in many cases. If the rock is rippable, the cost is much less.

A *ripper* is a pointed, curved hook or several hooks attached to the rear of a tractor or separately mounted for towing and used to loosen rock by ripping through it. The ripper is solidly mounted and, behind a powerful tractor, can break up surprisingly solid rock which is then pushed or hauled away.

A ripper is selected to break the rock into the correct sizes for whatever handling is planned. It may be pushed aside by bulldozer or hauled by scraper or truck. It may be kept on the site to be buried or used as rip rap. If it is to be hauled off the site, it might be sold as fill or rip rap (broken stone spread on a slope, stream bank, or shore line to resist erosion. Required size depends on water force to be resisted.)

Earthwork Control

The traditional method of providing control for earthwork is with surveyors' stakes placed to indicate the outer limits of excavation and embankment areas and to indicate the line separating excavation from embankment. Those at the outer limits are called *slope stakes* if they are at the top or bottom of a proposed slope. Slope stakes are inclined away from the work rather than being vertical.

If the finished surface is to be a fairly short, straight slope, cut or fill is marked on these slope stakes in feet and tenths. For slope stakes, *cut* is the vertical distance downward from the existing ground at a stake for the top of the slope to the proposed toe of the slope. A *fill* is the vertical distance upward from the existing ground at a stake for the toe of the slope to the proposed top of the slope (see Figure 4.2).

If the finished surfaces are to be irregular or if they are to be straight but longer than about 100 feet, intermediate vertical stakes are needed to indicate height or depth to finished surface. *Cut* or *fill* directly under or over the stake measured from the stake top or a horizontal line on the side of the stake vertically to finished surface is marked on each stake in feet and tenths.

These stakes are placed in a grid pattern with horizontal spacing of 25, 50, or 100 feet. They are removed or covered by grading and might be replaced several times. However, they can often be saved by reshaping the earth as close as possible to the stakes without disturbing them until the entire area, except for a small spot at each stake, is at finished elevation. Then depressions or mounds at the stakes are brought to finished elevation with no appreciable change in the surrounding ground.

Laser Control

A rotating laser beam provides the most efficient way to control rough grading (or fine grading). The laser is mounted on a tripod and powered by a 12-volt battery. It emits a continuous, narrow red beam of light that rotates rapidly so that, even though it passes any one point intermittently, for practical purposes it can be considered a plane of light. The laser beam cannot be seen in daytime unless it strikes something. In bright sunlight, it may be difficult to see at all.

The laser can be set to produce a plane of light either level or at the slope desired for the finished surface. When set correctly, the laser generates a plane all points of which are at the same distance above the desired finished surface.

This distance above finished surface, known as the *grade rod,* can be marked on a pole or board (also called a *grade rod*) and used to check the ground surface during grading. When the rod is vertical and the beam hits the mark, the bottom of the rod must be at finished grade. When the grade rod stands on the ground, the light beam inter-

Finished surface and original surface coincide at top and bottom of
hill. When a rod is placed at either place, the laser beam
strikes it at grade rod height. That height is then
used to indicate how much to cut or fill
throughout the area to be graded.

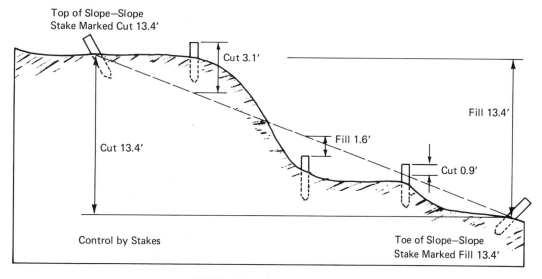

FIGURE 4.2 Grading Control.

cepts the rod above the mark if the ground is below finished grade and below the mark if the ground is above finished grade. Earth is added or removed until the light coincides with the mark on the grade rod, indicating that the ground at the bottom of the rod is at finished grade (see Figure 4.2).

The laser can be used to control grading only on a plane surface (straight slopes). It cannot be used at all if there are to be no finished plane surfaces and it cannot be used efficiently for very small plane surfaces. The finished surface of many subdivisions does not include any plane surfaces large enough to justify control by laser. The method is, however, far more efficient than any other when justified by the size of the job.

A laser receiver is available that can be attached to a calibrated level rod and moved up and down the rod. It indicates with sound signals or lights whether it is above, below, or at the beam. It can be moved by hand using the above and below signals until the signal indicates it is at the beam. Interpreting the signals is easier and more accurate than reading the laser beam crossing the rod.

Grade rod is determined by standing the rod on finished grade and noting the reading where the receiver indicates it is at the beam. Whenever the rod is placed on the ground afterward, the receiver indicates the height of the beam above the ground and the required fill or excavation can be determined by the difference between that reading and the grade rod (see Figure 4.2). The principle of operation is the same as without the receiver. Receivers are also available that home in on the beam automatically so that the operator needs only to read cut or fill.

Laser Safety

A laser (light amplification by stimulated emission of radiation) is a device that can produce an intense beam of light with the capability of cutting through steel or sending a beam in a straight line for miles. Lasers used for construction are not of such high intensity but do have the capability of sending a beam, which can damage the human eye, in a straight line for about a thousand feet. The beam is reflected in a new direction if it strikes a reflecting surface such as glass or metal.

Because of the danger from such a device, several states have regulations governing the use of construction lasers and even require them to be operated only by state-licensed operators who understand the dangers and the methods for avoiding them.

A laser beam, or any other light that enters the eye, is concentrated onto the retina by the lens of the eye. Because of the additional concentration, the retina can be damaged by a low-power laser that would not damage any other part of the body. Such damage is usually but not always permanent. Neither the laser beam nor its reflection should ever be allowed to strike any person's eye.

Earth-Moving Equipment

Almost all the equipment used for clearing, grubbing, and earth moving is tractor-mounted. Tractors are of two types—crawler and wheel. They are designed to push or pull a load but are also equipped with attachments for other purposes. The more common types of equipment are described here.

Crawler tracks are designed to prevent sinking into soft ground by spreading the weight of the tractor over a larger area than wheels can. The tracks are damaged less by sharp rocks than tires are. The crawler grips the ground better than a wheel tractor and so delivers more power on loose or slippery surfaces. Wheeled tractors travel faster and over longer distances and can travel on paved surfaces without damaging them.

A *bulldozer* is a crawler or wheel tractor with a heavy blade perpendicular to the direction of travel used primarily to push trees, stumps, earth, rock, aggregate, or other equipment that needs a push. A bulldozer is also used for shallow excavation. The blade can be raised and lowered and, in some cases, angled (see Figure 4.3).

A *front-end loader* is a tractor with a scoop bucket on the front designed to be pushed into loose material, hoist it, and dump it into a truck or carry it a short distance to be dumped. A front-end loader also can be used for the same chores as a bulldozer but does not perform as well because the bucket is light and not as well designed for pushing (see Figure 4.4).

A *scraper* is a tractor-pulled, self-loading, bottom-loading, earthmover that loads by scraping up the soil and unloads through the bottom in a uniform layer that often requires little or no further spreading (see Figure 4.5). Trucks can haul loads more efficiently than scrapers

FIGURE 4.3   Bulldozer [Courtesy of Deere & Company, Moline, Illinois].

FIGURE 4.4   Front-End Loader [Courtesy of Deere & Company, Moline, Illinois].

FIGURE 4.5   Scraper (Courtesy of Deere & Company, Moline, Illinois).

but must be loaded by other equipment and, therefore, overall efficiency is not better unless the haul distance is long.

Earthmovers, including bulldozers, front-end loaders, scrapers, or graders (discussed in Chapter 11) can be equipped with a laser receiver that signals a servo motor which raises or lowers the blade or cutting edge to produce the desired finished surface. The receiver is mounted on a mast attached to the blade or cutting edge.

The grade rod is determined by setting the cutting edge at finished grade and adjusting the receiver up or down the mast until it is aligned with the laser beam and then clamping it in place. Audio or visual signals indicate whether the receiver should be moved up or down as with the receiver on the hand-held level rod. The distance from receiver to bottom of blade is then the grade rod.

The receiver is then set to follow the laser beam. If the cutting edge on the ground rises or falls with the ground surface, the receiver quickly returns to the laser beam and the cutting edge follows, producing the desired finished surface (see Figure 4.6).

Soil Compaction

Compaction decreases the volume of void space between soil particles by forcing the particles closer together. The closeness of the particles prevents them from being pushed aside under traffic or other loads.

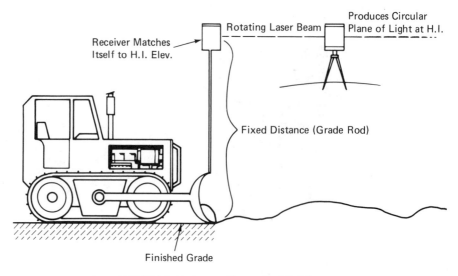

FIGURE 4.6   Laser-Controlled Bulldozer.

The decrease in volume of voids causes settlement. This controlled settlement prevents later harmful settlement under use. Pressure, impact, kneading, and vibration are used to compact soil where it occurs naturally and where it has been placed in fills. All compactors exert pressure and usually employ another means also. Fills are constructed in layers, called *lifts*, of varying thicknesses which are compacted before constructing the next lift.

Sheepsfoot rollers are useful for soil having a high percentage of clay. They use impact and kneading, penetrating to the bottom of lifts as deep as 1 foot, and compacting upward with each additional pass until the roller "walks out" of the soil (see Figure 4.7).

Smooth-wheel rollers are used to compact granular soil with a small amount of clay or without any clay in it. They employ pressure only and are limited to lifts of 8 inches. They are also used to smooth rough surfaces—rutted roads or areas finished with sheepsfoot rollers (see Figure 4.8).

Pneumatic rollers of ordinary size are used on soil types ranging from silty or clayey sands through clean sands to gravelly sands and also on sandy clays in lifts up to 8 inches. Large-tired rollers up to 20 tons in weight with tire air pressure up to 150 psi exert such great pressures that they are used for compacting all possible types of soil in lifts as great as 2 feet. Wheels are close to each other, on two axles, with as

FIGURE 4.7 Vibratory Sheepsfoot Roller [Courtesy of Ingersoll-Rand Company].

many as nine on one and eight on the other, arranged so that the rear tires cover the spaces between the front tires. Large-tired rollers have fewer wheels. Because of the tires' wobbling motion, compaction is obtained by kneading as well as pressure (see Figure 4.9).

FIGURE 4.8 Smooth-Wheel Roller [Courtesy of Hyster Company].

FIGURE 4.9   Pneumatic Roller [Courtesy of Hyster Company].

FIGURE 4.10   Vibratory Plate Compactor [Courtesy of Puckett Brothers Manufacturing Company, Inc.].

Vibratory compactors are used for all granular soils that are free of clay and do not contain too much silt. Sheepsfoot, smooth-wheel, and pneumatic rollers as well as plate or shoe-shaped vibrating compactors are used on lifts up to 6 inches. Vibration rate is variable to suit the natural frequency of the soil being compacted (see Figure 4.10). Manually operated vibratory compactors and impact rammers are available for work in areas too small for major equipment.

REVIEW QUESTIONS

4.1. Discuss the reasons for saving trees in a residential subdivision.

4.2. Discuss precautions to take to protect trees that are not to be removed.

4.3. How are trees removed?

4.4. How are tree remains disposed of?

4.5. Define the term *grade rod* as a physical entity and as an abstraction.

4.6. Describe how a grade rod is determined with a laser.

4.7. Grade rod is 1.3 feet below the rotating laser beam. Is cut or fill required? How much?

4.8. What is the difference in the meaning of *cut* and *fill* when marked on a stake in a grid pattern and when marked on a slope stake?

4.9. What is the basic principle of safe use of a construction laser?

4.10. What advantages has a tracked vehicle over a vehicle with wheels?

4.11. Rank the earthmovers described in the chapter by ability to excavate earth and to transport earth.

CHAPTER 5

Erosion and Sedimentation

The entire surface of the earth is constantly being leveled by wind, rain, flowing water, frost, and anything else that loosens or moves soil particles. Because of gravity, each loosened particle tends to move downhill, coming to rest at a lower elevation. The overall result is a very slow leveling of the earth's surface.

Storm Water Runoff

When one drop of rain lands on fine soil, the drop splashes upward and outward in an arc carrying particles uniformly in all directions. On level ground, the particles are carried the same distance radially in all directions. However, on a slope, particles that are carried downhill land farther from the center than particles that are carried uphill. The overall result from many drops is downhill movement of the soil. *Rain splash* alone results in the rearrangement of significant amounts of soil.

Every drop either evaporates, seeps into the ground, or runs off over the surface and is called *storm water runoff* or just *runoff*. Storm water runoff at the top of a slope flows in a thin sheet across the ground. Irregularities in the ground surface divert enough of the sheet flow to form *rills* or tiny streams of water as runoff proceeds downward. Rills wash out seeds and seedlings. Farther down the slope, larger channels and, eventually, gullies are formed.

Erosion, Transportation, and Redepositing

When the process of soil loosening and removal is vigorous enough to be a problem, it is known as *erosion*. Eroded particles are transported to another location and deposited there.

There are three distinct phases during which damage can be done. The three are listed here with some adverse results.

1. *Soil removal* prevents the growth of vegetation and leaves an unsightly mess.
2. *Soil transportation* by streams turns the soil into a water pollutant and may result in killing aquatic life and rendering the water unfit

for drinking or recreation. Transportation by wind causes the soil to become an air pollutant and may cause respiratory problems, damage to machinery, and dirty clothing and living spaces.

3. *Soil deposition* or *sedimentation* buries many things, from vegetation killed by wind-blown soil to water intakes or entire reservoirs rendered useless by water-born ''silt.''

The four factors that influence the amount of erosion, transportation, and redepositing (sedimentation) are:

1. *Weather, mainly rainfall and temperature.* Gentle rain and wind do not erode; intense rain and wind do. Dry weather causes fine-grained soil to dry out and become easily eroded by wind. Wet or frozen soil is not as easily eroded.

2. *Vegetation.* Growing leaves protect soil from rain splash and wind, stems slow the surface flow of water, and roots hold the soil particles in place. Roots and stems open the soil so that water is absorbed, thereby lessening the amount that flows over the ground.

3. *Soil, mainly grain-size.* The ease with which particles are loosened and moved is inversely proportional to grain size. However, clay, which has the finest grain size, is not easily eroded when wet because it is so cohesive that it forms one large mass. The soil most subject to erosion is silt which has a slightly larger grain size than clay but is not cohesive. Sand and gravel particles are larger than silt and, therefore, are not as easily eroded.

4. *Slope.* The capacity of flowing water to carry particles depends on its velocity and depth. Steeper slopes produce greater velocities. The greater the distance storm water runoff flows overland, the greater its depth. Therefore, longer slopes produce greater depths. Steeper and longer slopes produce more erosion.

Influence of Development

The natural leveling processes often take place without damage to the environment but can also be as destructive as tornadoes, floods, and earthquakes, which are all part of the natural leveling process. All the processes, whether naturally destructive or not, are made more disruptive by site development.

Site development increases erosion by the removal of vegetation, the increase in traffic, and the moving of earth. The protective covering of topsoil with its soil-anchoring root growth is removed and stockpiled as one of the first steps in development. Next, soil is excavated, hauled, and deposited elsewhere until the final contours are approximated. Heavy construction equipment travels rapidly back and forth raising clouds of dust and loosening and pulverizing the soil, making it more erodable. Steep slopes are exposed temporarily while earthwork proceeds. Many times, finished slopes are also steeper than the natural ones.

Although erosion cannot be prevented, it can be kept within reasonable bounds by thorough planning. The planning board or other reviewing agency may require that a plan for erosion and sedimentation control be submitted for approval.

A variety of measures are needed to reduce erosion and to manage that which cannot be avoided. Conduits are needed to carry away concentrations of water to areas where they can be released without damage—flat land with soil not easily eroded, or a natural body of water. Sediment carried by the water must be held back especially if the conduit discharges to a body of water. Before water enters the conduit, as much sediment as possible is held back. Sediment may also be collected at spots along the conduit. Erosion must be prevented at the point of discharge from the conduit. Figure 5.1 shows the elements of a complete system to control erosion, transportation, and sedimentation.

Watering the traveled areas is a common method of keeping the dust down and is preferable to using waste oil for this purpose. The oil pollutes the soil and storm water runoff and, in sufficient quantities, could pollute the ground water. Although further discussion of preventive measures deals specifically with water, much of the discussion also applies to wind.

Control of Erosion

One way of reducing erosion is to work on one small section of the site at a time, finishing one section and protecting it from erosion before starting work on the next section. The steeper the finished surface, the more important it is to protect it quickly. Local government officials may require protection of each section before another section is exposed.

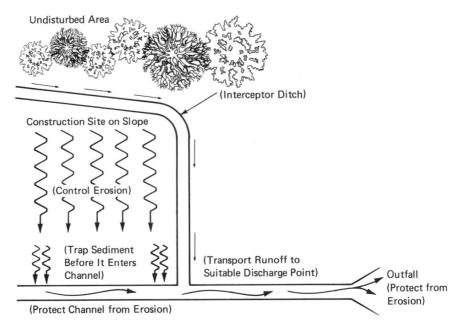

FIGURE 5.1   Construction Site Erosion, Transportation, and Sedimentation.

The most effective protection against erosion is to establish growing vegetation over all disturbed earth. Grass or legumes are the fastest growing and are not likely to be objectionable, once they are established, as some of the larger plants may be. They are often kept as permanent cover.

Topsoil that has been stockpiled is spread and more is brought in if necessary to obtain a 3- to 6-inch final depth, depending on the type of topsoil and underlying soil. A layer of topsoil 6 inches deep as placed settles 1 or 2 inches. The subsoil should be *scarified* (dragged or gouged by construction equipment to form grooves) before placing topsoil to bind the topsoil to it. Topsoil may not be needed where appearance is unimportant.

The type of grass or legume to be planted depends on climate, soil, slope, overland or channel flow to be expected, future use, amount of maintenance planned after the vegetation is growing, and other factors. Bluegrass, rye, clover, and crownvetch as well as many others are used. A landscape or agricultural expert should determine what is best for different cases and also whether fertilizer and lime are needed.

Slopes of 1 on 3 or flatter can be seeded by tractor-drawn spreading equipment. The cost of seeding increases for steeper slopes which require seed to be shot from adjacent flatter areas or to be scattered by hand.

Mulch is spread over seeds to hold moisture, reduce erosion, and protect seeds from wind and birds. Straw, pulverized leaves, or similar materials are useful as mulch. Spraying with drops of emulsified asphalt adds weight to hold mulch in place and absorbs heat from the sun, causing faster plant growth.

Nets of jute, cotton, or paper may be needed to hold soil and seeds on steeper slopes and may be used to hold mulch in place or used without mulch. The nets are anchored to the ground with wooden pegs or metal staples.

Sod may be placed in some areas that are subject to concentrated water flow. Spot sodding may be adequate. Grass spreads over the bare spaces through root growth. Sod requires daily watering for 30 days after being placed.

Unfinished slopes, unless fairly short and flat, must be protected from excessive erosion before construction is finished and plant growth can be started. One protective method is surface roughening which reduces the amount of runoff and slows its velocity. Scarifying with a harrow in a direction parallel with contour lines (therefore, perpendicular to the direction of runoff flow) produces grooves and ridges that hold runoff until it overtops each little ridge. Larger grooves may be needed on steeper slopes and are cut with an angled bulldozer blade and spaced as required to perform the same function on a larger scale.

Tracking or driving a tracked vehicle with cleats up and down the slope compacts the soil and produces holes that hold runoff. Compaction reduces erosion but looser soil would be better for future plant growth. Scarifying results in very loose soil; cutting with the bulldozer blade changes soil density the least. Tracking can be done on steeper slopes than scarifying or cutting by bulldozer. All the methods form little ponds that collect and hold all runoff from small rainstorms and slow the velocity of runoff from larger storms.

Sedimentation Control

Eroded soil particles are suspended in the runoff if they are small and rolled or bounced along by the runoff if they are large. It is best to intercept these particles close to where they come from and allow the water to flow on. A greater distance of travel results in a greater buildup of water and, therefore, a more difficult job of removing sediment. In addition, if the collected sediment is to be returned to where it eroded from, closer is better. It is not returned if it will be easily eroded again or if returning it will damage growing vegetation.

Filters and dams are used to collect sediment. *Filters* trap solid particles and allow water to flow through. Dams form ponds in which the water velocity is so slow that particles settle to the bottom before the water flows over the dam.

Natural vegetation or sod in the path of runoff catches some particles by a filtering action and slows the flow enough to cause others to settle. These barriers are useful in strips across the path of runoff, along the banks of a stream that runoff enters, or at the entrance to a conduit or channel. This type of barrier is satisfactory for fairly small amounts of sediment and should be raked clean after every rainstorm.

A filter of coarse crushed stone or gravel piled across the path of flow holds back particles smaller than the particles it is made of and allows water to flow through easily. Filters made of smaller particles are able to catch smaller particles but do not allow water to flow through as easily. They also become plugged sooner. This type of filter is placed at the entrance to a conduit or channel. A plugged filter acts as a dam and may continue to work satisfactorily for a time.

Hay bales or sand bags are used the same way as stone but operate as dams and form sedimentation basins which slow the water so that particles settle and clear water flows over the top. Bales should be anchored with stakes driven through them into the ground to prevent being floated and pushed aside and should be set into trenches 6 inches deep to prevent undermining. Either the stone filters or dams may be installed at intervals within a ditch.

Transportation

Large flows must be intercepted before they can damage a bare slope. Ditches or dikes are constructed at the top of the slope and terraces or benches are constructed part way down long slopes if needed. These are shown in Figure 5.2. Their surfaces require stone, sod, asphalt, or portland cement concrete lining if they collect large flows, if they are constructed in easily eroded soil, or if their slopes are steeper than 2 percent. They are generally left in place and continue to function as permanent installations.

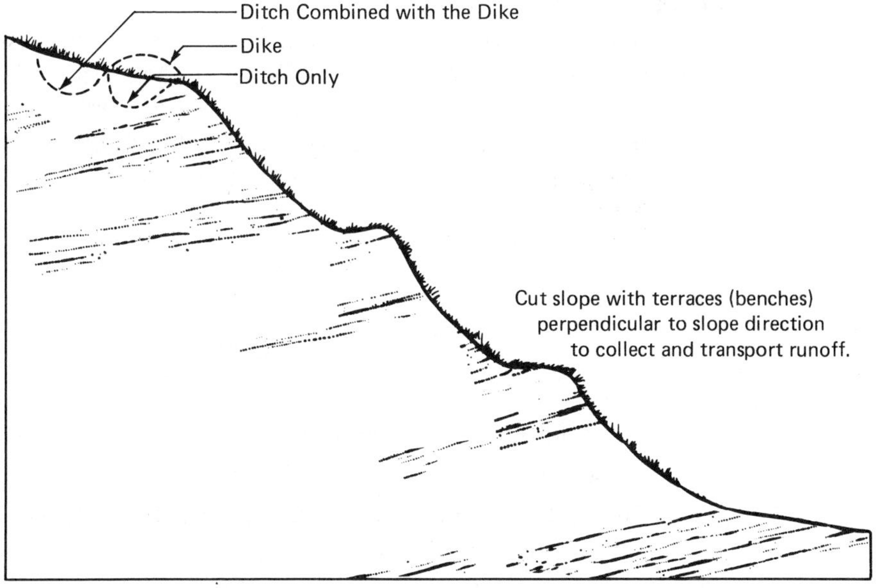

Interceptor ditch, dike, or combination carries runoff across top of slope.

FIGURE 5.2   Runoff Control for Long, Steep Slopes.

The intercepted water must be conducted to a location where erosion will not take place. As a temporary measure, a flexible fabric pipe with corrugated metal pipe end sections is used to carry collected water across easily eroded slopes to a level area. Corrugated metal pipes may be used as a part of a permanent installation but are more expensive to install and not usually justified for temporary use. They must be placed on a prepared base. The fabric tube is simply placed on the ground. The upper end section must be well bedded so that water does not undermine it. (See Chapter 6 for pipeline construction.)

Paved ditches are useful to carry away the intercepted water across flatter topography. Asphalt pavement is often used. Metal half-pipe flumes are commercially available for this purpose.

The velocity of the flowing water must be reduced before the water leaves the conducting device and flows onto the ground. A common means of doing this is to dump stones or broken concrete just upstream from the point where water leaves the device. Such a mass of material slows the velocity by causing the water to flow in conflicting directions, thereby reducing the energy available to erode the soil. The individual pieces must be large enough so that they are not swept away by the flowing water and they must not be so close together that they raise the water level above the sides of the conduit. Flowing water necessarily becomes deeper (backs up) when its velocity is reduced and it could overtop the sides.

The soil at the outlet requires protection from erosion. Rip rap, sod, or vegetation growth are all effective. The methods used to prevent erosion at the construction site are used to prevent erosion at the discharge end of ditches or conduits because the situation is similar. However, the greater discharge from a ditch is capable of causing more severe erosion.

REVIEW QUESTIONS

5.1. Draw an elevation view sketch of rain splash showing that it results in downhill movement of soil.

5.2. Of the four factors that influence erosion, discuss how construction influences three of them to cause increased erosion.

5.3. Discuss what harm can be caused by depositing of soil by wind or water.

5.4. Explain how surface roughening deters erosion.

5.5. Explain the operation of a filter and dam used to prevent the carrying away of eroded soil.

5.6. Discuss the advantages of a flexible fabric pipe compared to a metal pipe.

CHAPTER 6

Pipelines

Pipelines below the surface conduct water and gas to homes and conduct sewage and storm water away from them. In addition, underground conduits contain telephone, electric, and television cables. Sanitary sewers, storm drains, and waterlines are usually installed by the subdivider and are the only ones discussed in detail in this chapter.

General

Pipe is designated in inches by its nominal inside diameter. It is further designated as pressure or nonpressure pipe according to whether the pipe, especially the joint, is designed to carry liquid flowing under pressure or flowing under the influence of gravity without pressure. Only the types most commonly used for sanitary sewers, storm drains, and waterlines are discussed here. Sanitary and storm lines are gravity lines with a few exceptions and waterlines are pressure lines.

Asbestos-cement is a mixture of portland cement mortar with randomly distributed asbestos fibers for reinforcement. Nonpressure pipe is manufactured in sizes from 4 to 6 inches in 1-inch increments; from 8 to 20 inches in 2-inch increments; from 24 to 36 inches in 3-inch increments; and in lengths of 5, 6½, 10, and 13 feet. Pressure pipe is manufactured in sizes from 4 through 20 inches in 2-inch increments, 24 inches, 30 inches, and 36 inches and the same lengths. Pipe can be field cut with an ordinary hand saw.

Vitrified clay pipe is made of finely ground clay or shale mixed with water, extruded through a die under great pressure and fired to a temperature at which some of the material melts to a dense vitreous condition while the particles with high heat resistance do not melt but form a stiff matrix that maintains the shape of the pipe.

Clay pipe is manufactured in sizes from 6 to 12 inches in 2-inch increments and from 15 to 36 inches in 3-inch increments and in lengths up to 10 feet. In some areas, it is available in 3- and 42-inch sizes. Only nonpressure pipe is made. It is cut in the field by chiseling and breaking.

Nonreinforced concrete pipe is made by tamping very dry concrete into steel molds. It is made in sizes from 4 through 12 inches in 2-inch increments and from 15 through 36 inches in 3-inch increments and in lengths of 3, 4, 6, 7½, and 10 feet. Only nonpressure pipe is made of nonreinforced concrete. It may be cut in the field with a chisel or concrete saw.

Reinforced concrete pipe is manufactured by depositing concrete over a steel wire reinforcing cage within a single cylindrical form rotated so rapidly that the concrete is compacted against the form by centrifugal force. Nonpressure pipe is made in sizes from 12 through 36 inches in 3-inch increments and also in larger sizes. Lengths are 4, 5, 8, and 12 feet. Pressure pipe is made in sizes of 12, 15, 16, 18, 20, 21, 24, 27, and 30 inches and beyond in lengths up to 24 feet. Reinforced concrete pipe is usually ordered to exact length for the job because of the difficulty of cutting pipe in the field.

Corrugated aluminum pipe is manufactured of rectangular flat plates corrugated perpendicular to the pipe axis, curved, and riveted or welded longitudinally to form 2-foot lengths of pipe which are then riveted or welded together to attain the desired length; or it is made of one long narrow strip wound continuously barber-pole-style and joined by one continuous weld or lock seam to form a length of helical pipe.

Pipe is made in sizes from 6 to 12 inches in 2-inch increments, from 15 to 24 inches in 3-inch increments, and from 30 to 66 inches in 6-inch increments and also in larger sizes. Lengths are available in 2-foot increments up to 40 feet. Inside diameter is measured as the smallest diameter between corrugated surfaces. Only nonpressure pipe is made. Pipe can be cut in the field with an ordinary hand saw.

Corrugated galvanized steel pipe is manufactured the same way as aluminum pipe in the same sizes and lengths. Size is measured the same way and only nonpressure pipe is made. *Galvanizing* is coating with zinc for protection against corrosion. Corrosion protection is further improved by pressing a felt made of asbestos fibers into the molten zinc galvanizing coating on both surfaces and saturating the felt with a bituminous coating before corrugating. Another method of improving corrosion resistance is by coating with aluminum. The pipe can be cut in the field with a hack saw.

Ductile iron pipe is cast by pouring molten metal into a rapidly spinning cylindrical mold where centrifugal force causes it to solidify as a hollow cylinder. Pipe is made in sizes of 2 and 3 inches, from 4 to 20 inches in 2-inch increments, and from 24 to 54 inches in 6-inch increments and in lengths of 18 and 20 feet. Shorter lengths can be ordered. It is suitable for nonpressure or pressure pipe. Pipe is cut in the field with a pipe saw or cutting torch.

Three types of *plastic pipe*—ABS (Acrylonitrile-Butadiene-Styrene), PE (Polyethylene), and PVC (Polyvinyl Chloride)—are in common use for sewers, storm drains, and waterlines. All are manufactured by extrusion. They stiffen and soften with temperature change and become weaker at higher temperatures. Underground temperature changes are not great and remain cool enough to cause no difficulty. Their surfaces may be damaged by long exposure to sunlight. Pipe can be cut with a hand saw.

Plastic pipe is made in sizes from 3 to 48 inches and in lengths up to 35 feet. PE pipe may be purchased in coils of even greater length. *Truss pipe* is made of ABS with spaces filled with a weak portland cement mortar in 8-, 10-, 12-, and 15-inch sizes in 6¼ and 12½ foot lengths. It is shown in Figure 6.12.

Location of Pipelines

Pipelines must be built within public rights of way or easements and must be far enough from right-of-way lines or easement lines so pipe can be repaired without excavation or construction equipment encroaching on private property. Easements are often established through entire blocks, centered on rear property lines, to serve lots or houses on both sides. There are advantages to either the right-of-way or easement location. The chief advantage to the easement location is the ease of uncovering pipes for repairs. No pavement need be removed before excavation nor replaced afterward. However, access may not be as readily available as it should be according to the easement agreement. Fences, gardens, and other beautification projects may be in the way even if prohibited by the agreement. Valves, manholes, and grates may be deliberately hidden by these beautification projects. There may be more delays to making repairs and more hard feelings among the residents over damages than if utilities are under the street pavement. Usually, not all utilities are placed in an easement because of the excessive width required.

The chief advantage to the street location is the ease of locating the valves, manholes, or grates when it is necessary to make repairs. However, those within the pavement may be covered by asphalt resurfacing and be very difficult to find. Proper maintenance procedures prevent this from happening. All castings should be raised to the new finished surface before resurfacing.

Disadvantages include the expense of raising castings for resurfacing and replacing them when they are kicked out or broken by traffic; the hazards to traffic caused by the missing or broken castings and by the slippery surface of the castings in the pavement; and the noise caused by traffic over the castings.

Pipes should be placed underground according to a standard arrangement to protect public health and safety and to facilitate locating the pipes to make repairs. A typical arrangement is shown in Figure 6.1. A sketch of this kind is part of subdivision design standards in some municipalities.

The sanitary sewer and waterline should be separated by at least 10 feet (clear space) horizontally and at least 18 inches (clear space) vertically when they must cross. It is preferable for the waterline to be above the sewer when they cross but that cannot always be arranged. It is possible for sewage leaking into the soil from a broken sewer to be drawn into a waterline where it would seriously endanger public health.

Both sanitary sewer and storm drain should be separated from the gas main. Both serve as conduits to collect gas that leaks into the soil and conduct it up slope where it may become concentrated enough to explode if accidentally ignited. It is more likely to happen in a storm drain because gas main and storm drain are often at the same level while the sanitary sewer is normally below so that leaking gas does not reach it. There are no deliberate openings from the sanitary sewer to the surface as there are with the storm drain so that flames from the surface cannot ordinarily ignite gas in a sanitary sewer.

Water in the waterline is normally under pressure so that gas cannot enter. If it does enter, it cannot explode and is not a hazard to the health of those drinking the public water.

Pipe Materials

Pipe materials are of two kinds—rigid and flexible. Rigid pipe does not change its shape under load. If it fails, it fails by breaking or cracking. Flexible pipe deflects under load, changing its cross-section from round to oblong. It fails by deflecting excessively, buckling, or collapsing. The most commonly used rigid pipe materials include asbestos-cement, clay, plain concrete, and steel-reinforced concrete. Flexible pipe materials commonly used include corrugated aluminum, galvanized corrugated steel, ductile iron, and plastic.

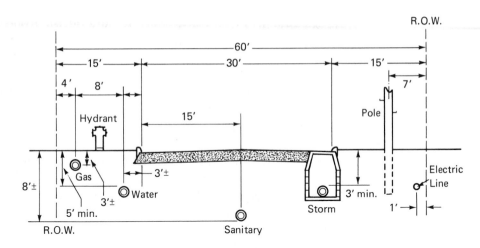

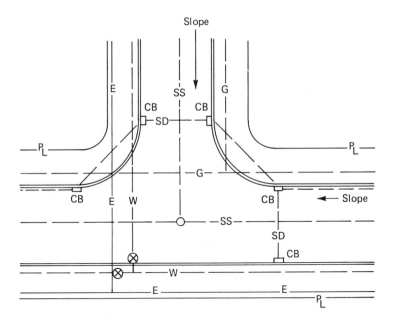

FIGURE 6.1 Typical Utility Locations.

Characteristics to be considered when selecting pipe material are strength, smoothness of the interior where liquid flows, resistance to corrosion from the soil, resistance to abrasion and corrosion on the inside, imperviousness to liquid, weight that must be lifted during handling, pipe length, cost, and type of joint.

Pipe of any of the materials could be made strong enough to support any weight of soil above it but some may then be too heavy or too expensive for practical use. Clay, concrete, and ductile iron pipes are much heavier to handle in comparable sizes than aluminum, galvanized steel, or any of the plastics and asbestos-cement is of intermediate weight. There is little difference in the interior smoothness or friction factor of pipe made of these materials with the exception that corrugated metal has a much higher resistance to flow but can be lined with portland cement concrete or asphalt to achieve comparable smoothness.

Corrosive soils attack steel and ductile iron, both of which can be protected by a loose, watertight wrapping of polyethylene. Soils corrosive enough to damage pipe do not often occur naturally but may be found where waste such as cinders has been dumped.

All the pipe material is resistant enough to abrasion for use as sanitary sewers, storm drains, or waterlines.

Ordinarily sanitary sewage, storm water, and domestic water do not corrode pipe except ductile iron which is, therefore, often protected inside with a coating of portland cement when used for sewage or for water distribution. If protection is necessary because of characteristics of the liquid, a coal tar epoxy or plastic coating might be used inside concrete pipe. An asphalt coating might be used inside a corrugated steel pipe for corrosion resistance as well as flow improvement.

Loads on Pipe

The load on underground pipes comes from the weight of the fill over the pipe. Pipe is usually installed in a narrow trench dug through undisturbed soil and is covered with the soil that was excavated from the trench. The maximum load that acts on this pipe is directly proportional to the specific weight of the backfill soil and to the square of the trench width at the top of the pipe even though the trench may be wider above this level.

The load is greater for deeper trenches but is affected more by specific weight of soil and width of trench. The increase in load due to depth becomes less and less at greater depths and there is a depth, depending on trench width at the top of the pipe, beyond which depth makes no difference in load on pipe.

An explanation of the importance of the trench width is that, over the years, soil at the sides of the pipe settles slightly more than the pipe and the load across the entire trench width is transferred to the pipe instead of the soil at the sides of the pipe. The wider the trench, the greater this load.

If the pipe is rigid, it carries nearly all the load because the fill between the pipe and trench will settle more than the rigid pipe no matter how well it is compacted. If a flexible pipe has fill at the sides so well compacted that the fill settles no more than the pipe, the proportion of the backfill load supported by the pipe is the same as the proportion of outside pipe width to trench width at the top of the pipe.

The reason the depth of trench is not so influential is that friction between the backfill trying to settle downward and the immobile, undisturbed soil at the sides of the trench holds back part of the backfill load. The friction is caused by the active lateral pressure of the backfill against the trench walls.

The factors that determine the load indicate that a narrow trench is preferable to a wider one as long as it is wide enough to install the pipe without hardship. If a trench has wide, sloping sides there will be less load on the pipe if it is installed in a narrow trench at the bottom of the wider excavation as shown in Figure 6.2.

Pipe is sometimes placed on the ground and fill is piled over it. An example is a culvert to carry a stream under a street embankment. Loads may be greater or less on pipes installed this way than in a trench as deep as the height of the fill. The load on such a pipe is proportional

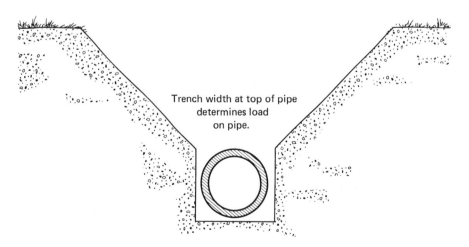

Trench width at top of pipe
determines load
on pipe.

FIGURE 6.2   Method of Reducing Load on Pipe in a Wide Trench.

to the specific weight of the fill and is proportional to the square of the outside pipe width instead of trench width.

The way height of fill affects this load depends on the amount of settlement of the top of the pipe compared to the amount of settlement of the adjacent fill. The load is proportional to the height of fill if soil and pipe settle the same amount. However, if one is more resistant to settlement, it takes more of the load.

Load on the pipe is greater if the soil settles more than the pipe and less if the pipe settles more. Therefore, good compaction of the fill is important in order to minimize soil settlement. The use of flexible pipe is advantageous to allow the top of the pipe to settle and transfer load to the soil.

Strength of Pipe

The ability of pipe to resist a load depends on pipe size, wall thickness, material or materials, and method of manufacture. However, it depends even more on how it is installed. *Pipe strength* means the load in pounds per linear foot of pipe that just causes the pipe to fail. Strength of rigid pipe is determined by testing pipe samples on the apparatus depicted in Figure 6.3 until they fail. A force uniformly distributed along the length of pipe is increased at a standard rate until the

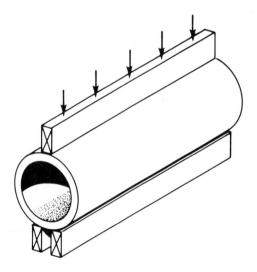

FIGURE 6.3   Three-Edge Bearing Test for Pipe Strength.

pipe fails. The force in pounds per linear foot of pipe at failure is the *three-edge bearing strength* of the pipe.

A rigid pipe is considered to fail when it breaks. A reinforced concrete pipe will not break until it has cracked extensively so is considered to fail when any crack in the pipe reaches a 0.01-inch width over a length of 1 foot.

Flexible pipe is considered to fail when it deflects (reduces its original height) to the extent that its usefulness as a conduit is impaired. Allowable deflection is often set at 5 percent of its original height. The force required in pounds per linear foot of pipe is a measure of the stiffness of the pipe. Some flexible pipe may be nearly flattened without breaking or cracking.

Flexible pipe stiffness is determined by the parallel-plate loading test. A short length of pipe is compressed between two horizontal rigid plates in a manner similar to that of the three-edge bearing test. The deflection is noted as the load is increased up to the failure load in pounds per linear foot of pipe at 5 percent deflection.

A pipe properly installed in a trench is better able to resist failure than the same pipe on the three-edge bearing or parallel-plate testing machine. Pipe imbedment terminology is illustrated in Figure 6.4. Factors by which various types of bedding increase the strength of rigid pipe in a trench are given in Figure 6.5. The factor for each type of bedding represents how much stronger the pipe is with that bedding than it is according to the three-edge bearing test. Proper placement

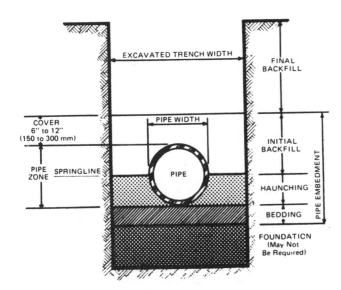

FIGURE 6.4 Pipe Installation Terminology [Copyright ASTM. Reprinted with permission].

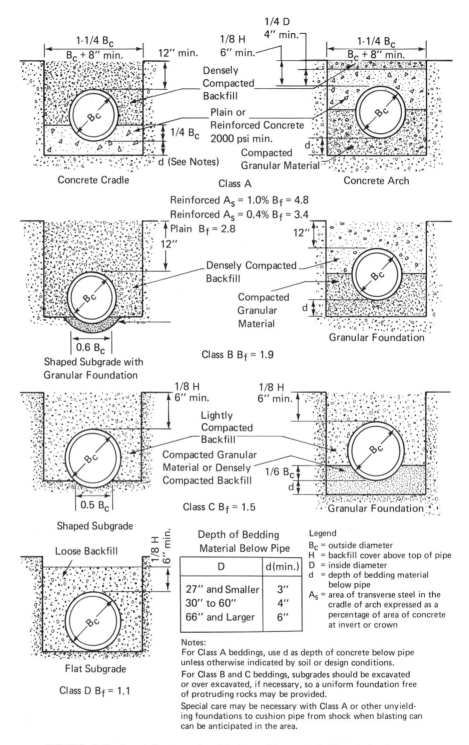

FIGURE 6.5 Load Factors for Various Classes of Pipe Imbedment
[Pipe Strength Equals Three-Edge Bearing Strength Multiplied by B_f]
[Courtesy of the American Concrete Pipe Association].

and compaction of all imbedment material is necessary to achieve the load factor.

Bedding for ductile iron pipe installed in trenches is shown in Figure 6.6. Bedding factors are not used. Instead, bending stress in the pipe wall and deflection of the pipe caused by the soil load are kept within allowable limits by selection of the laying condition and the pipe wall thickness. Relationships between bedding and stress or deflection depend partly on modulus of elasticity of pipe material and so are different for different pipe materials. Factors are available for calculating stress and deflection for ductile iron pipe for each laying condition shown.

Pipe installed on the ground with fill over it (designated as the

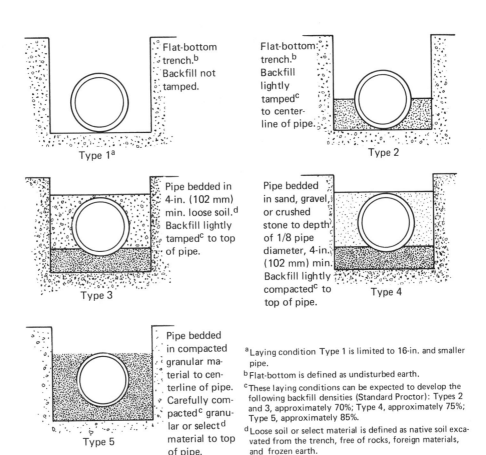

FIGURE 6.6 Standard Imbedment Conditions for Ductile Iron Pipe [Copyright ASTM. Reprinted with Permission].

projecting pipe condition) is also better able to resist failure than the same pipe on the three-edge bearing or parallel-plate testing machine. Bedding used for rigid pipe installed this way is shown in Figure 6.7. Because active soil pressure acts horizontally on the sides of the pipe, a projecting pipe can support a greater load than the same pipe in a trench.

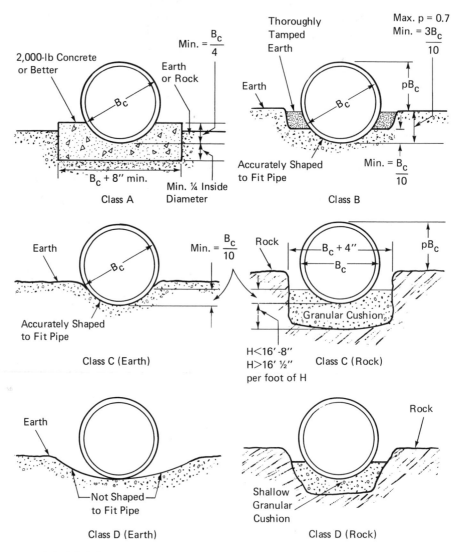

FIGURE 6.7 Classes of Bedding for Projecting Conduits [Courtesy of the American Society of Civil Engineers].

The load factor for projecting rigid pipe depends on class of bedding, the proportion of height of the pipe projecting above bedding into the fill, and the extent of the active soil pressure against the pipe sides. Active pressure varies with the height of fill, diameter of pipe, and strength of soil. The soil must be strengthened by compaction to achieve its potential active pressure.

Each manufacturer lists strengths of pipes based on the three-edge bearing test or parallel-plate loading test. The installed strength equals the listed strength multiplied by the factor for the bedding used.

A safety factor is used in calculating the allowable load on a buried pipe. A safety factor equals the failure load divided by the allowable load or

$$SF = \frac{\text{Three-edge Bearing Strength} \times \text{Factor}}{\text{Allowable Load}}$$

Safety factors varying from 1.0 to 1.5 are used by designers for rigid pipe in trenches and larger safety factors ranging up to 2 are used for flexible pipe.

The design of a pipeline involves selection of a type of pipe and type of bedding that together provide the strength needed to resist the load caused by the installation (trench or embankment), width of trench, specific weight of fill, and depth of fill. None of these conditions may be changed in the field without permission of the engineer in charge of construction supervision.

Figure 6.8 shows how failure is prevented in properly bedded pipe and also two ways in which improperly placed bedding causes loads beyond the strength of the pipe. The bedding and backfill must distribute the load uniformly along the top and bottom of the pipe or the pipe is subjected to stresses it is not built to take.

Rigid pipe material is weak in tension and strong in compression. Although flexible pipe is not weak in tension, it is designed to keep its shape under compression from all directions and is not strong enough to hold its shape when compression from top and bottom greatly exceeds that from the sides.

A pipe subjected to a uniformly distributed load is subject to *arch loading*. If it fails because of excessive load, the top deflects causing the top and bottom to be closer and the sides to bulge outward. Tension is caused at the inside of top and bottom and at the outside of the sides.

Excessive tension causes longitudinal breaks in rigid pipe and lon-

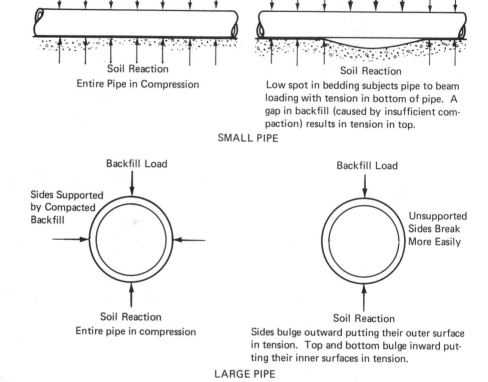

FIGURE 6.8   How Bedding and Backfill Strengthen Pipe.

gitudinal deflection in flexible pipe. Well-compacted fill at the sides of all pipe helps to prevent bulging of the sides and, therefore, deflection of the top. For flexible pipe, side support is definitely counted on to resist failure.

Pipe shape is not designed to withstand beam loading, and rigid pipe easily breaks on the bottom or tension side when subjected to it. Because of the rigidity, the break extends around the pipe resulting in a transverse break. Flexible pipe flattens transversely at the section where excessive beam load occurs. Large pipe is not likely to be subjected to damaging beam loading because it is large compared to most gaps that occur in bedding.

A stone in the fill is subjected to a load from the column of soil above it much the same as a pipe is subjected to a load caused by the prism of soil over it. If the stone is next to a pipe, it concentrates the load at a point on the pipe. This may break a rigid pipe and puncture or dent a flexible pipe that would not otherwise be overloaded. A stone near the pipe may settle with the rest of the fill until it contacts the pipe and may even work its way down through the surrounding soil because of the downward force on it. A stone under the pipe exerts a concentrated load because the smaller particles near the stone settle by compaction more than the stone, leaving a large portion of the pipe's weight (and the weight of backfill) on the stone.

Pressure within a pipe, such as exists in a waterline, produces tension throughout a pipe wall, and the load from fill produces tension in part of the pipe wall. The stress in the pipe wall is the sum of the two; and, therefore, a pipe cannot support as great an external load when subjected to internal pressure.

Pipes are manufactured in various strength classes. For gravity pipe, the class number often indicates the minimum load in pounds per linear foot of pipe that can be supported without failure during the three-edge bearing test. For pressure pipe, the class number indicates the recommended maximum operating pressure in psi. The American Water Works Association sets standards for crushing strength, flexure strength, and impact strength in addition to bursting pressure, which is far above the indicated operating pressure, for pipes made of various material.

For example, asbestos-cement nonpressure pipe is manufactured in the following classes: 1500, 2400, 3300, 4000, and 5000 indicating minimum strength in pounds per linear foot of pipe in the three-edge bearing test. Larger-size pipes bear the weight of a wider mass of soil above them than small ones do and are thus subject to greater loads under the same conditions. Therefore, a higher class of pipe may be needed for larger pipe than for smaller pipe under the same loading conditions. Asbestos-cement pressure pipe is made in 100, 150, and 200 classes.

Clay pipe and plain concrete pipe are nonpressure pipe and are available in two classes: standard strength and extra strength. Manufacturers' literature lists three-edge bearing test strengths for all sizes in each class. Larger-diameter pipe has greater strength in the same class because it must support a wider load.

Pipe Joints

Adjacent pieces of pipe are connected by joints that are simply and quickly assembled and are designed to minimize leakage. The most common method of sealing the joint is with a hard rubber or plastic ring within a groove that encircles the pipe. The cross-section of the ring varies from one manufacturer to another. The ring is compressed when the pieces of pipe are joined. Compression takes place between the two pipe ends, one inside the other in a bell-and-spigot joint or tongue-and-groove joint or modification thereof (see Figure 6.9). A *mechanical joint* is a bell-and-spigot joint with a ring that is compressed into the space between bell and spigot by a metal ring around the spigot that is drawn toward the bell by bolting the ring to the bell.

In some cases, a collar compresses two rings from outside, one against each pipe (see Figure 6.10). Pipe is delivered to the job with the collar in place on one end of each piece so it is installed the same way as bell-and-spigot pipe. All these joints are made by installing the ring, lubricating it, and simply pushing the next piece of pipe into the pipe already in place.

One connecting band is tightened around the two adjoining ends of corrugated metal pipe (see Figure 6.11). The band includes a gasket when greater watertightness is needed. The two pipes are set in place and the band is tightened around them.

A collar is used to join two pieces of ABS or PVC pipe by solvent welding. The solvent dissolves a thickness of the spigot and the collar, they are placed in contact, the solvent evaporates, and the two parts are fused into one homogeneous piece. The pipe is delivered to the job with a collar solvent welded to one end of each piece of pipe, so the joint is a variation of the bell-and-spigot joint (see Figure 6.12).

Sections of PE pipe may be fused similarly by heating with metal plates or may be fused end to end without the collar. Special equipment and training are needed.

The following types of joints are in common use:

Asbestos-cement pressure and nonpressure pipe—collar and ring gasket, push on.
Clay nonpressure pipe—bell-and-spigot and ring gasket, push on.
Plain concrete nonpressure pipe—bell-and-spigot and ring gasket, push on.

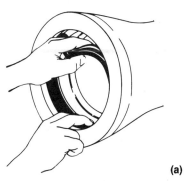

(a)

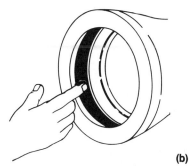

(b)

(a) Insertion of Gasket

All foreign matter in the socket must be removed. Foreign matter in the gasket seat may cause a leak. The gasket must be wiped clean, flexed, and placed in the socket with the large round end entering first, so that the gasket is seated evenly around the inside of the socket with the heel of the gasket fitting snugly in the retainer seat.

(b) Application of Lubricant

A thin film of lubricant should be applied to the inside surface of the gasket. The plain end of the pipe must be cleaned of all foreign matter on the outside from the end to the stripes. In some cases, it is desirable to apply a thin film of lubricant to the outside of the plain end from about 3 inches back from the end. Lubricant other than that furnished with the pipe should not be used.

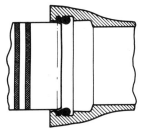

(c)

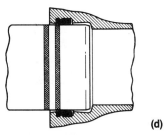

(d)

(c) Initial Entry of Plain End into Socket

The plain end of the pipe should be aligned so it just makes contact with the gasket. This is the starting position for the final assembly of the joint. Note the two painted stripes near the plain end.

(d) Completely Assembled Joint

Joint assembly should then be completed by forcing the plain end past the gasket (which is thereby compressed) until the plain end makes contact with the bottom of the socket. Note that the first painted stripe will have disappeared into the socket and the front edge of the second stripe will be approximately flush with the bell face.

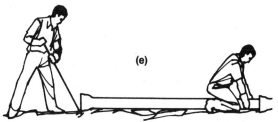

(e)

(e) Crowbar Method of Assembly

Eight inch and smaller pipe may be joined by pushing against the face of the bell of the entering pipe with a crowbar or spade.

FIGURE 6.9   Installing Push-On Joint Ductile Pipe. Bell and Spigot Are Called Socket and Plain End [Courtesy of U.S. Pipe and Foundry Company].

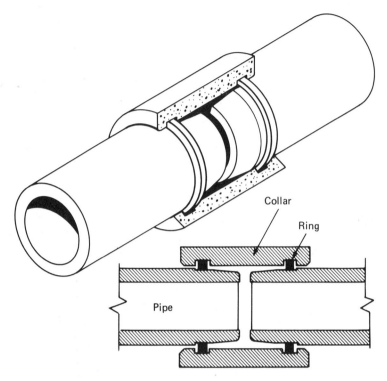

FIGURE 6.10 Section Through a Typical Collar Joint with Compressed
Rings.

Reinforced concrete pressure pipe—bell-and-spigot and ring
gasket, push on.

Reinforced concrete nonpressure pipe—bell-and-spigot, tongue-
and-groove, modified tongue-and-groove all with ring gaskets,
push on.

Corrugated galvanized steel nonpressure pipe—connecting band
with or without gasket.

Corrugated aluminum nonpressure pipe—connecting band with
or without gasket.

Ductile iron pressure and nonpressure pipe—bell-and-spigot and
ring gasket, push on and mechanical joint with ring gasket.

ABS pressure and nonpressure pipe—solvent weld, push on, and
bell-and-spigot and ring gasket, push on.

PE pressure and nonpressure pipe—heat fusion.

PVC pressure and nonpressure pipe—solvent weld, push on, and
bell-and-spigot and ring gasket, push on.

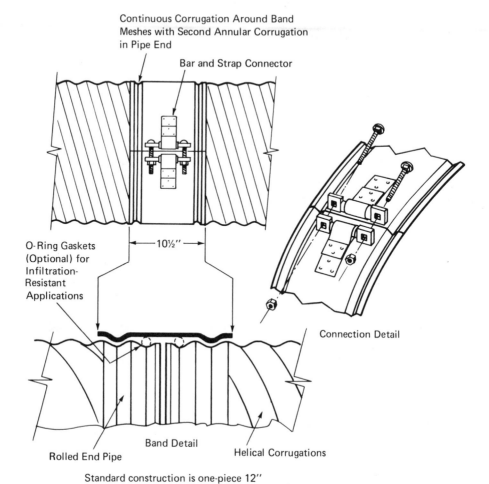

Continuous Corrugation Around Band
Meshes with Second Annular Corrugation
in Pipe End

Bar and Strap Connector

O-Ring Gaskets
(Optional) for
Infiltration-
Resistant
Applications

|← 10½" →|

Connection Detail

Band Detail

Rolled End Pipe

Helical Corrugations

Standard construction is one-piece 12"
through 48" and two-piece 54" and above.

FIGURE 6.11 Connecting Band at Corrugated Metal Pipe Joint [Courtesy of Contech Construction Productions, Inc., Formerly Armco Construction Products, Inc.].

Construction Control

Construction drawings show pipeline locations in plan and profile views and in typical bedding cross-sections (see Figure 6.13). The developer builds according to the drawings as guided by construction stakes. The stakes are offset an agreed upon distance from the centerline of the proposed pipe opposite the side where excavated soil will be placed.

I Storage and Handling

1. Store truss pipe on a smooth bed to prevent point loading.
2. Never stack over 8 feet high (6 feet is recommended).
3. Don't drop truss pipe from truck or drag it across sharp objects.

II Primer and Cement

1. Keep both primer and cement away from open flames.
2. Avoid prolonged inhalation of vapors.
3. May be fatal if swallowed.
4. Keep all containers of primer and cement closed to avoid evaporation.

III Chemically Welded Joints

1. Remove dirt and mud from bell and spigot with rag or scraper.
2. Apply primer liberally to outside of spigot and inside of coupling. "Johnny Mops" have proven very effective for applications.

3. Apply cement immediately to the same surfaces.

4. Make joint immediately (within one minute) by shoving home with ¼ rotation.

IV Chemically Welded Saddle—Fittings

1. Stick template on truss pipe to mark outline of hole.
2. Use keyhole or saber saw or other instruments to cut hole.
3. Apply primer and cement liberally to entire area of pipe and underside of saddle.

4. Immediately place saddle firmly on pipe and tighten two stainless steel bands around pipe and saddle.

FIGURE 6.12   Installing Plastic Truss Pipe or Solid Wall Pipe [Courtesy of Contech Products, Inc., Formerly Armco Construction Products, Inc.].

FIGURE 6.13 Typical Plan and Profile of a Sanitary Sewer [see Figure 6.4 for a Typical Cross-Section].

The developer selects an offset distance that will provide enough work area to avoid disturbing the stakes.

Pipelines are of two kinds—gravity and pressure. The gravity lines, sanitary sewers and storm drains, are built to flow partially full and must be constructed to the design slope to carry liquid satisfactorily. Waterlines carry water under pressure and are built with a specified soil (or soil and pavement) cover over the pipe for protection from traffic and freezing. They follow the proposed finished surface up and down hills at the correct depth below the surface.

Gravity lines are built to line and grade from surveyor's stakes. *Line* means horizontal direction and *grade* means elevation. Line and grade of gravity pipelines are indicated by notes on the stakes or are tabulated on a sheet of paper called a *grade sheet* or *cut sheet*. The pipeline is built on a straight slope from one elevation to the next and, therefore, will be at the designated slope. The word *grade* is often used to mean slope.

The surveyor determines elevation at the top of each stake using surveying procedures. The elevation of the pipe *invert* (inside bottom) opposite each stake is determined from the construction drawings. The vertical difference between the two elevations is the *cut* at each stake (see Figure 6.14). Stakes are set at stations, at 25- or 50-foot intervals, at changes in slope or direction, and at manholes or stormwater inlets.

Horizontal offset distances and cuts for gravity lines are measured from a nail flush with the stake top to the pipe invert. The *invert* is the lowest point inside the pipe and is, therefore, on the center line. It is the surface the liquid flows on and good construction results in a smooth invert for least resistance to flow. Using the invert as a control surface assures that it will be smooth.

Surveyors' stakes set for waterlines must provide an accurate line, but no elevation control is needed. The pipes are set in place at the offset distance with a horizontal measurement using a tape or straight board at each stake and proceeding on a straight line between stakes. The trench is made deep enough to provide the required cover over the pipe and depth is checked from the ground surface at the edge of the trench.

There are several kinds of control systems that can be set up for gravity lines from the surveyors' stakes. One often-used system requires batter boards to hold a string centered over the proposed pipeline, parallel with it and at a preset distance above the invert (see Figure 6.15).

A batter board is built across the trench opposite each surveyor's stake. A level line is brought from the stake top out to the batter board

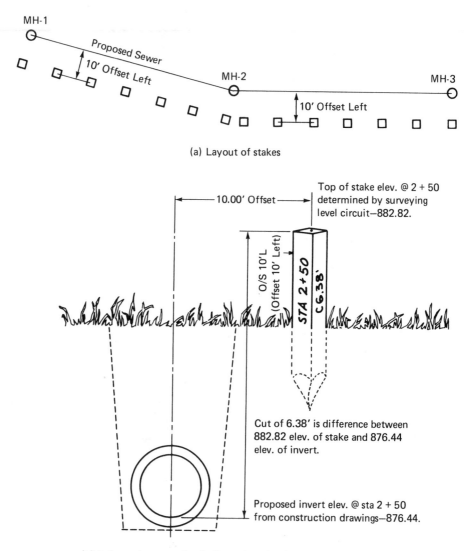

(a) Layout of stakes

Top of stake elev. @ 2 + 50 determined by surveying level circuit—882.82.

├──────── 10.00' Offset ────────┤

O/S 10'L
(Offset 10' Left)

STA 2 + 50
C 6.38'

Cut of 6.38' is difference between 882.82 elev. of stake and 876.44 elev. of invert.

Proposed invert elev. @ sta 2 + 50 from construction drawings—876.44.

(b) Information on stakes indicates location for proposed pipe line.

FIGURE 6.14 Construction Stakes.

and the batter board is set level at a distance above the level line that will put the batter board a convenient whole number of feet (called *grade rod* or *story pole*) above the proposed invert. All batter boards are built with the same grade rod until depth of trench makes it inconvenient and a new grade rod is chosen (see Figure 6.16).

A *grade rod,* marked with the preset distance above a *shoe* (metal

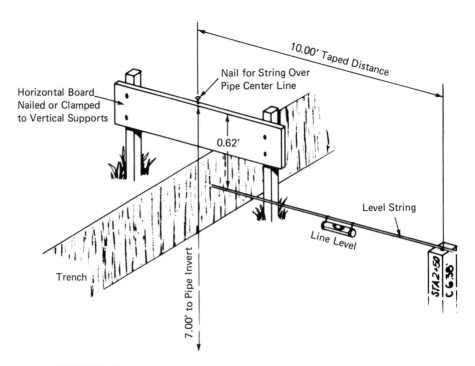

FIGURE 6.15 Setting Batter Boards 7 Feet above Finished Grade.

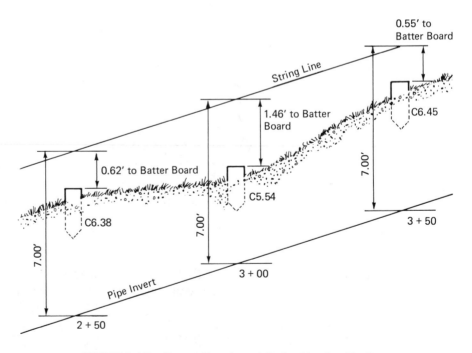

FIGURE 6.16 Batter Boards and String Line for Pipeline.

shelf bracket or similar right-angle shape) at the bottom of the rod, is used to set each piece of pipe under the string line at the correct distance with the shoe on the pipe invert. Note that the term *grade rod* is used to refer to the vertical distance from control line to finished construction and also to refer to the stick used to measure that distance.

A plumb bob is hung from the string to center the pipe. Line (by plumb bob) and grade (by grade rod) must be checked separately because the string line sags when the plumb bob is hung from it. Line and grade are adjusted alternately by moving the pipe until both line and grade are correct (see Figure 6.17).

The string line must be straight where the pipeline is to be straight and, if three or more batter boards are in place, a quick look down the length of the string line reveals any error, even a small one. If only two batter boards are up, the line is straight no matter how inaccurate it is. Therefore, the experienced developer keeps at least three batter boards up to provide a check on the string line.

Usually, the most efficient way to control pipeline construction is

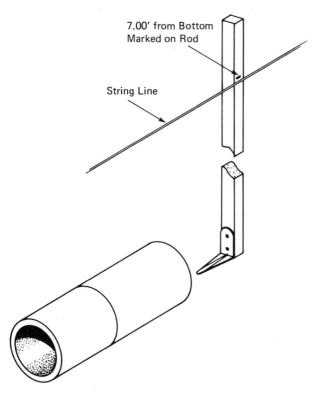

7.00′ from Bottom
Marked on Rod

String Line

FIGURE 6.17 Grade Rod or Story Pole in Use.

to set a laser beam as the control line and build the pipeline centered on the beam. A *laser* is a device that projects a very narrow, straight-light beam over a long distance. The light beam is seen as a red dot on any surface it hits. The laser has been adapted specifically for pipeline construction.

Construction stakes are needed only at laser setups which are usually at manholes or storm water inlets typically spaced 400 feet apart. Figure 6.18 shows a typical set of stakes for a laser setup. Direction and distance to the center of the manhole or storm water inlet are indicated and cut from the stake top to the pipe invert at that point is also indicated.

The laser is mounted on a stand that can be leveled and adjusted up and down. The laser beam can be rotated horizontally and vertically about one center point the same as the line of sight of a transit. The laser setup must meet four criteria:

1. The laser must be level or the horizontal and vertical motions will not be accurate. It is equipped with leveling adjustments and a level bubble.
2. The laser center must be on the center line of the proposed pipeline. A mark provided on top of the laser is on a vertical line over the laser center when the laser is level. A flat seat is built into the laser and is at a predetermined vertical distance above the laser center when the laser is level.
3. The beam must be pointed in the correct direction or ''on line.''
4. The beam must be inclined at the correct slope taken from the construction profile drawings.

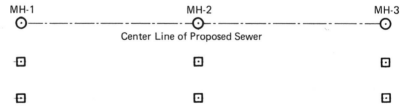

Two stakes form a line perpendicular to sewer at each manhole. Stakes are 10 and 20 feet from the center of the manhole. Manhole construction is centered 10 feet from near stake on the extension of a line connecting the two stakes. Cut is marked from the near stake.

FIGURE 6.18   Stakes for Laser Control of Sewer Construction.

The laser is set up on a reasonably level base approximately at the desired elevation. Concrete blocks or boards are satisfactory as a base. The laser will settle and change the location of its beam if it is set directly on the ground. The laser is then adjusted until it is level, centered under a plumb bob at the correct direction and distance from the construction stakes, and raised or lowered to the elevation of the center line of the pipeline as indicated by the cut from the construction stake (see Figure 6.19).

The cut is the vertical distance from stake top to pipe invert. The rod is read with a level at a height above the stake top equal to the backsight. The laser beam is above the invert at the pipe center and the bottom of the level rod is at the designated point on top of the laser at a predetermined distance, called the *laser constant,* above the beam.

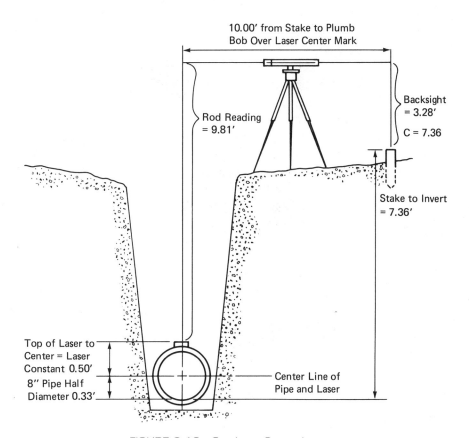

FIGURE 6.19 Setting a Sewer Laser.

Some arithmetic is needed to determine the number that must be read on the rod to indicate that the laser center is at the pipe center line elevation:

$$\text{Rod reading} = \text{cut} + \text{backsight} - \text{one half pipe diameter} - \text{laser constant}$$

The rod reading required in Figure 6.19 is $7.36 + 3.28 - 0.33 - 0.50 = 9.81$ feet.

The next step is to direct the laser beam in the direction of the proposed pipeline. There are several ways of doing this. The most accurate way requires that a transit be centered over the laser center by means of a plumb bob or optical plumb line. The transit can be set up on the manhole or storm inlet wall if there is one already in place. If not, a temporary platform for the transit is built across the excavation.

The transit line of sight is set on line as shown in Figure 6.20. The backhoe excavating the trench must be moved out of the way for this operation. If there is no change in pipeline direction at this point, the transit can be set on line by sighting to the rear, and then reversed so that the telescope points ahead on an extension of the back line. If the pipeline changes direction at this point, the angle is generally not known and the method shown in Figure 6.20 must be used.

Once the transit is on line, the laser beam is lined up in the same direction. The transit cross hairs are focused on a convenient stationary smooth surface in the trench. A section of pipe, hand shovel, or the backhoe bucket can be used. Following signals from the transit operator, the laser operator directs the laser beam to coincide with the transit cross hairs. The laser beam is then on line. The pipe slope taken from the construction profile drawing is set into the laser, pointing the beam upward at the required slope. The beam is then on the proposed pipe center line.

Translucent templates sized for each pipe diameter with their centers marked are inserted into both ends of the first pipe to be laid. The laser beam shines through the templates and so is visible at both ends. The first pipe is centered on the beam. Succeeding pipes are fitted into the preceding one and the far end is aligned on the beam with a template. For large pipe, the laser and templates are set at a prescribed small distance above the invert to avoid handling very large pipe-size templates.

A difference in temperature along the path of the laser beam causes it to change direction. A change in temperature is inevitable

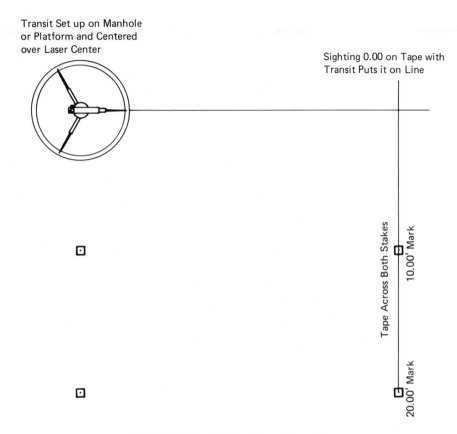

Transit Set up on Manhole
or Platform and Centered
over Laser Center

Sighting 0.00 on Tape with
Transit Puts it on Line

Tape Across Both Stakes

10.00' Mark

20.00' Mark

FIGURE 6.20   Sighting Transit on Line.

when sun-warmed pipe from alongside the trench is added to pipe in place in a deep, cool trench. A blower that forces air through the pipe will maintain a constant temperature and a straight beam.

Construction

The following discussion applies to the three types of pipeline except that controlling the slope does not apply to waterlines.

The trench is excavated with a backhoe, starting with an approximate center line such as a line made on the ground using a bag of lime with a hole in it, and finishing the trench bottom as accurately as possible by using the laser beam on the backhoe bucket (see Figure 6.21). A

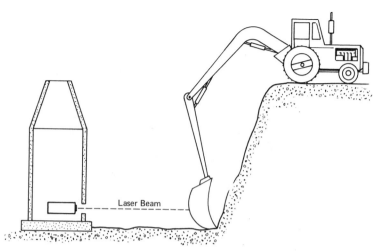

FIGURE 6.21   Trench Excavation for a Pipeline.

backhoe is a crawler or wheel-mounted excavating dipper designed to excavate below the level of the equipment's operating surface by pulling the dipper toward the equipment. Its primary purpose is trench excavation and it can deposit the excavated material at trenchside or load it into a truck.

The final trench bottom elevation can be controlled with a grade rod of the distance from pipe center line to bottom of bedding and finished with a backhoe or hand shovel. The hand shovel can be marked to serve as a convenient grade rod.

If no shoveling is done by hand, the trench must be deeper on the average than shown on the drawings in order to be deep enough at all points for minimum bedding depth because the backhoe cannot finish the trench bottom accurately. A hand shovel can be used more efficiently than the backhoe to clean out loose chunks and can be used to scrape a little deeper where necessary behind the backhoe, allowing the backhoe to excavate closer to the correct depth and thereby saving bedding material.

Granular bedding material is dumped into the finished trench with a front-end loader (shown in Figure 4.4) or by hand shovel. It is smoothed to the proper depth with hand shovels marked for the laser beam. Figure 6.22 shows how marks are aligned with the laser beam to control trench bottom and top of bedding.

Pipes are lowered into the trench by construction equipment (usually the excavating backhoe with a cable attached to the bucket) for heavy pipe or by hand for light pipe (see Figure 6.23). Pipe should be inspected for cracks before being lowered. Cracks that cannot be seen

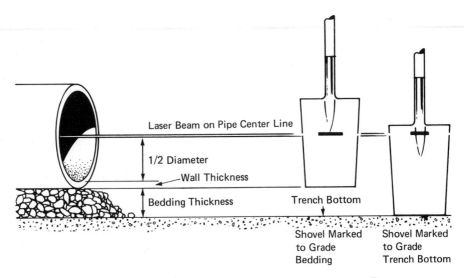

Laser Beam on Pipe Center Line

1/2 Diameter

Wall Thickness

Bedding Thickness

Trench Bottom

Shovel Marked
to Grade
Bedding

Shovel Marked
to Grade
Trench Bottom

FIGURE 6.22   Hand Shovels Marked to Match the Laser Beam.

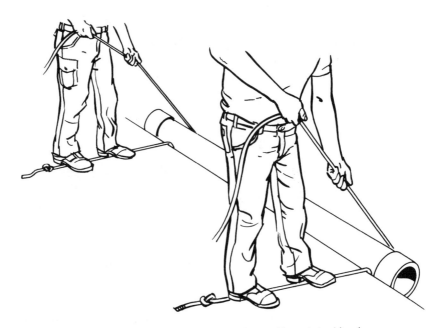

FIGURE 6.23   Lowering Pipe into a Trench by Hand.

can be detected by tapping the pipe with a hammer or similar object. An uncracked pipe rings and a cracked pipe sounds like a cracked bell.

The first piece of pipe is aligned on the laser beam by inserting a template into each end of the pipe, shoveling enough granular material under the pipe to raise it a little higher than it should be, and working the pipe back and forth down into the bedding material until the pipe is firmly bedded and the two templates are centered on the laser beam.

The next pipe is jointed to the first one without moving it and is firmly bedded with one template at the far end of the pipe aligned with the laser beam. The entire reach of pipeline is constructed this way, pipe by pipe (see Figure 6.24).

If the work is controlled by string line, the pipes are aligned with the grade rod from string line to invert and the plumb line from string line to the center of the top of the pipe, alternating the two controls until alignment is satisfactory.

Bedding material or other specified material is thrown into the trench by hand against the trench sides to avoid jarring the pipe out of alignment. It is pushed under the haunch of the pipe with shovels, brought up evenly on both sides of the pipe so the pipe is not forced to either side, and is tamped with hand tampers. The rest of the imbedment material is also thrown in by hand and tamped to the height specified. Above that, backfill may be pushed or dumped in by machine.

Pipe is laid uphill whenever possible. In fact, most construction proceeds uphill so that gravity acting downhill tends to consolidate the work rather than loosen it. An additional reason in the case of pipelines is that rainwater entering the trench flows away through a sanitary

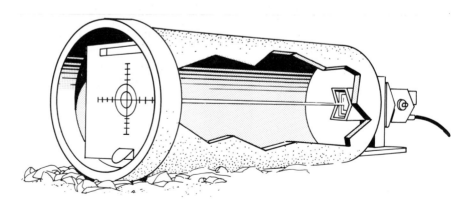

FIGURE 6.24 Section of Pipe Alined on a Laser Beam [Courtesy of Spectra Physics].

sewer or storm drain when building uphill and stands at the low end of the trench and must be pumped out when building downhill. However, trench water may not be allowed in a sanitary or storm line if it is too muddy and it is never allowed in a waterline.

Pipe will float in water. Even the heaviest pipe, when the entire hollow volume is included, is not so heavy that it cannot be floated by water in the trench. A pipeline tightly capped at both ends, as often required whenever the work is not in progress, is readily floated by water standing in the trench. Even if a pipeline is open at one or both ends, a section of it can be floated by water trapped in the trench by partially completed backfill. A pipeline that has been floated does not settle to its previous position when water is removed from the trench, but must be completely rebuilt. Therefore, it is inadvisable to leave any pipeline overnight without enough backfill over it to hold it down.

Pipes are joined by inserting the end of one pipe into the larger end of another pipe that is already in place. (See the section on pipe joints for more details.) The first pipe is always placed with the large end in the laying direction (uphill for gravity lines). As the smaller end is pushed toward the stationary larger end, it does not scoop loose ma-

FIGURE 6.25 Trench Box in Use [Courtesy of Griswold Machine and Engineering, Inc.].

STABLE SOIL

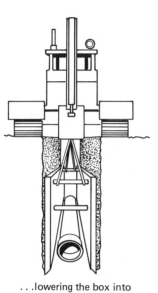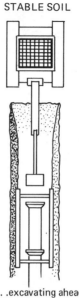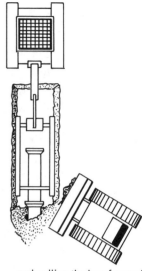

. . .lowering the box into the trench for installing pipe. . .

. . .excavating ahead of the box for the next length of pipe. . .

. . .and pulling the box forward into the new excavation while backfilling at the rear. . .

UNSTABLE SOIL

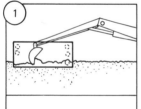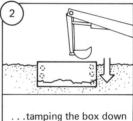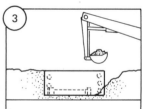

1 Place the box in line and dig from inside. . .

2 . . .tamping the box down after each bucketful.

3 When the box attains grade, install pipe.

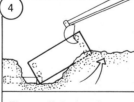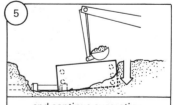

4 Then, pull the box forward and up approximately 45 degrees. . .

5 . . .and continue excavating inside, tamping the front of the box again to grade for setting the next length of pipe.

FIGURE 6.26 Excavating Techniques with a Trench Box (Courtesy of Griswold Machine and Engineering, Inc.).

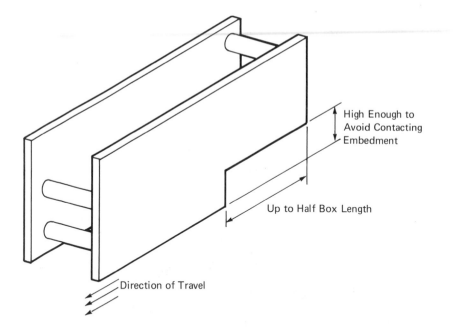

FIGURE 6.27   Trench Box Modified to Prevent Disturbing Pipe Imbedment.

A difficulty with a trench box is that the sides of the box extend to the bottom of the trench and pipe imbedment is placed inside the box with the sides of the box between the pipe imbedment and the natural soil. When the box is dragged forward, a gap is left which must be filled or the imbedment material, which was so carefully compacted, will be loosened by shifting laterally into the gap. Dragging the box may disturb the imbedment so much that it cannot be filled satisfactorily. It is always difficult to fill the gap from within the box, but workers are not protected outside the box.

Bedding is disturbed less if the box is lifted clear of imbedment vertically, moved ahead, and then lowered vertically. However, dragging is often necessary. A box modified as shown in Figure 6.27 allows pipe and imbedment to be placed toward the rear of the box where the lower part of the box is cut away with no danger of disruption when the box is dragged forward. The box is supported on the trench bottom by the front part where excavation takes place.

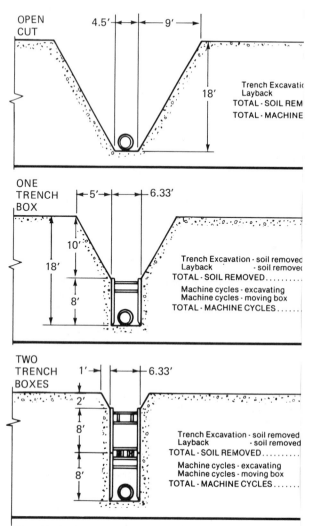

Note: Earth volume and cycles are for a trench 12 feet long in stable soil

FIGURE 6.26 *Continued*

terial into the joint as the larger end would i
smaller. Some corrugated metal pipe is made of
with overlapping joints. This pipe should be plac
the direction of flow and water flows over the j

The trench must be prevented from collapsi
it. There are various methods to brace trenches. .
is often used for construction of subdivision pip
shown in Figure 6.25 and Figure 6.26 shows ho

REVIEW QUESTIONS

6.1. What is the basic difference between pressure and nonpressure pipe?

6.2. What are the differences in the way pressure and nonpressure pipelines are built?

6.3. Indicate which lines are made of pressure pipe and which of nonpressure pipe: television cable conduit, storm drain, waterline, natural gas line, telephone cable conduit, sanitary sewer, conduit for street lighting.

6.4. Explain why gravity lines are separated from natural gas lines.

6.5. Describe the different ways flexible and rigid pipe support external loads. Explain why backfill at the sides of flexible pipe must be well compacted.

6.6. Why are sewer lines and waterlines separated? What are the separation requirements?

6.7. Explain the two factors to consider in order to decide on bottom trench width.

6.8. If a pipe is marked with the strength "2200," what does it mean? If that pipe is bedded with a load factor of 1.9, what is its failure strength? What is the allowable load if a safety factor of 1.3 is desired?

6.9. Explain why large stones must not be allowed near the pipe when it is being bedded or backfilled.

6.10. A surveyor's stake is marked C7.34. How far above the top of stake is a batter board built for a grade rod of 9 feet?

6.11. A surveyor's stake is marked C7.94. What rod reading is needed to set a laser with a constant of 0.50 foot for a 10-inch pipe with a backsight of 4.57?

6.12. Discuss how to set up a laser to control sewer construction.

6.13. At what height would you mark a hand shovel to control trench bottom using a laser set up for 15-inch pipe with 4-inch bedding and pipe wall thickness of ½ inch?

CHAPTER 7

Sanitary Sewers

Sanitary sewers collect plumbing wastes from buildings and conduct them to a plant where they are treated to remove most of the harmful constituents and discharged back to nature. The smallest diameter sewer allowed by sanitary codes is 8 inches and in residential developments they are usually not much larger than that. Materials commonly used for these pipes are vitrified clay, asbestos-cement, ductile iron, concrete, and plastic. Joints must be tight to prevent ground water from entering and overloading the sewer and to prevent sewage from escaping and polluting the ground water.

Ground water that enters the sewer may be very costly because it contributes to overloading the sewer from the point of entry to the pollution control plant, which may include miles of sewer, and because it must be treated at the same cost as sewage when it reaches the pollution control plant. Infiltration of ground water is discussed further in Chapter 8.

Sewers in much of the United States are designed and constructed according to the standards in Appendix C.

Gravity Sewers

Sanitary sewers are gravity pipelines wherever possible. They are usually the deepest of the pipelines that serve a subdivision and are, therefore, installed first after rough grading. Deeper trenches are more likely to collapse than shallower ones and the likelihood of any trench collapsing is increased by having the disturbed soil of a backfilled trench near it. Therefore, it is better to finish the deeper pipelines first so that their already greater tendency to collapse will not be increased by backfilled trenches nearby.

Pipelines must be constructed deep enough so that waste water from buildings flows to them by gravity through service lines. The *service lines* or *house sewers* are 4- or 6-inch pipe installed deep enough to collect waste water from the lowest part of the building and carry it at a minimum slope of ¼ inch per foot to the main sewer.

The main sewer must be at least as deep as the lower end of the house sewer and the farther the building is from the main, the deeper the main must be. The main sewer elevation is set for houses built at the zoning setback line. The main sewer is usually in the center of the street (or at the rear lot line) because this site requires the least depth of excavation when opposite houses are at approximately the same elevation (see Figure 7.1). A sewer at the rear must usually be deeper than one in the street because it is farther from the building and because the lot slopes toward the street if possible.

Because a gravity sewer must flow continually downward, it often becomes quite deep, even in level terrain, before it reaches the water pollution control plant which may be many miles away. Unlike a storm drain, the sanitary sewer carries grossly polluted water and cannot discharge its contents to the nearest body of water or gully. It may become very deep and expensive if it cuts through a hill.

Pressure Sewers

An alternative is to collect the sewage at the end of a gravity sewer and pump it under pressure through a pipe called a *force main* or *pressure sewer* to another gravity line (see Figure 7.2). The force main is constructed and tested the same way as a waterline. In the 4- and 6-inch sizes common in subdivisions, plastic, asbestos-cement, or ductile iron pipe is usually used. A gravity sewer must be installed parallel with the force main for service connections because service lines are not connected to the force main. Most designers try to avoid pumping because of the continuous power costs; the consequences of a power failure; and the higher maintenance, repair, and replacement expenses.

Service Lines

Tee or wye fittings are installed as part of the main sewer at points where service lines will be connected when houses are built. These must be fitted with watertight plugs to keep ground water out of the main sewer and soil out of the fitting. If pavement is to be built over the sewer before houses can be connected, service lines are installed from the main far enough to clear the pavement and their trenches are backfilled. The ends must be watertight. Pipe suppliers stock watertight plugs for tees or wyes and service pipes. Station and offset from the sewer are recorded so the ends can be located when the houses are built. A marker stake, preferably one that extends above the ground surface

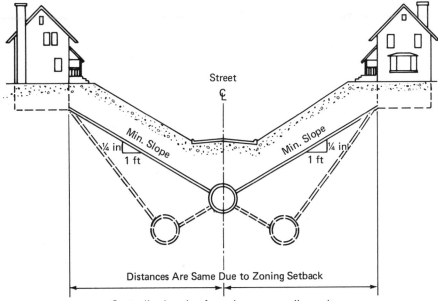

Center line location for main sewer usually results
in least trench depth for main and services.

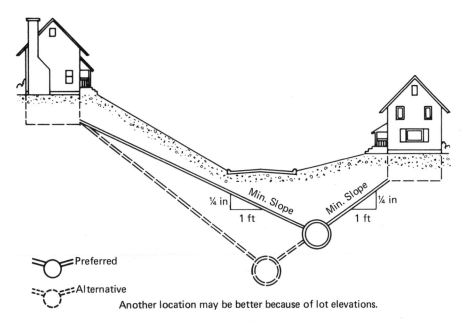

Another location may be better because of lot elevations.

FIGURE 7.1 How Main Sewer Location Affects Trench Depth.

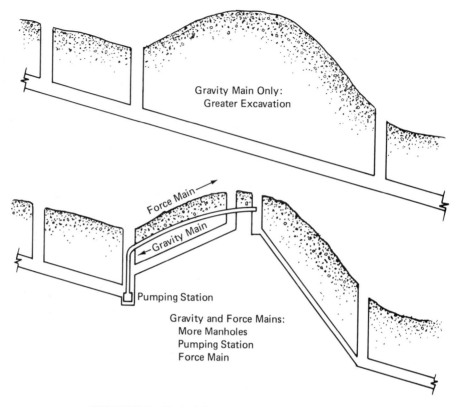

FIGURE 7.2 Typical Sewage Collection Alternatives.

and down to the fitting or pipe end and has the cut or depth to the connection point noted on it, makes location easier (see Figure 7.3).

Only waste water is allowed to enter the service line. No basement floor drains, footing drains, or roof drains are allowed to be connected.

Manholes

Access is required (via manholes) to inspect, clean, and repair the sewer main. State or subdivision regulations govern the maximum allowable spacing between manholes. Four hundred feet is a common maximum for small sewers. This spacing is about the farthest a person crouched down in a manhole could push a cleaning rod in the days when sewers were cleaned by hand. A greater length can be cleaned with modern

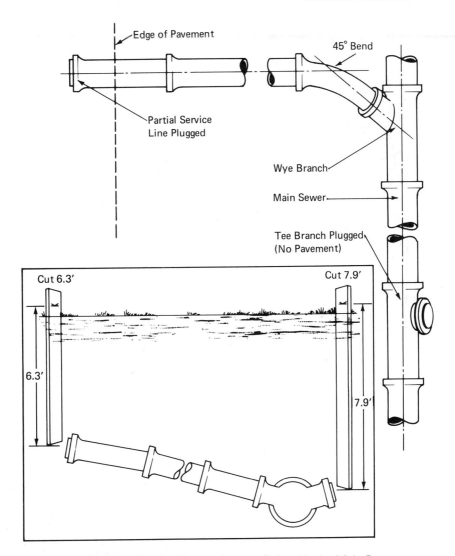

FIGURE 7.3   Service Connections as Built with the Main Sewer.

power equipment and many times no one needs to enter the manhole to do it.

The manhole is a vertical, cylindrical structure with a 4-foot inside diameter and top tapering to the size of the cast iron frame on which the cover fits (see Figure 7.4). The joint between cover and frame should be gasketed watertight if the cover is located where it can be covered with water. Manholes on street center lines are at the top of

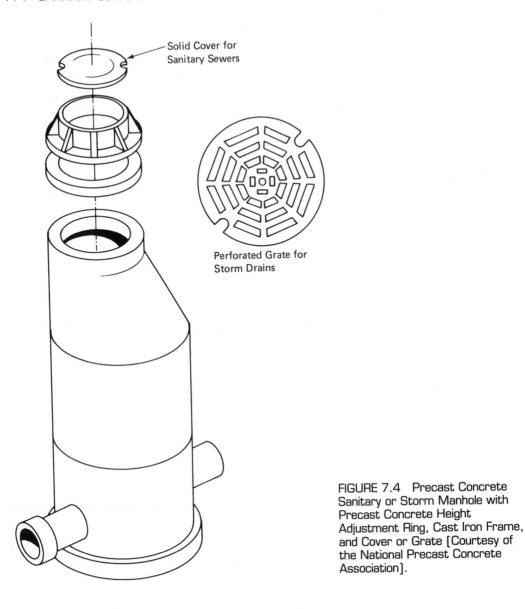

Solid Cover for
Sanitary Sewers

Perforated Grate for
Storm Drains

FIGURE 7.4 Precast Concrete
Sanitary or Storm Manhole with
Precast Concrete Height
Adjustment Ring, Cast Iron Frame,
and Cover or Grate [Courtesy of
the National Precast Concrete
Association].

the street crown and need not be watertight because water drains away
from the crown.

Manholes are built of brick or curved concrete block at the site or
are cast of reinforced concrete and brought to the site in sections ready
for installation. The first section of a precast manhole is the base which
includes a circular spread footing that encloses the bottom. Other sec-

tions are cylinders similar to large concrete pipe and are stacked above the base one on top of the other with the top one being a cone with a top the size to support the frame. The supplier determines the number and sizes of sections needed for the correct height according to the construction drawings.

Steps may be built into the walls or included in the precast sections. Some municipalities prefer to use a portable ladder. Manholes are coated on the outside with a bituminous coating to prevent the entrance of ground water. Precast manholes have tongue-and-groove joints and a butyl rubber gasket between sections.

If the manhole is built in place, a concrete spread footing is required to support its weight on the soil. A smooth channel is formed in the footing to connect incoming and outgoing pipes or the bottom half of a pipe is embedded in the footing to serve as a channel. Pipe in the shape of a trough (no top half) is manufactured for this purpose. A precast base may include a precast channel or the channel may be formed on the job in fresh concrete placed on top of the footing. The surface of the concrete should slope slightly toward the channel.

Holes are precast in the manhole walls so that pipes fit into them at correct line and grade. The precast manhole supplier determines hole locations from construction plans and profiles. On some jobs, manholes are delivered to the site with no sewer holes. The walls must be broken, pipe inserted, the hole mortared, and the gasket installed between the mortar and the pipe. Precast holes are preferred unless their locations cannot be accurately determined.

The joint between manhole and pipe must be watertight to keep ground water out of the sewer system and it must be flexible enough to allow differential settlement of the heavy manhole and the lighter pipe. See Figure 7.5 for a method used to accomplish this.

Manhole and footing may be set in place first, a laser set up inside, and pipe built upstream starting with the pipe connected to the manhole. Alternatively, pipe may be installed first leaving a gap requiring one pipe or less on each side of the manhole location.

A short vertical drop may be designed at a manhole to impart additional energy to the flowing sewage because of energy lost there. If a vertical drop is shown on the construction profile, it is built as follows: The pipe downstream from the manhole is built the usual way, centered on a laser beam from the downstream manhole. Then the upstream pipe is built centered on a beam from a laser in this manhole set up higher by the amount of the vertical drop. Each pipe is connected to the manhole centered on its beam. After the laser is removed, the

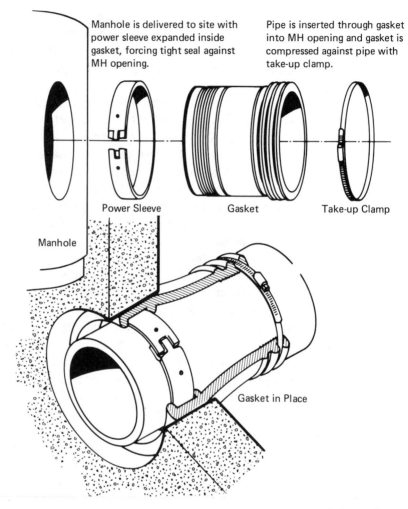

Manhole is delivered to site with power sleeve expanded inside gasket, forcing tight seal against MH opening.

Pipe is inserted through gasket into MH opening and gasket is compressed against pipe with take-up clamp.

Power Sleeve

Gasket

Take-up Clamp

Manhole

Gasket in Place

FIGURE 7.5 Pipe-to-Manhole Connection [Courtesy of Press-Seal Gasket Corporation].

channel through the manhole is built on a straight slope from one wall to the other, instead of a vertical drop, as shown in Figure 7.6.

Exfiltration/Infiltration Testing

The municipality usually requires a test to prove that the sewer joints will not allow excessive infiltration. Manholes and service lines are tested at the same time. This is an additional reason for plugging the

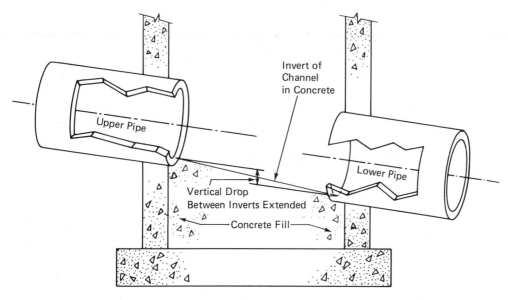

FIGURE 7.6 Pipe Construction Through a Manhole.

ends of service lines. If the line is above the water table, an *exfiltration test* may be run in which the line is filled with water and the amount that leaks out is measured (see Figure 7.7). The sewer must be plugged at two points; inflatable rubber stoppers can be used.

The sewer must be filled with water to the specified height in the manhole. The greater the height, the greater the exfiltration will be. A large amount of water is required (approximately 1800 gallons for 400 feet of 8-inch pipe and one manhole) and may not be readily available unless there is a waterline with a hydrant nearby.

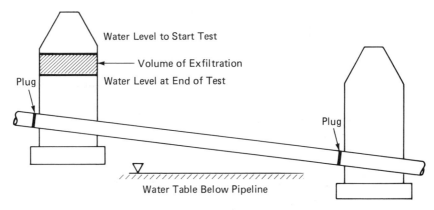

FIGURE 7.7 Exfiltration Test.

The starting water level is marked with chalk or crayon on the inside of the manhole and, after a suitable period of time for the water level to fall, the level is marked again. The missing volume has leaked through pipe joints, service line joints or plugged ends, manhole, sewer-to-manhole joints, or a crack in a pipe. If a pipe is cracked, the water level will drop quite rapidly. The trench should not be completely back-filled before testing so that it will be possible to see a concentrated leak (cracked pipe) and to repair it without excavating. However, some backfill might be needed to avoid floating the pipe (see Chapter 6).

Total leakage allowed is determined according to the pipe size and length, length of test, and the specified maximum leakage or *allowable leakage*. No additional leakage is allowed for the manhole (this practice may vary) or the plugged ends of the service lines. The allowable leakage from Appendix C, Sec. 24.8, is 200 gallons per inch of pipe diameter per mile of pipe length for a day-long or 24-hour test. Less may be allowed under the regulations of a particular municipality and more may be allowed in cases of unusual construction difficulty.

If a greater volume is missing from the manhole than the total allowable leakage, the sewer is not acceptable and the builder must repair it. If the pipe in Figure 7.7 is tested for 8 hours using the standard of Appendix C and the water level drops 9 inches, the following calculations indicate whether or not the sewer is acceptable:

Actual Exfiltration

$$M.H. \text{ Depth } \times \text{ Cross Section Area } = \text{ Volume}$$
$$0.75 \text{ ft } \times (\pi \times 4^2 \text{ ft}^2)/4 = 9.42 \text{ ft}^3$$
$$9.42 \text{ ft}^3 \times 7.48 \text{ gal/ft}^3 = 70.5 \text{ gal actual}$$

Allowable Exfiltration

$$200 \text{ gal/in. mi day } \times 8 \text{ in. } \times (400/5280) \text{ mi } \times (8/24) \text{ day}$$
$$= 40.4 \text{ gal allowed}$$

Actual > allowable ∴ unacceptable

If eight partial service lines, each 20 feet long are included in the test, the allowable exfiltration is increased by the amount determined as follows:

$$200 \text{ gal/in. mi day } \times 6 \text{ in. } \times (8 \times 20/5280) \text{ mi } \times (8/24) \text{ day}$$
$$= 12.1 \text{ gal allowed}$$

$$40.4 + 12.1 = 62.5 \text{ gal allowed}$$

Actual $>$ allowable $\therefore$ unacceptable

If the sewer is below the water table it is subjected to outside water pressure as if it were submerged in water with the surface where the water table is. Infiltration takes place and an *infiltration test* can be run by measuring the flow of water at the lower end of the section to be tested. A dam with a built-in weir can be used to measure the flow. Flow must be stopped above the section being tested by a dam or an inflatable rubber stopper at a manhole.

A weir reading is converted to flow in cubic feet per second which must be compared to the allowable flow in gallons per inch per mile per day. For a 90° vee-notch weir, the flow in cubic feet per second is $2.5\,H^{2.5}$, where H is the height of flowing water above the weir (see Figure 7.8).

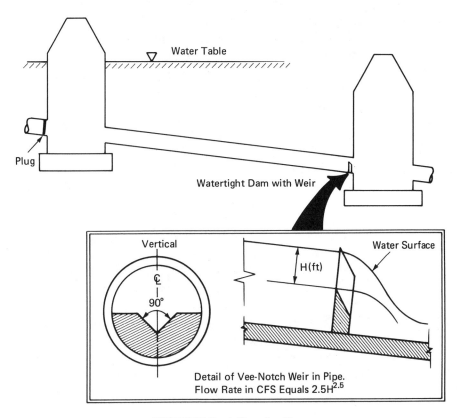

FIGURE 7.8   Infiltration Test.

If infiltration measured at the weir is 0.001 cubic foot per second for 600 feet of 24-inch sewer, the following calculations indicate whether or not the sewer is acceptable:

Actual Infiltration

$$0.001 \text{ ft}^3/\text{sec} \times 7.48 \text{ gal/ft}^3 \times (24 \times 60 \times 60) \text{ sec/day}$$
$$= 646 \text{ gal/day actual}$$

Allowable Infiltration

$$200 \text{ gal/in. mi day} \times 24 \text{ in.} \times (600/5280) \text{ mi}$$
$$= 545 \text{ gal/day allowed}$$

$$\text{Actual} > \text{allowable} \therefore \text{ unacceptable}$$

There are several ways the calculations can be made. Allowable and actual rates may be converted to the same units by any convenient means and compared.

It is difficult to measure small flows accurately with a weir and, therefore, it is difficult to test small pipes reliably this way. The water table fluctuates with the seasons and, unless the test is made when the water table is high, it is not an accurate indication of pipe joint performance.

Low-Pressure Air Test

The low-pressure air test is performed by sealing a section of sewer to be tested, subjecting it to a pressure of 3.5 pounds per square inch and determining the time for the pressure to drop one pound per square inch due to air leakage (see Figure 7.9). Air pressure is started at 4 pounds per square inch and decreases as the air cools in the pipe. (The pipe is always cooler than the compressed air.)

If the pressure stabilizes between 4 and 3.5 pounds per square inch, the test may be started. A stopwatch is used and the stabilized air pressure is noted. If the pressure loss is less than 1 pound per square inch after a time in minutes equal to 0.472 multiplied by the inside pipe diameter in inches, the sewer joints are satisfactory.

It may be necessary to run a low-pressure air test on a sewer that is below the water table. In this case, the sewer is subject to outside

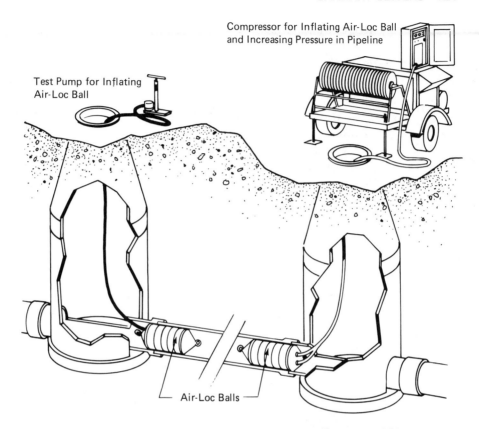

FIGURE 7.9 Low-Pressure Air Test of a Pipeline [Courtesy of Cherne Industrial, Inc.].

water pressure determined by the height of water over it. The air pressure in the sewer must be 3.5 pounds per square inch greater than outside pressure at the beginning of the test. A pressure of 1 pound per square inch is exerted by a height of 2.31 feet of water.

A small pipe is installed through the manhole wall at the top of the sewer and plugged until the test is to be run. With plug removed, a clear plastic tube is attached to the pipe at the inside of the manhole and held up to allow ground water to rise to the level of the water table. This height in feet above the top of the sewer, divided by 2.31, indicates the pressure in pounds per square inch exerted by the water on the outside of the sewer. Air pressure is built up to exceed this amount by 3.5 pounds per square inch and the test is run as previously described.

Low-pressure air tests are made quickly and need not be made at a manhole. This is a convenience for the inspector and developer. Any length of sewer can be checked immediately after installation and back-filled if it passes. This eliminates the problem of whether to backfill or leave the trench open if a section of pipeline cannot be tested that day. A disadvantage of the method is that manholes are not included in the testing.

If a test shows excessive leakage, it is usually due to one bad joint or one cracked pipe and the plugs can be used to locate the bad spot. One plug is shifted to the middle and a quick check indicates which half the bad spot is in. One half of that half is checked and the process is continued until the spot is located within a few feet.

Other Tests

A test for straightness is sometimes required using an angled mirror on a stick to reflect a sight line through the sewer, shining a flashlight through the sewer, or projecting a laser beam. The usual requirement is that the inspector's line can extend from one manhole to the next.

A more stringent requirement is that a video camera that records the entire trip be pulled through the sewer on a cable. The video may be viewed live on a screen at the surface and may also be recorded on film for a permanent record. Stations appear in a corner of the screen as the camera proceeds.

Pressurized System

A system completely under pressure is sometimes used and may be far more economical to install in hilly terrain or where bedrock or ground water are near the surface (see Figure 7.10). Each house has an enclosed tank in which sewage is collected and pumped periodically through a pressure service line to the pressurized main.

The intermittent operation of these service pumps forces the sewage through the main to a pollution control plant or to a point from which it can flow by gravity sewer to the plant. Original construction is inexpensive because the pressure lines are small and are installed at a constant, shallow depth below the surface and no manholes are needed. They are built and tested the same as waterlines. Three feet of

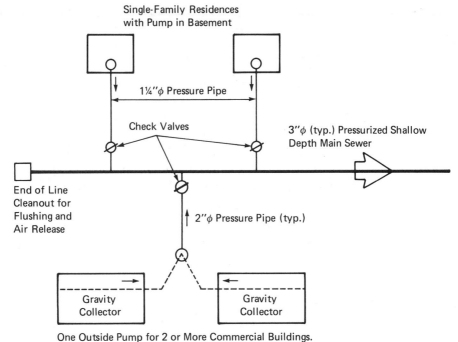

Single-Family Residences
with Pump in Basement

1¼"φ Pressure Pipe

Check Valves

3"φ (typ.) Pressurized Shallow
Depth Main Sewer

End of Line
Cleanout for
Flushing and
Air Release

2"φ Pressure Pipe (typ.)

Gravity
Collector

Gravity
Collector

One Outside Pump for 2 or More Commercial Buildings.

FIGURE 7.10   Pressurized Sewage Collection System.

cover is sufficient. Because sewage is fairly warm when it leaves a residence, there is little danger of freezing and the pipe need not be below the frost line in most climates.

REVIEW QUESTIONS

7.1. Discuss why a sanitary sewer is likely to be deeper than other pipelines.

7.2. R.O.W. width is 60 feet, zoning setback distance is 50 feet, the basement floor is 6 feet below the front yard, and the yard has a slope of 1.0 percent down to the edge of the 24-foot pavement. What is the approximate depth of the sewer trench at the pavement center line?

7.3. Building lots are 200 feet deep, zoning setback distance is 60 feet, the basement floor is 7 feet below the backyard, and the yard has a slope of 0.8 percent up to the rear property line. What is the approximate depth of the sewer trench on the back property line? Use 25 feet for the width of a house.

7.4. Give two reasons why ground water and other clean water should not be allowed in sanitary sewers.

7.5. Describe the ways ground water enters a sewer system.

7.6. What leakage is allowed per hour in 360 feet of 16-inch pipe if the allowable rate is 125 gal/in./mi/day?

7.7. If exfiltration of 250 gal/in./mi/day is allowed in 335 feet of 12-inch pipe and water level in a manhole drops 5 inches in 3 hours, is the sewer acceptable?

7.8. If infiltration of 100 gal/in./mi/day is allowed in 570 feet of 48-inch pipe and measured infiltration is 0.008 CFS, is the sewer acceptable?

7.9. What is the starting pressure for a low-pressure air test of a sewer with the water table 6 feet above it?

7.10. What is the maximum length of time for a low-pressure air test of a 15-inch sewer that is 400 feet long? 300 feet long?

7.11. Discuss the advantages of low-pressure air tests over exfiltration/infiltration testing.

CHAPTER 8

Storm Drainage

Storm water is removed from around buildings by grading the lots so that they slope away from the buildings toward the street or a drainage easement. Water that flows to the street is intercepted by a roadside ditch or flows over the curb and into the gutter. The pavement slopes longitudinally so that water in the gutter flows downhill until it reaches a grate through which it flows into a storm water inlet from which a pipe carries it underground to the nearest watercourse. Pavement contains a *crown* or a slope from the center to the gutter so that all rain that falls on the pavement flows to the gutter. Water that flows in an easement may flow overland to a street or watercourse or may enter a storm drain in the easement through a grate.

Design

Storm drainage facilities are designed with the expectation that they will be overloaded at times. An acceptable frequency of overloading called the *design frequency* is selected. The facility is designed for the greatest storm of this frequency called the *design storm.* Any greater storm overloads the facility and causes some flooding. Rainfall intensity-duration-frequency tables or graphs based on statistical analysis of past rainfall gaging records are used to determine a design rate of flow.

Design frequencies are selected on the basis of a comparison between the cost of the expected inconvenience and damage from overloading and the cost of building a larger facility to obtain less frequent overloading. It is not economical to try to build facilities large enough so that they are never overloaded. Design frequencies for residential subdivisions vary from 5 to 25 years and may be specified by subdivision regulations. It is estimated that drainage structures will be overloaded an average of once per design period.

Overloading the drainage system in a residential subdivision means that some streets and intersections will be flooded for several hours during and after a rainstorm. It may be bad enough so that streets cannot be used for some time. Some basements or garages may even be flooded. The cost of ever larger drainage facilities is weighed against the benefits obtained by reducing the frequency of flooding until a balance is reached between cost and benefits. The cost must not exceed the value of the benefits.

Splashing water is hazardous to traffic and a nuisance to pedestrians. Two requirements are in common use to avoid deep water in traveled areas of the pavement. Water flowing in the gutters is prevented from entering intersections by storm water inlets at the uphill sides of all intersections. Inlets are spaced about 400 feet apart between intersections depending on the maximum spacing allowed by subdivision regulations.

General Standards

Drains are of 12-inch or 15-inch minimum size allowed and are provided with a minimum of 3 or 3½ feet of cover, depending on the subdivision regulations. Drains are sometimes built in the center of the street with manholes to which water is delivered by branch drains running from inlets at the gutters. As an alternative, which is less expensive, the drain is built from inlet to inlet along one side of the street and water from inlets on the opposite side of the street is carried by branch drains to the inlets on the main drain. See Figure 8.1 for sketches of the two systems.

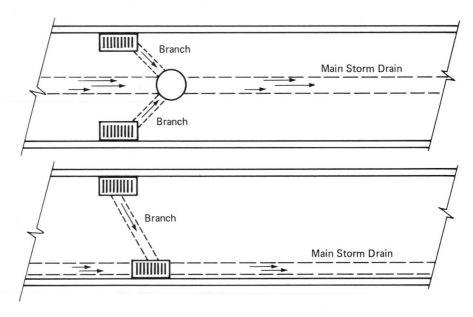

FIGURE 8.1   Typical Layouts of Street Drainage Systems.

Water from roof drains and footing drains should be run to a storm water inlet unless it can be disposed of elsewhere without causing a nuisance. It can be piped to a tee or wye connection in the storm drain similar to the sanitary sewer connections described in Chapter 7. Storm drains should not be broken open to connect pipes.

Clean water is never allowed in sanitary sewers even if it must be pumped to reach the elevation of the storm drain. Avoiding the possibility of such pumping is one of the advantages of designing streets lower than adjoining lots. Some subdivision regulations require a storm water inlet or other connection to be available at each lot for drainage of roof or ground water.

Inlet Grates

A storm water inlet includes a grate and frame, structure, and connection to a drain. Typical grates for two different shaped curbs are shown in Figure 8.2. Water is admitted through the curb and gutter. The curb box or curb hood forms a continuation of the concrete, asphalt, or stone curb. The grate and box are held in place by a frame that is seated on the inlet structure. The box is often adjustable to match the curb height and is available to match any curb cross-section. Grates for use where traffic at the gutter is too heavy to be supported by a grate are made with no grate extending into the gutter and opening in the side of the curb. Flat grates with no curb box are available for use in drainage easements.

One of the requirements of a curbside grate is that its hydraulic capacity match that of the drain. If several inlets, including all inlets upstream, lead to one drain they should together admit the rate of flow the drain is designed for.

The grate openings should allow small objects that will not block the drain to pass through, but should hold back those that could block or partially block the drain. The grate openings should be small enough or oriented in such a direction that they do not catch bicycle wheels but allow them to cross safely.

The grate should have the strength to carry heavy traffic and the durability to resist corrosion from street salt and other contaminants and to resist erosion due to grit. Frames and grates are made of cast iron, ductile iron, or galvanized steel. Grate sizes for residential streets are on the order of 2 feet parallel with the curb by 1½ feet.

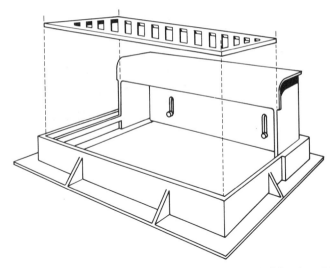

Diagonal ''bicycle safe'' openings,
for vertical curb (adjustable height
curb box); rectangular frame for
rectangular structure.

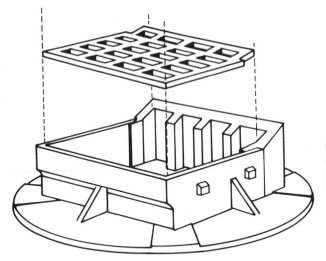

Rectangular openings, for rolled
curb; round frame for round
Rectangular openings, for rolled curb;
round frame for round structure.

FIGURE 8.2   Typical Storm Water Frames and Grates.

The frame and grate, which are flush with each other, may be depressed slightly below the pavement or built flush with the pavement, depending on the municipality's standards. A depression is desirable on steep slopes to slow the water so that more of it enters the inlet, but is not needed on flat slopes. A depression on flat slopes tends to collect debris and plug the inlet because of the slow velocity; but on steep slopes, where water velocity is greater, it does not collect debris provided some water flows by to carry the debris. Traffic, especially bicycles and high speed traffic, near the curb could be hampered by depressions.

The usual practice for slow-moving residential street traffic is to install the grate level even though the curb and gutter slope. The center of the grate is set at or slightly below the elevation of the gutter. This provides a little drop at the uphill edge of the grate and a flat area for the water to pond momentarily, which increases the flow into the inlet.

The grate should be covered after the inlet is finished so that construction waste does not enter. This is especially important during paving when asphalt or portland cement concrete will fall through the grate unless it is covered. Pavement is placed right up to the frame so the temporary cover should fit snugly with no extension beyond the frame. The grate can be left off and the cover substituted temporarily. The temporary cover is usually cut from plywood, fiberboard, or whatever material is available.

Inlet Structures

The inlet structure is often made from the same mold as precast concrete manholes (see Figure 7.4) or built with the same curved concrete block as built-in-place manholes having 4-foot inside diameters. They are also made in rectangles of various sizes. Rectangular structures should be of reinforced concrete.

The sides of rectangular structures are subject to tension toward the inside surface due to horizontal earth pressure, and concrete block walls have no appreciable resistance to tensile stress. Concrete blocks reinforced with wire mesh at the horizontal joints or nonreinforced precast or poured concrete boxes may be used for shallow inlets.

The concrete structure is installed a little lower than needed so that when the frame is set it can be shimmed with brick or small concrete block to the correct elevation. The frame may rest on the brick but the space between structure and frame must be mortared so that it is watertight. If, through field error, the grate is installed slightly low there is no great harm caused. However, if the grate is even the slightest amount higher than the finished pavement will be, it cannot be left that way or it will not serve its purpose (to allow surface water to enter). Concrete must be chiseled or sawed from the top of the structure to lower the frame and grate and this is expensive work.

Structures made of galvanized corrugated steel are sometimes used with corrugated steel pipes. The structure is a section of pipe 4 feet in diameter or of another specified diameter, delivered to the job with pipe stubs welded at the openings in correct locations to connect to the drains. The connections of pipes to inlet are very efficiently made. A concrete footing is used and the frame with grate may be bolted to the galvanized steel or installed on a concrete pad at the top of the structure.

Catch Basins

A *catch basin* is an inlet structure with a sump below the pipe or pipes for the purpose of causing sand and gravel to settle by slowing the velocity of the water. The usual storm water inlet at the end of a drain has the bottom partially filled with concrete to form a smooth surface, entirely sloping toward the outgoing drain. The usual inlet with a drain passing through has a smooth channel formed in the bottom of the structure. The purpose of a smooth channel is to keep debris of any kind moving with the water.

The flow of water in a storm drain varies quickly when rain stops, from a full pipe with the capacity to carry and bounce large gravel to a trickle that leaves the gravel where it settles. The gravel and smaller particles may eventually reduce the capacity to an unacceptable rate of flow or plug it altogether. This heavy material is expensive to remove from a pipeline.

The purpose of catch basins is to catch the heavy material where it is easier to remove—in the sump under a removable grate where it is accessible to a clam shell bucket or suction hose. The sump (2 feet deep or more is typical) increases the cost of the inlet and should not be built unless the extra cost is justified (see Figure 8.3).

Catch basins are mosquito-breeding sites between rainstorms and may be the source of objectionable odors. Cleaning them involves a recurring expense that could outweigh the expense of the infrequent drain cleaning that would otherwise be required. If a catch basin, once built, is determined not to be needed, it is simply left uncleaned and

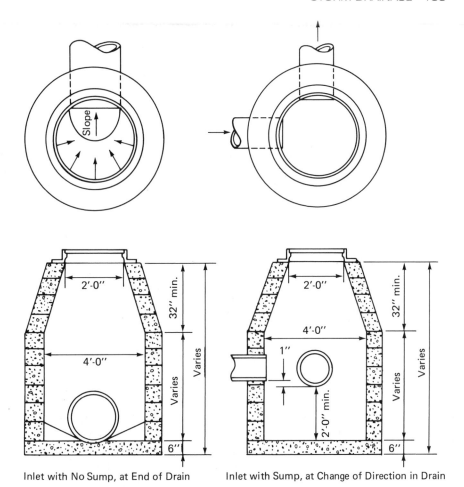

Inlet with No Sump, at End of Drain   Inlet with Sump, at Change of Direction in Drain

FIGURE 8.3 Typical Storm Water Inlets (Concrete Block).

the sump fills up eliminating the mosquito and odor problem and causing no harm to the structure.

Catch basins are useful downhill from unpaved streets or gravelly areas, especially in localities of sudden, intense rainstorms that are capable of carrying large particles and dropping them when the rain stops. An inlet followed by a steep drain is less likely to need a sump than one followed by a drain on a flat slope because the swifter flow of water in the steep drain carries larger particles. Therefore, a flat section of drain downstream is more likely to collect debris. If there is no sump, grate openings should be small enough to keep large particles out and no curb opening should be provided unless it is grated. To avoid reduction in the capacity of the grate to admit water, a larger grate and, therefore, a larger structure may be needed.

Drains

Pipelines for carrying storm water (known as *drains*) are gravity lines and are constructed for gravity flow. However, at times they will flow under the pressure of inlets full of water because they are designed to be overloaded at the design frequency. If pipe joints and pipe-to-inlet connections are not watertight, water will be forced out of the pipe into the bedding where it might develop its own channel through the permeable bedding material and eventually carry away enough particles to undermine the pipe.

The purpose of storm drains is to remove surface water, not ground water. *Infiltration* or ground water that enters at the joint between structure and frame, at the pipe-to-inlet joint, or through joints in the drain takes up part of the carrying capacity of the drain that is intended to be available to carry storm water runoff. Some municipalities require these joints to be as watertight as those for sanitary sewers. However, many do not.

Infiltration, which also occurs in sanitary sewers, results in soil particles being carried into the inlet or drain and, over a period of time, undermining pavement. In the older parts of some cities, most inlets have broken pavement or curbs around them because of undermining. Occasionally, a vehicle breaks through pavement that can no longer bridge the gap and the vehicle settles into a hollowed-out cavern.

Alternative Systems

Where soil is sufficiently permeable, storm water can be disposed of in the soil through *seepage pits* or *dry wells* which are a variation of the storm water inlet. They are built in the same locations as storm water inlets and have the same frames and grates. However, the structure, of precast concrete, concrete block, or galvanized corrugated steel, has holes in the sides, no bottom other than a footing, no pipe outlet, and is normally larger than an inlet structure. They are built in the same way as seepage pits for sewage disposal shown in Figure 10.7.

The structure is built with sufficient wall and bottom area for water to seep into the soil at a fast rate and sufficient volume to hold the runoff from the design storm while seepage takes place. Spacing, depth, and diameter of these pits are based on *percolation rate* (vertical movement of water through the soil), *permeability* (horizontal movement of water through the soil), and on location of the water table. The subject is discussed in more detail in Chapter 10 under "Seepage Pits."

In certain cases, this system is substantially less expensive than piping the storm water and it has the added advantage of recharging the ground water (see the discussion under "Detention Basins" in this chapter).

A similar method of disposing of storm water is to carry it in drains from standard storm water inlets to a large open pit. The pit, called a *ground water recharge basin* or *percolation pond,* is designed on the same basis as seepage pits—recharge area and holding volume. Storm water runoff carries fine soil particles that will eventually plug the soil of the recharge basin or the seepage pits. Both must be cleaned periodically by raking—a difficult task in the case of the seepage pits.

The recharge basin holds water for some time after a rainstorm and must be fenced and locked as a safety precaution. Subdivision regulations may require bushes to screen the view because the large pit (typically occupying a full building lot) may not be considered compatible with residential living.

Drainage Basins

A *drainage basin,* sometimes called a *watershed,* is the area that slopes downward to one point and, therefore, is the area from which storm water runoff flows to that point. Every point on the ground has its own unique drainage basin; therefore, locations for storm water inlets should be carefully selected. Each inlet has a unique drainage basin for which it should be designed. Each runoff drain also has its own drainage basin made up of inlet drainage basins. The direction of overland water flow is perpendicular to contour lines and, therefore, lines separating basins are parallel and perpendicular to contour lines (see Figure 8.4).

Each subdivision is located on a drainage basin or basins that are part of larger basins and its development influences and is influenced by other developments within those basins. Common law and common sense and sometimes subdivision regulations dictate that a developer may not change natural storm water drainage to the detriment of other property owners.

Upstream development should not increase runoff to the detriment of lower properties and lower properties should allow a reasonable rate of runoff to flow through. A municipality may require one developer to slow the rate of runoff to protect lower property and another may be required to provide drainage facilities larger than

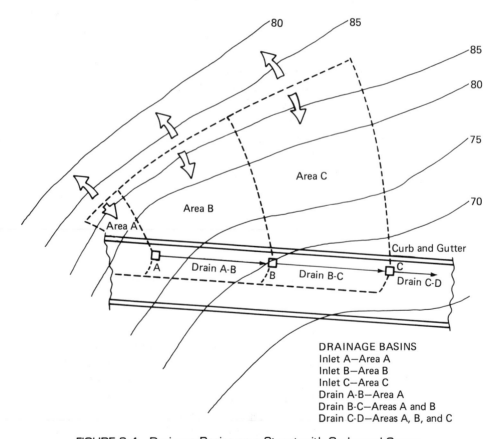

DRAINAGE BASINS
Inlet A—Area A
Inlet B—Area B
Inlet C—Area C
Drain A-B—Area A
Drain B-C—Areas A and B
Drain C-D—Areas A, B, and C

FIGURE 8.4   Drainage Basins on a Street with Curbs and Crown.

needed within that development in order to handle the flow of water from a development upstream.

Detention Basins

Rain evaporates, percolates into the ground, or runs off over the ground surface. The portion that runs off from natural terrain is often on the order of 10 percent. Subdivision development increases the quantity that runs off to 30 or 50 percent by greatly reducing the portion that enters the soil although slightly increasing the amount that evaporates.

Roofs and pavement built where grass and trees once were accomplish most of this. In addition, rough ground and depressions that held the rainwater, allowing more percolation and reducing the total amount of runoff as well as its velocity, are replaced by compacted, smoothly sloping lawns.

The increased total volume and velocity mean that a larger quantity arrives downstream from the developed area when it rains and it arrives sooner than it did before development. Runoff that used to arrive after rainfall from the immediate area had left now arrives at the same time, overloading drainage facilities and possibly flooding properties.

Some subdivision regulations prohibit the developer from discharging water from the subdivision at a greater rate of flow (cubic feet per second) than existed before development. Unless ground water recharge is feasible, the only way to avoid doing this is by detaining the water in a *detention basin* and releasing it at a rate no greater than the allowed rate.

If the basin contains a permanent pool that is enlarged temporarily each time it receives runoff, it is called a *retention* basin. This usage is not standardized and the terms are sometimes used interchangeably. Either basin performs the function of returning more water to the ground than if the water flowed freely and might be considered a recharge basin. A retention basin returns more to the ground. In areas of low ground water, recharging the ground water may be its main purpose. Lowering of the water table is a serious problem in many areas and one of the causes of it is the increase in runoff due to development. In many cases, the production of water supply wells is decreased and, in rare cases, the ground surface settles because of the lack of ground water.

A natural bowl-shaped basin with a narrow outlet is the ideal site for one of these basins. A small dam is built to hold back the water and a pipe having a carrying capacity no greater than the rate of flow allowed downstream is installed under the dam. No matter how rapidly water reaches the basin by overland, stream, or pipe flow, it can leave at no greater rate than the capacity of the outgoing pipe.

If there is to be no permanent pool, the pipe is installed at ground level, the same as any other culvert. The area behind the dam will be flooded occasionally for short periods of time and can be used as a recreation area at other times.

If a permanent pool is desired, an intake tower is built at the upstream end of the pipe with the opening at the low water level desired for the permanent pool. The water will fall below this level during a dry spell unless a permanent stream flows into the pool. A permanent pool should not be planned without a continuously flowing stream because it will become stagnant between rainstorms (see Figure 8.5).

Culverts

A *culvert* is a short storm drain laid at ground level with an embankment built over it. Culverts are often needed in subdivision development to carry streams under streets or to carry ditch flow under driveways. They are bedded and backfilled as discussed in Chapter 6 for projecting pipes.

If a natural stream is to be piped it is important that the upper and lower ends of the culvert coincide with the stream bed. If either end is low, the stream will deposit soil in the culvert and if either end is high, the stream will undermine that end. Changing the course of a stream to suit a desired culvert location is likely to result in a washout of the embankment or stream bank.

The embankment is protected at each end by rip rap, gabion, or a concrete wall. Aluminum pipe should not be placed in contact with a portland cement concrete wall because of the corrosive chemical reaction between the two materials. Aluminum reacts with lime in the concrete to create hydrogen gas, increasing voids in the concrete and sub-

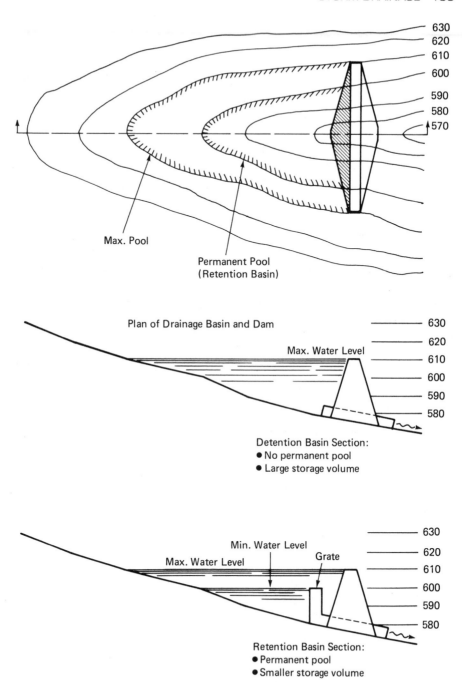

FIGURE 8.5 Storage of Storm Water Runoff.

stantially reducing concrete strength. A layer of building paper is sufficient separation.

Corrugated metal pipe is often used for culverts and, as with any flexible pipe, it is important that initial backfill be brought up evenly on both sides to prevent any imbalance and that it be well compacted to provide strength.

The upper end of a culvert or storm drain that encloses a natural stream may have to be protected with a large grate called a *trash rack*. It is built across the opening like a fence, of timber or structural steel, with vertical posts imbedded in concrete and horizontal rails spaced to catch debris considered too large for the conduit.

Streams carry trees, logs, stumps, and other trash at times of high water. The trash rack is intended to stop things of this type and should let leaves and sticks pass through. It should stop boulders but not gravel. If openings are too small they are plugged with debris much of the time and prevent the free flow of water.

The trash rack is subject to heavy shock loads when hit by debris. The magnitude of the loads is difficult to estimate. A logical assumption is that the maximum load on the trash rack takes place if it is completely plugged and water has backed up and is flowing over the top. The entire area is then subject to unbalanced hydrostatic pressure and this is probably the greatest load it can receive. If the trash rack is cleared of debris on a regular basis, it will never be subjected even to that load.

REVIEW QUESTIONS

8.1. Discuss the requirements of a storm water grate.

8.2. Discuss the factors to consider before deciding whether to include a sump in the storm water inlets.

8.3. How does the expected street traffic affect the choice of a grate and the elevation of the grate?

8.4. Explain why inlet structures are usually round in horizontal cross-section.

8.5. Why is the inlet structure never installed slightly high, although it can be slightly low?

8.6. What are the four types of construction used for storm water inlets?

8.7. At what points does water pass from the seepage pits or dry wells to the soil?

8.8. Explain ways in which development increases runoff.

8.9. Explain how a retention or detention basin decreases the rate or magnitude of runoff. It also decreases the total volume of runoff. Explain this.

8.10. Explain how to backfill at the sides of a culvert (or any large flexible pipe).

8.11. Explain the purpose of a trash rack.

CHAPTER 9

Waterlines

Waterlines carry water from a storage tank to be withdrawn through small service lines leading to each house. They follow the finished surface with a specified depth of cover over the top of the pipe to protect it from traffic or from freezing or both. Water in the waterline is likely to have a temperature of about 55°F and in small pipes freezes solid fairly easily if surrounded by frozen soil. In northern climates, waterlines are placed below the normal frost line. Four- or 6-inch pipes are the smallest permitted and subdivision waterlines are seldom larger than 20 inches. Ductile iron and plastic pipe are probably the most common in subdivisions. A waterline intersection and appurtenances are shown in Figure 9.1.

Design

High points, low points, and any dead ends along the waterline are fitted with valved blowoff pipes of small size. Dissolved air in the water is released in the line and collects at high points where it obstructs the flow of water. The air pocket is released periodically by opening the blowoff until a steady flow of water indicates the air is gone.

There is always some sediment in the water and it settles at low points in the line and at dead ends. That reduces the capacity of the line and causes the water to become dirty if disturbed by a surge in the flow as at the time of a fire. Dead ends are usually prohibited, unless they cannot be avoided, because of the sediment and because the water develops a flat taste. Both are due to the fact that the water has very little movement. The sediment is flushed periodically by opening the blowoff until the flow of water is clear. Often hydrants rather than blowoffs are placed at the points where flushing is needed and are used for flushing.

Valves are needed in waterlines to shut off the flow of water to sections needing repair. They are installed at each intersection as well as spaced at 800 feet maximum so that any block can be isolated and water service continued beyond the block (see Figure 9.2).

Several kinds of valves may be used but the gate valves shown in Figure 9.1 are the most common. A valve is needed on the branch line to the hydrant to shut off flow if hydrant repairs are needed.

Hydrants are installed near each street intersection as well as

145

FIGURE 9.1   Intersecting Waterlines and Appurtenances (Courtesy of
Mueller Company, Decatur, Illinois)

spaced at 600 feet maximum. They are set at side property lines for
aesthetic reasons and to avoid possible conflict with a driveway.

General Construction

Pipe and all appurtenances should be kept clean while stored alongside
the trench and while being installed. They are going to be in contact
with drinking water. Loose dirt should be removed from inside before
the pipe is lowered into the trench. If pipes or appurtenances are in
standing water or otherwise subjected to unusual contamination, the
insides should be swabbed with a chlorine solution before they are lowered into the trench.

Open ends of installed pipe should be closed when pipe laying is

Four valves at each intersection—each line can be shut off without affecting other service.

Acceptable

Three valves—each line can be shut off without affecting other service at reduced cost.

Best

Three valves—middle line cannot be shut off without shutting off all lines.

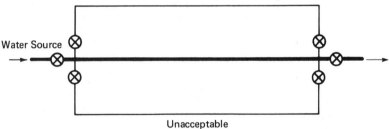

Unacceptable

FIGURE 9.2   Values for Three Water Mains Serving Subdivision Blocks.

not in progress to prevent any contaminants, including trench water or animals, from entering the pipe. As pipe laying proceeds, the pipe is backfilled enough to prevent its flotation if the trench becomes flooded; but all joints, fittings, and valves are left exposed for testing as described in this chapter under ''Waterline Testing.''

Flowing water forced to change direction exerts a force (*centrifugal force*) against the surface that turns it toward a new direction. For pipelines, that surface is the pipe wall at the outside of the bend. The force is greater for larger pipes, for greater velocity, for greater change in direction, and for more abrupt change in direction.

Because the usual pipe joints are not designed to resist a longitudinal pull, they could eventually be pulled open because of the centrifugal force. A *thrust block* of concrete is poured between the pipe and undisturbed trench wall to transfer the centrifugal force of the water against the pipe to the earth alongside the trench. Figure 9.3 shows where thrust blocks are needed. A type of pipe called *anchoring* pipe, which resists opening of the joints, or tie rods welded to the pipe across the joints may be used.

Waterline direction is changed by the installation of a fitting called a *bend* or *elbow* shown in Figure 9.4. Bends have the same kind of joint as the straight pipe they connect and they are installed in the same way. The change in direction is rather abrupt and not always suitable.

Waterlines may be "curved" gradually to follow the curve of street pavement. The cost of bends is saved and the pipeline is then easy to locate by offset distance from the curb when repairs are necessary. The "curve" is made of straight sections of pipe with deflections at each joint so that a curve is approximated. Manufacturers provide tables of maximum allowable deflections for each type of pipe and joint. A sample table is shown in Figure 9.5. Joints are designed so that they do not leak when deflected up to this amount.

In calculating joint deflections for pipeline curves, an angle of 80 percent of the manufacturer's listed maximum should be used to allow for the inaccuracies of construction methods. Seldom do full-length pipes and 80 percent of the listed deflection angle result in a satisfactory pipe curve. Usually, the angle must be smaller or the pipe must be cut to shorter lengths. Typical calculations follow.

Example 9.1

$$8 \text{ in. pipe} \quad R = 350 \text{ ft} \quad \Delta = 35°$$

$$\max \phi = 0.80 \times 5° = 4°$$

$$N = \frac{35°}{4°} = 8.75 \text{ (use 9)}$$

$$\phi = \frac{35}{9} = 3.89°$$

$$N - \ell = 8$$

$$\ell = 2 \times 350 \tan \frac{3.89°}{2} = 23.77 \text{ ft}$$

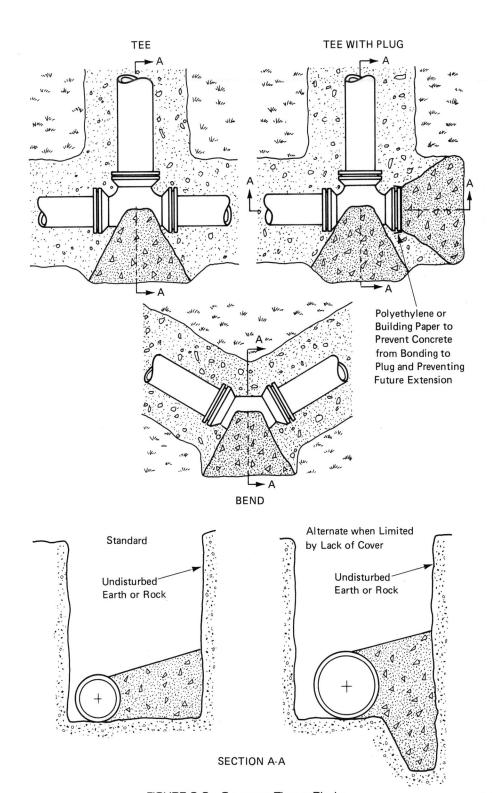

TEE

TEE WITH PLUG

Polyethylene or
Building Paper to
Prevent Concrete
from Bonding to
Plug and Preventing
Future Extension

BEND

Standard

Undisturbed
Earth or Rock

Alternate when Limited
by Lack of Cover

Undisturbed
Earth or Rock

SECTION A-A

FIGURE 9.3   Concrete Thrust Blocks.

149

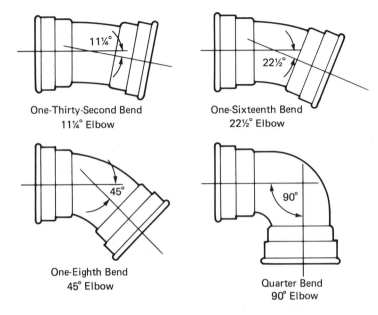

One-Thirty-Second Bend
11¼° Elbow

One-Sixteenth Bend
22½° Elbow

One-Eighth Bend
45° Elbow

Quarter Bend
90° Elbow

FIGURE 9.4 Typical Water Line Bends.

but maximum pipe length is 20 ft (from table); use 20 ft pipe lengths

$$\phi = 2 \tan^{-1} \frac{\ell}{2R} = 3.27°$$

use eight pieces of pipe 20 ft long and nine deflections of 3.27°

Example 9.2

$$14 \text{ in. pipe} \quad R = 360 \text{ ft} \quad \Delta = 16°$$

$$\max \phi = 0.80 \times 3° = 2.4°$$

$$N = \frac{16}{2.4} = 6.67 \text{ (use 7)}$$

$$\phi = \frac{16}{7} = 2.29°$$

$$N - 1 = 6$$
$$\ell = 2 \times 360 \tan \frac{2.29°}{2} = 14.39 \text{ ft}$$

use six pieces of pipe 14′-4″ long and seven deflections of 2.29°

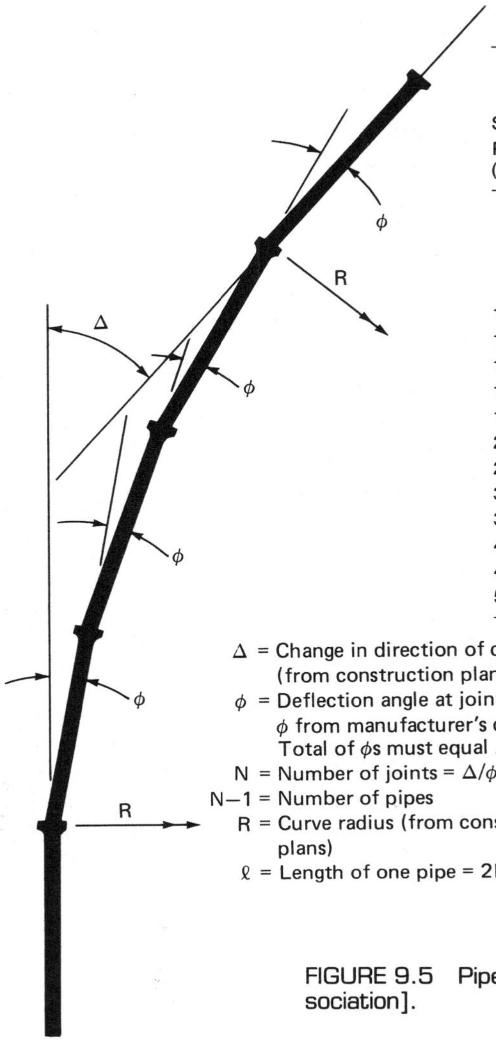

MAXIMUM DEFLECTION FULL-LENGTH PIPE PUSH-ON-TYPE JOINT PIPE

Size of Pipe In. (mm)	Deflection Angle Deg.	Maximum Deflection In. (mm)		Approx. Radius of Curve Produced by Succession of Joints—ft. (m)	
		18-ft. length (5.5 m)	20-ft. length (6.1 m)	18-ft. length (5.5 m)	20-ft. length (6.1 m)
3 (76)	5°	19 (483)	21 (533)	205 (62)	230 (70)
4 (102)	5°	19 (483)	21 (533)	205 (62)	230 (70)
6 (152)	5°	19 (483)	21 (533)	205 (62)	230 (70)
8 (203)	5°	19 (483)	21 (533)	205 (62)	230 (70)
10 (254)	5°	19 (483)	21 (533)	205 (62)	230 (70)
12 (305)	5°	19 (483)	21 (533)	205 (62)	230 (70)
14 (356)	3°	11 (279)	12 (305)	340 (104)	380 (116)
16 (406)	3°	11 (279)	12 (305)	340 (104)	380 (116)
18 (457)	3°	11 (279)	12 (305)	340 (104)	380 (116)
20 (508)	3°	11 (279)	12 (305)	340 (104)	380 (116)
24 (610)	3°	11 (279)	12 (305)	340 (104)	380 (116)
30 (762)	3°	11 (279)	12 (305)	340 (104)	380 (116)
36 (914)	3°	11 (279)	12 (305)	340 (104)	380 (116)
42 (1,067)	2°	7.5 (191)	8 (203)	510 (155)	570 (174)
48 (1,219)	2°	7.5 (191)	8 (203)	510 (155)	570 (174)
54 (1,372)	1.5°	5.5 (140)	6 (152)	680 (207)	760 (232)

Δ = Change in direction of curve (from construction plans)

ϕ = Deflection angle at joints (max. ϕ from manufacturer's catalog) Total of ϕs must equal Δ

N = Number of joints = Δ/ϕ

N−1 = Number of pipes

R = Curve radius (from construction plans)

ℓ = Length of one pipe = 2R tan $\phi/2$

FIGURE 9.5 Pipeline Curve Table [Courtesy of the Ductile Iron Pipe Research Association].

151

Each pipe is first assembled in a straight line and then the joint is deflected by moving the free end laterally a predetermined distance laid off with an ordinary rule perpendicular to the original pipe position. The offset distance is calculated as the tangent of the deflection angle multiplied by the pipe length. After a pipe has been deflected, the next pipe is joined and deflected the same way. The deflection distances listed in Figure 9.5 are for the pipe lengths and angles listed. Deflection distances for the field must be calculated using the actual pipe length and angle decided on. Deflection distances for the previous two examples follow.

Example 9.3

$$\text{Deflection distance} = 20 \text{ ft tan } 3.27° = 1.14 \text{ ft or } 13.7 \text{ in.}$$

Example 9.4

$$\text{Deflection distance} = 14.39 \text{ ft tan } 2.29° = 0.58 \text{ ft or } 6.9 \text{ in.}$$

A combination of sections of pipe and bends may be used to approximate a sharp curve. Standard bend angles are 90°, 45°, 22½°, and 11¼° called one quarter, one eighth, one sixteenth, and one thirty-second bends for ductile iron pipe; and 45° and 3° for plastic truss pipe and solid-wall plastic pipe. Allowable deflections at joints between bends and pipe are the same as for the same type of joint between pipes.

Valves are somewhat heavier for their bearing area than the pipe is and may be set on small concrete footings to prevent unequal settling unless soil is very firm. A removable long-stemmed key is used to open and shut valves from the ground surface. A hollow metal or plastic cylinder, called a *valve box,* is set so that it rests on the valve and extends to the surface to provide an opening to operate the valve. It is sealed at the top with a screw-on cap flush with the pavement or ground. Valve and valve box are shown in Figure 9.1.

Hydrant Construction

Because of the great weight of a hydrant for its small bearing area, the hydrant may settle more than the pipe over the years and snap the pipe. To prevent this, the hydrant is set into or on a concrete spread footing.

After being used, a hydrant is full of stagnant water which may pollute the water supply or freeze and break the hydrant. The hydrant is equipped with a drain hole that opens to the soil when the hydrant valve to the waterline is closed. Unless the soil is very permeable, a pit must be available under the hydrant to hold one hydrant full of water until it drains away through the soil.

The pit is filled with coarse aggregate that has sufficient void space to hold the water. The entire pit should be lined with permeable fabric and the top of the pit covered with it to prevent soil from creeping into the voids. If the drain hole is below the water table, it should be plugged and the hydrant will have to be pumped dry after each usage.

Direction of water flow is changed from horizontal to vertical to reach the hydrant; therefore, a concrete thrust block is installed behind the hydrant. It is important for appearance that the hydrant be vertical before the thrust block is poured and also important that fresh concrete does not plug the hydrant drain nor seep into the water storage pit under the hydrant (see Figure 9.6).

Service Construction

Service lines are 3/4 inch or 1 inch in size. Copper and plastic are probably the most commonly used materials. The main waterline is tapped at an angle above the horizontal and a connection called a *corporation* that includes a *corporation stop* (valve) is threaded into the tap.

The stop remains closed until a service line is connected and extended to the property line, or other point if specified by the municipality, where it is connected to another valve called a *curb stop*. A valve box called a *curb box* is set on top of the curb stop with its cover flush with the lawn. A key with arm extending to the surface may be part of the installation. A service is shown in Figure 9.7.

A small concrete footing is often required under the curb stop to prevent unequal settling and a curve called a *gooseneck* is built in to guard against kinking the pipe and to allow some differential settling without breaking the connection.

The corporations may be factory installed or tapped and installed on the job. Factory connections are made better and are less expensive, but some crews may not get them installed in front of the future houses and facing upward. In that case, it is less expensive and, in fact, necessary to tap the pipe in the field.

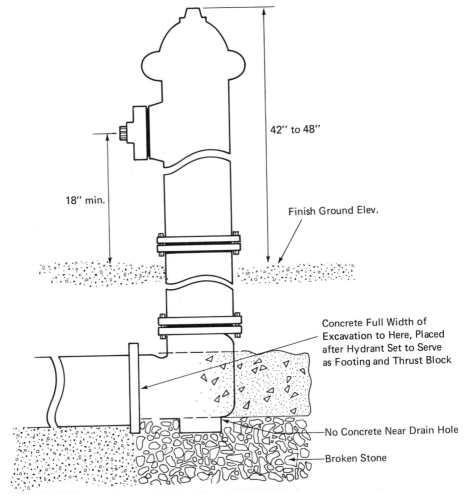

42" to 48"

18" min.

Finish Ground Elev.

Concrete Full Width of
Excavation to Here, Placed
after Hydrant Set to Serve
as Footing and Thrust Block

No Concrete Near Drain Hole

Broken Stone

FIGURE 9.6   Hydrant Installation.

Waterline Testing

The completed waterline is subjected to two tests, a pressure test and a leakage test, prescribed by the American Water Works Association. The tests are run on sections of the line separated from the rest of the system by closed valves.

A hole is drilled into the upper end of the pipe and the pipe is filled with water. Additional holes fitted with corporation cocks may

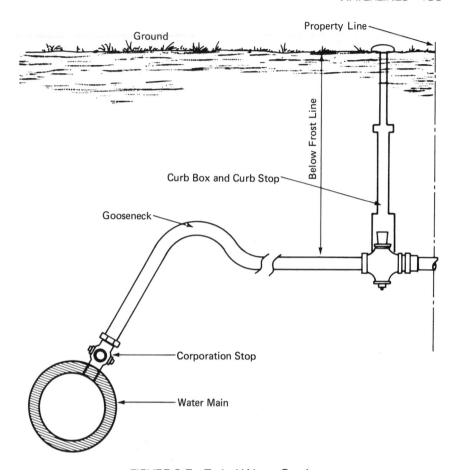

FIGURE 9.7 Typical Water Service.

be needed at high points to release all air. An air pump furnished by the developer and pressure gage furnished by the inspector are attached to the hole. Pressure specified for the tests applies at the lowest point of the line. If the gage is at a higher elevation, the gage test pressure should be less than specified test pressure by 0.433 psi for each foot difference in elevation.

The pressure test is run first in order to locate any large leaks. Pressure, which is usually one and one half times the expected operating pressure, is maintained for at least an hour. During that time, all exposed parts of the system, including joints, fittings, valves, and hydrants, are examined for leakage and all leaks are repaired.

The leakage test follows to determine whether or not the loss of water due to small, unavoidable leaks is below the specified maximum.

The leakage test runs for two hours at a specified pressure, usually the expected operating pressure. At the end of the test, the water lost is made up with a measured amount which represents the leakage. A table of allowable leakage based on pressure, pipe size, and spacing of joints is shown in Figure 9.8.

Disinfection

The waterline is disinfected after the leakage test before customers use the water. *Disinfection* means the killing of all disease-causing microorganisms, not necessarily all microorganisms. The line is first flushed from one end to the other through hydrants or taps made for the previous tests. Larger openings may be needed to maintain a flushing velocity of at least 2.5 feet per second through the pipe. This velocity will not carry chunks of clay or other large masses that may be in the line. It is adequate to remove small particles that unavoidably entered the line even though care was taken to keep the pipes clean during construction.

The velocity is calculated by using the formula $V = Q/A$. Q is the rate of flow in cubic feet per second and A is the cross-section area of the pipe. The velocity for a flow of three CFS through a 10-inch pipe is computed as follows:

$$A = \pi D^2/4 = \pi(10/12)^2 \times 1/4 = 0.545 \text{ ft}^2$$

$$V = (3 \text{ ft}^3/\text{sec})/0.545 \text{ ft}^2 = 5.5 \text{ ft/sec}$$

The velocity can be determined by collecting the discharge for a period of time. The rate of flow may then be adjusted so that the time of collection indicates the desired velocity. For example, if a 14-inch line is to be flushed and velocity determined by collecting the discharge in a 55-gallon drum, the maximum length of time to fill the drum is determined as follows:

$$A = \pi D^2/4 = \pi (14/12)^2 \times 1/4 = 1.07 \text{ ft}^2$$

$$55 \text{ gal} \times 1 \text{ ft}^3/7.48 \text{ gal} = 7.35 \text{ ft}^3$$

RECOMMENDED ALLOWABLE LEAKAGE PER 1000 FEET OF PIPELINE (Gallons per Hour)

Avg. Test Pressure PSI	Nominal Pipe Diameter, Inches																	
	2	3	4	6	8	10	12	14	16	18	20	24	30	36	42	48	54
450	0.32	0.48	0.64	0.95	1.27	1.59	1.91	2.23	2.55	2.87	3.18	3.82	4.78	5.73	6.69	7.64	8.60
400	0.30	0.45	0.60	0.90	1.20	1.50	1.80	2.10	2.40	2.70	3.00	3.60	4.50	5.41	6.31	7.21	8.11
350	0.28	0.42	0.56	0.84	1.12	1.40	1.69	1.97	2.25	2.53	2.81	3.37	4.21	5.06	5.90	6.74	7.58
300	0.26	0.39	0.52	0.78	1.04	1.30	1.56	1.82	2.08	2.34	2.60	3.12	3.90	4.68	5.46	6.24	7.02
275	0.25	0.37	0.50	0.75	1.00	1.24	1.49	1.74	1.99	2.24	2.49	2.99	3.73	4.48	5.23	5.98	6.72
250	0.24	0.36	0.47	0.71	0.95	1.19	1.42	1.66	1.90	2.14	2.37	2.85	3.56	4.27	4.99	5.70	6.41
225	0.23	0.34	0.45	0.68	0.90	1.13	1.35	1.58	1.80	2.03	2.25	2.70	3.38	4.05	4.73	5.41	6.03
200	0.21	0.32	0.43	0.64	0.85	1.06	1.28	1.48	1.70	1.91	2.12	2.55	3.19	3.82	4.46	5.09	5.73
175	0.20	0.30	0.40	0.59	0.80	0.99	1.19	1.39	1.59	1.79	1.98	2.38	2.98	3.58	4.17	4.77	5.36
150	0.19	0.28	0.37	0.55	0.74	0.92	1.10	1.29	1.47	1.66	1.84	2.21	2.76	3.31	3.86	4.41	4.97
125	0.17	0.25	0.34	0.50	0.67	0.84	1.01	1.18	1.34	1.51	1.68	2.01	2.52	3.02	3.53	4.03	4.53
100	0.15	0.23	0.30	0.45	0.60	0.75	0.90	1.05	1.20	1.35	1.50	1.80	2.25	2.70	3.15	3.60	4.05

Table is for 18-foot pipe lengths. Allowable leakage is inversely proportional to pipe length. For 20-foot lengths, multiply table value by 0.9.

FIGURE 9.8 Allowable Leakage for Ductile Iron Water Pipes [Courtesy of the Ductile Iron Pipe Research Association].

$$Q = AV$$

$$7.35 \text{ ft}^3/\text{T sec} = 1.07 \text{ ft}^2 \times 2.5 \text{ ft/sec}$$

$$T = 7.35/(1.07 \times 2.5) = 2.7 \text{ sec}$$

After flushing, the line is filled with chlorinated water which is allowed to stand for 24 hours. During that time, the chlorine, which is a very active chemical, reacts with many substances in the water in addition to being used up by killing microorganisms. At the end of 24 hours, 10 parts per million (ppm) of chlorine must remain in the water as proof that microbes have been killed without coming close to depleting the chlorine. Valves should be worked open and shut during this time to disinfect them. The proportion of remaining chlorine is determined by comparing the color of the water with the color of comparator discs.

One ppm means one part by weight of the substance (chlorine in this case) to one million parts by weight of water. A strength of 50 ppm is usually sufficient to achieve the residual 10 ppm after 24 hours. One ppm is also called *one milligram per liter*. Because of the specific weight of water (1000 grams per liter), the ratio is the same.

The weight of chlorine needed is proportional to the weight of water needed to fill the line. If 600 feet of 14-inch line is to be treated with 50 ppm, the weight of chlorine is calculated this way:

Vol of water = length × cross-section area
$$= 600 \text{ ft} \times 1.07 \text{ ft}^2 = 642 \text{ ft}^3$$

Wt of Water = Vol × Specific Wt
$$= 642 \text{ ft}^3 \times 62.4 \text{ \#/ft}^3 = 40060 \text{ lb}$$

Wt of Chlorine $= 50/1,000,000 \times 40060 \text{ lb} = 2 \text{ lb}$

Water is allowed to flow slowly through a valve from the existing system to the new pipeline. Chlorine solution is added through a corporation near the entrance point of the water. Chlorine gas may be used directly or in water solution and chlorine-bearing compounds, usually calcium hypochlorite or sodium hypochlorite, may be used in solution. The weight of compound to be added is determined by dividing the weight of chlorine required by the percentage (by weight) of available chlorine on the manufacturer's label.

After chlorination, the line is flushed with water from the existing system while valves are operated to rid them of chlorine. Flushing continues until there is no evidence (by test) of the chlorine used for disinfecting.

Bacteriological tests for coliform bacteria (indicators of the presence of sewage) and for excessive microbes of any type are made and must be negative before the water is considered suitable for human consumption.

REVIEW QUESTIONS

9.1. At what locations should water be bled from a waterline and why?

9.2. Explain how pressure tests and leakage tests are run.

9.3. What function do thrust blocks perform?

9.4. What is the purpose of a gravel-filled pit below a hydrant?

9.5. What is the velocity through an 8-inch pipe if 40 gallons of water flow in 7 seconds?

9.6. What depth of water must be collected in a drum of 3 feet in diameter in 5 seconds to indicate a velocity of 2.5 feet per second in a 10-inch pipe?

9.7. What weight of chlorine is needed for 40 ppm in 570 feet of 20-inch line?

9.8. What weight of $CaHCl_2$ at 65 percent available chlorine is needed?

CHAPTER 10

Subsurface Sewage Disposal

It may be more economical to build a subsurface sewage disposal system on each building lot than to install a sewer main and service lines. This is likely to be the case if the sewer main must be extended a great distance to connect to an existing system. Even if they do not cost less in the long run, the individual systems may be preferred because the subdivider is paid for them as houses are sold, whereas the entire sewer system must be built and financed before the first house can be sold. An alternative is to build one central subsurface sewage disposal system with sewer mains and service lines. Individual systems are discussed in this chapter. Larger systems for disposal of sewage from more than one house are designed and built on the same principles but are not discussed specifically.

Sewage Disposal Principles

Sewage includes all waste water from the house—kitchen, bathroom, and laundry. It does not include water from roof drains or footing drains. Sewage contains less than 1 percent waste material; the rest is water. However, the waste material includes *pathogenic* organisms, meaning those that cause disease. Nearly all the waste material is biologically degradable (changeable to a harmless substance by microscopic organisms or *microbes*).

Sewage water is disposed of primarily by percolation but also through evaporation and transpiration. Evaporation takes place throughout the depth of penetration by air. *Transpiration* is the passing of water through plant roots and into the air through the leaves. Both are dependent on climate and season but are significant in nearly all locations.

The soil to which sewage is discharged acts as a filter, holding back solid particles and allowing water to percolate deeper into the soil. The water is cleaned through various mechanisms in the soil, but mainly by filtering. In a very short distance (usually a matter of inches, depending on the soil) domestic sewage is cleansed and ready to be part of the ground water that is used for drinking.

If the sewage flows into the ground water, along rock crevices, or on an impervious surface such as clay or rock before it has been adequately filtered, it will not easily be filtered but might carry its organic matter and pathogenic microbes a hundred feet or more before losing its polluting ability.

Particles filtered out of the sewage must be removed or they will eventually plug the soil. They are removed by microbes that consume them, converting them to carbon dioxide and water.

Because of this biological consumption, the soil is cleaned and is able to continue to process sewage indefinitely as long as the rate of application is not too great and sufficient periods of no application are available for the microbes to keep up with their food supply. Different soils have different capacities to assimilate sewage. Some soil is, however, too fine to allow water to pass through freely enough and a few soils are too coarse to hold the organic particles back.

There are two types of microbes and two different types of decomposition. The microbes of the preceding paragraph are *aerobic*. They require oxygen and their decomposition is rapid and produces no offensive odor. *Anaerobic* microbes thrive only in the absence of oxygen and their anaerobic decomposition is comparatively slow and produces offensive odors.

If the organic material begins to plug the soil so that the aerobic microbes use up the little air that can get through, anaerobic decomposition begins with its objectionable odor. The situation can only get worse if the flow of sewage remains as great as before because anaerobic decomposition is slower than aerobic and the solid waste material in the soil will increase. Anaerobic decomposition will clean the soil in time if the sewage flow ceases. Therefore, a failed system can recover but only if it is not used.

Sewage contains enough solids to overload any soil and a settling tank is needed to collect solids before sewage is delivered to the soil. Sewage is held in the tank for at least 24 hours with very little movement, causing heavy solids to settle to the bottom and light material such as soap and grease to rise to the top.

Decomposition of such large amounts of material depletes oxygen and the process becomes anaerobic or *septic* so such a tank is called a *septic tank*. It is closed to the atmosphere because of the objectionable odor. The quantity of septic matter is reduced by anaerobic decomposition; but the accumulation of nonbiodegradable matter must be cleaned out periodically.

Septic tanks are generally made of precast concrete or concrete blocks, but are also made of fiberglass or steel coated inside and out for protection from corrosion.

General Design

The lot should be graded so that sewage can flow by gravity from the house to the subsurface disposal site. Pumping increases the cost substantially and decreases the reliability because of the possibility of pump breakdowns.

Individual disposal systems may eventually pollute the ground water or become anaerobic so that they must be replaced by a public sewer and central disposal. The pipe from house to septic tank should be located so that it can serve as part of the house sewer to a future public main sewer. If possible, the future sewer location should be planned between lots rather than in the street where pavement removal and replacement will be required. If subsurface disposal and future sewer must be at opposite ends of the house, original plumbing should be installed to facilitate the changeover.

The daily quantity of sewage is proportional to the number of people living in a house and is determined for design by multiplying the number of people by the design figure of gallons per person per day. This figure varies from 75 to 100 in different areas, depending on state or local government regulations. Because the ultimate number of dwellers cannot be known, the assumption is made when the house is built that there will be a maximum of two people per bedroom and the sewage flow is estimated accordingly.

A septic tank, shown in Figure 10.1, is selected of a size to hold sewage for the length of time required by the regulating agency (24 hours or longer) before letting it flow to the soil. Longer times are required for smaller quantities because of the larger fluctuations of smaller flows.

The required septic tank capacity is calculated by multiplying the daily quantity of sewage by the required detention time in days. The septic tank volume required for a four bedroom house with design quantity of 100 gallons per person per day and a required detention time of 36 hours is calculated as follows:

$$4 \text{ bedrooms} \times 2 \text{ persons/bedroom} \times 100 \text{ gal/person/day} \times 1.5 \text{ day}$$
$$= 1200 \text{ gal}$$

Additional capacity is required to collect solids between times of cleaning and the total capacity required is based on government regulations.

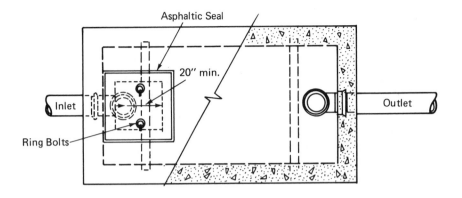

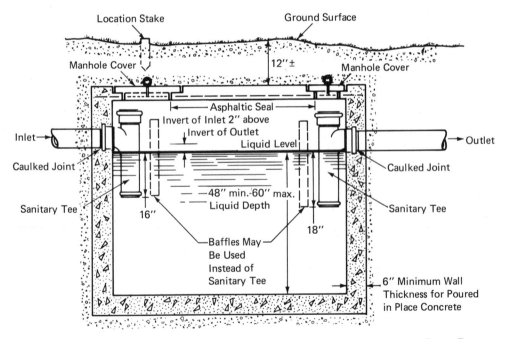

FIGURE 10.1 Typical Concrete Septic Tank [Courtesy of the New York State Department of Health].

The inlet to the septic tank is baffled or provided with a tee to direct the flow downward and under the scum layer. The outlet is baffled or provided with a tee to prevent floating solid waste from being carried out. The baffle or tee should not be so deep that solids from the tank bottom are carried out. The outlet opening is located so that, when the tank is holding its maximum capacity of heavy and floating solids, it will be in the clean space between them.

The inlet should be at least 2 or 3 inches above the outlet to prevent the backing up of sewage in the inlet pipe. This could cause solids to begin settling in the pipe. Open space is provided above liquid level for scum storage with access for gases to pass to the inlet pipe and out the house vent. Access should be available at inlet and outlet for inspection and cleaning. These access openings should be sealed airtight.

It is important that the tank be set level for proper flow. It is placed on an aggregate base so that it does not settle unevenly. A two-compartment tank with tanks in series causes more solids to settle than a single-compartment tank of the same size and is used for large installations.

Site Investigation

Site evaluation for subsurface sewage disposal is an important part of the investigation that is made before the site is purchased. Nearby surface water and wells must not be contaminated by sewage disposal. A safe separation is shown in Figure 10.2. The capacity of streams to assimilate waste is important if a subsurface sand filter is needed for sewage disposal. Bedrock or other impervious material near the surface, a high water table, or steep slopes increase the cost of subsurface systems and could make the entire subdivision project uneconomical. The water table varies in elevation seasonally and it is the highest level that is significant.

Well-drained soil is needed. Simple observations can be helpful in identifying it. Certain trees and crops require well-drained soil and others grow only in poorly drained soil. Swamp grass indicates a location where water stands at times even if none is there now. Stream banks or road cuts may indicate what kind of soil lies near the surface. Rock outcrops indicate more rock below the surface. Soil maps have been prepared for some areas by government agencies such as the U.S. Soil Conservation Service. These indicate, in a general way, the suitability of the soil for waste disposal but do not eliminate the need for field investigation.

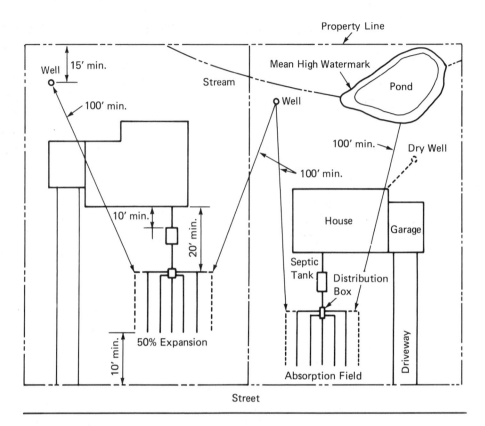

FIGURE 10.2 Clearances Required to Safeguard Public Health (Courtesy of the New York Department of Health).

Although surface observations are helpful, the suitability of soil for sewage disposal can be determined for certain only by subsurface investigation and testing at the point where the sewage is to be applied. However, the general suitability of the soil in the area can be judged by subsurface investigation and testing at several points throughout the area.

Subsurface conditions can be investigated by boring an auger hole and examining the earth brought up. A better examination can be made by excavating a pit with a backhoe and climbing down into it. Bedrock can be located by either method, although a boulder that stops the auger might seem to be bedrock. The water table can also be located by either method but more reliably in the pit.

The color of the soil often indicates whether or not it is suitable for sewage disposal. Rich brown or reddish colors indicate that iron in the soil is oxidized and, therefore, that the soil is well aerated and suitable. Gray indicates that no air reaches the soil, meaning that it is often below the water table or overlain by soil so tight that air does not reach it. In either case, it is unsuitable.

A *percolation test* of the soil produces the best evidence of the suitability of the soil for sewage disposal. It involves placing water into a hole in the ground and timing its rate of percolation into the soil. The test is performed in a hole of 4 to 12 inches in diameter with vertical sides.

The soil being tested is that at the bottom of the hole, so the bottom should be at the level at which sewage disposal will take place. However, that is seldom known at the time of preliminary investigation so the tests are usually made at about a 30-inch depth.

The sides and bottom of the hole are scraped with a knife or other tool to remove any smears caused by shovel or auger while excavating. A smear tends to block the entrance of water into the soil. Stones or gravel placed on the bottom reduce scouring when water is poured in. If the bottom is not protected, fine soil particles will be loosened and suspended in the standing water. They settle, with the finest ones settling last and forming a thin film that may reduce the percolation rate.

Presoaking the hole is required so that when the test is run the adjacent soil will be in the condition it will have during the wettest season of the year. It may be necessary to maintain as much as 12 inches of water in the hole for as long as 24 hours to complete the presoaking.

The test begins with 6 inches of water in the hole measured from the top of any layer of gravel or stones placed to prevent scouring. The percolation rate is the time it takes in minutes for the water level to drop 1 inch. The test must be repeated until the rate becomes stabilized. Often, each run takes longer than the previous one until, after several runs, two in succession are the same, indicating a stable condition.

The percolation rate is used to indicate the maximum allowable rate at which sewage may be applied to the soil. Figure 10.3 shows allowable application rates in gallons per day per square foot of soil.

General Construction

All surfaces of excavations should be raked to remove any smeared soil. Excavation should take place when soil is fairly dry to prevent excessive smearing. Heavy equipment cannot be driven over any excavation even after backfilling because of the danger of compacting the soil and decreasing the percolation rate or knocking the installation out of position.

Clearance must be maintained between the disposal surface and the water table or bedrock. These clearances can be seen in the illustrations of the various types of disposal systems.

Steps should be taken to facilitate evaporation and transpiration of sewage and to prevent the entrance of any surface water into the system. The ground surface over disposal areas should be graded so that storm water runoff flows away from them. A dike or ditch might be needed to divert surface water. No pavement should be built over the disposal area as that would reduce evaporation.

On hillsides, a *curtain drain* or *intercepting drain* may be required above the uphill side of the disposal area to lower the water table or as a precaution against a possible high water table. A curtain drain is built by the same method as an underdrain, which is described in Chapter 11. The intercepted ground water must flow by gravity to an outlet.

The area should be planted with grass for transpiration. Planting bushes or trees over the system or even near it should be avoided because the roots tend to plug the aggregate next to the disposal soil. Plant roots grow into the aggregate to obtain water during dry weather and also to obtain the nutrients that are in the sewage.

Absorption Fields

The effluent that flows from the septic tank contains disease-causing microbes and other pollutants and must be given further treatment. The preferred method is in *absorption trenches* which are constructed below the ground surface. The trench bottom is flat in cross-section and is flat or sloping slightly longitudinally.

Sewage is distributed along the length of the trench through a perforated pipeline or a pipeline made of pipes of short length with ¼-inch open joints covered at the top to keep aggregate out. Clay, bituminous fiber, rigid plastic, and corrugated plastic pipe of 4-inch diameter are commonly used. Corrugated plastic pipe is delivered in rolls and must be fully straightened when installed. The sewage is spread across the width of the trench by trickling over crushed stone or washed gravel. Figure 10.3 shows details of an absorption trench.

The bottom of the trench is the design surface and the total square

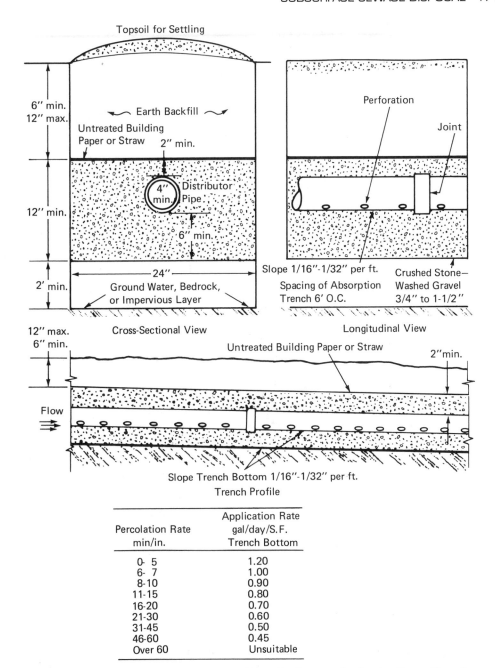

Percolation Rate min/in.	Application Rate gal/day/S.F. Trench Bottom
0- 5	1.20
6- 7	1.00
8-10	0.90
11-15	0.80
16-20	0.70
21-30	0.60
31-45	0.50
46-60	0.45
Over 60	Unsuitable

FIGURE 10.3 Absorption Trench with Allowable Sewage Application Rates Based on Soil Percolation Tests [Courtesy of the New York State Department of Health].

footage of bottom area needed is based on production of sewage in gallons per day divided by the allowable loading rate in gallons per day per square foot.

The trench bottom must be at the same level and in the same soil formation as the bottom of the percolation test hole and the average of several tests throughout the area of the absorption field must be used if the design loading is to be valid. A change in soil appearance indicates a possible change in percolation rate and additional tests are then needed.

In designing and constructing the trenches, the most important principle to keep in mind is that the sewage must be spread as evenly as possible over the trench bottom. The square footage of bottom area is based on the rate at which the soil can assimilate sewage. If any part of the soil is burdened with more than its allowable loading, it is likely to become plugged and turn anaerobic. Sewage that cannot percolate into that plugged soil will spread over the trench bottom, overloading adjacent areas and causing widespread failure.

It is important that distributor pipe and trench bottom are built with a constant slope. Variations in slope cause concentrations of sewage at the flatter slopes. If the overall slope is too steep, excessive sewage flows to the far end and, if too flat, excessive sewage runs out the pipe perforations at the front end and very little reaches the far end.

If sewage is distributed uniformly from the pipe, a level trench bottom will receive uniform loading. However, a sloping trench spreads the sewage by causing it to flow downhill until it enters the soil, thereby making up for small inequalities in the flow from the perforations.

Some regulations require the trench bottom to have the same slope as the pipe and some require a level trench. A level pipe will not produce equal distribution at low flows because sewage will flow out the first few perforations. A level pipe will produce better distribution at high flows because the sewage will quickly fill the entire pipe to the same level before any significant amount flows through perforations.

Because of the nature of sewage flows from a residence, compromises must be made in the attempt to maintain uniform distribution over the entire trench area. Sewage flows from the septic tank to the soil disposal area at the same rate as it enters the tank from the house. The flow rate varies from a prolonged high rate of flow, such as caused by the emptying of a bathtub full of water, to the small flow caused by washing your hands.

If a distributor pipe is too long, sewage will seldom reach the far end and the forward section will be constantly overloaded. Therefore, the sewage is distributed to several pipes of limited length such that the total trench bottom area equals or exceeds the required design area. One hundred feet is a common maximum length and shorter lines are preferred. All pipes are the same length.

Equal-length trenches require equal quantities of sewage to avoid overloading any one trench. This is assured by the installation of a distribution box shown in Figure 10.4. The box has an inlet from the septic tank and an outlet to each distributor. A baffle at the inlet separates the flow into two equal parts and the outlets must be arranged symmetrically to receive equal flows. The distribution box must be set

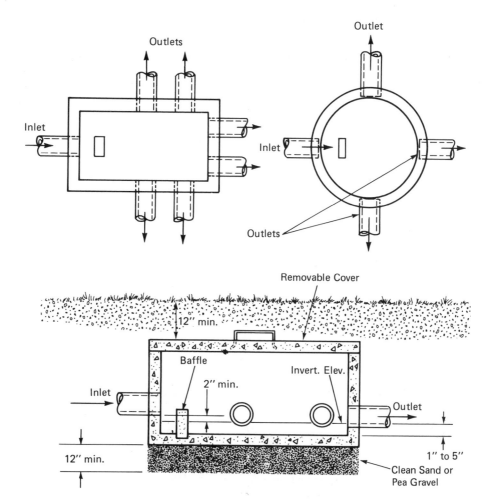

FIGURE 10.4   Distribution Box [Courtesy of the New York State Department of Health].

level to assure equal flows to the outlets which must all be at the same elevation. It must be well bedded on an aggregate base to assure that it remains level.

The construction of the trenches and pipes requires careful control. Batter boards and a string line are used for trenches and pipes as shown in Figure 10.5. The batter boards are set to hold the string line at the same slope as the pipe or trench is to be. The difference in elevation between two adjacent batter boards is the desired slope in inches per foot multiplied by the horizontal distance between batter boards in feet.

For a slope of $\frac{1}{16}$ inch per foot, the elevation difference is $\frac{1}{16}$ inch for each foot of horizontal separation. It is $\frac{10}{16}$ inch for a 10-foot separation, $\frac{30}{16}$ inch for a 30-foot separation, etc. For a level trench, the batter boards are at the same elevation.

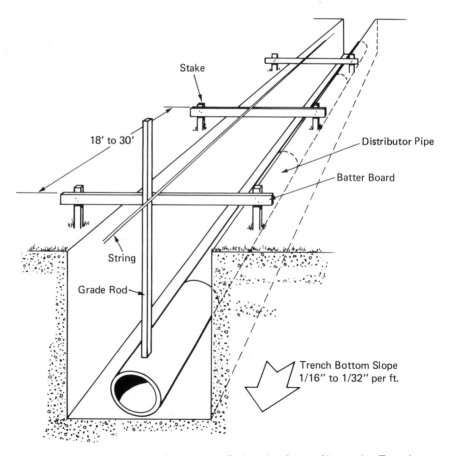

FIGURE 10.5 Batter Boards and String Line for an Absorption Trench [Courtesy of the New York State Department of Health].

The string line may be set at a random distance above the proposed construction. The first batter board is built at a convenient height and the others set lower or higher by the calculated amount. A builders' level is used as illustrated in Figure 10.6. Trench bottom and pipe are started under the string line at the distribution box. A straight stick is placed vertically on the finished work and the point at which it coincides with the string line is marked. The rest of the work is built at the same distance below the mark on the stick so that it is parallel with the string. The marked stick is called a *grade rod.*

Another method used to obtain accurate slopes requires the use of a straight board with a small block nailed to one end. The block height is the correct vertical distance at the desired slope for a horizontal distance the length of the board. For example, the block is $\frac{1}{16}$ inch in height for each foot of board length if the slope is to be $\frac{1}{16}$ inch per foot. A 6-foot board has a $\frac{3}{8}$-inch block. The board is placed on the pipe with the block downstream with a carpenters' level on the board. The pipe is installed with the board level and the pipe at the correct slope.

Seepage Pits

Seepage pits or *leaching pits* are covered pits used for sewage disposal. They have liners of perforated concrete or open-jointed concrete blocks and bottoms are open to the soil. The block is laid with staggered joints

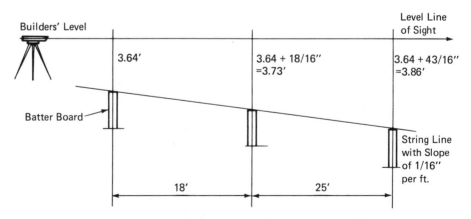

Each batter board varies from the adjacent one by 1/16 inch in elevation for each foot of horizontal distance between them.

FIGURE 10.6   Setting Batter Boards.

without mortar. For structural stability, blocks are set tight against each other with no opening between blocks. Some health departments require straight blocks laid with the cells horizontal to provide more openings to the soil. Others consider the openings caused by imperfections in the blocks to be sufficient.

Footings may be poured in place or made of precast concrete. However, a ring of blocks laid on their sides (for greater soil bearing) in a single layer with the long direction perpendicular to the direction of the wall is adequate to support structures of ordinary depth. See Figure 10.7 for an illustration of a seepage pit.

Seepage pits are useful where absorption trenches are not practical because the available area is too small or the soil near the surface has an unsatisfactory percolation rate. A rate greater than 60 minutes is considered unsatisfactory for absorption trenches or seepage pits and a rate in excess of 30 minutes may be considered unsatisfactory for seepage pits in some states. See Figure 10.8 for seepage pit separation requirements.

Seepage pits are much deeper than absorption trenches with correspondingly greater danger of contaminating ground water. Aeration is not as thorough in the pits as it is in the shallower trenches and sewage is not spread as uniformly throughout the soil because the bottom of a pit is in almost continuous use and the upper part is in use only when the sewage is deep enough to reach it. For these reasons, absorption trenches are preferable when conditions are suitable for either type to be used.

The outside surface of the liner from the bottom of the inlet pipe to the top of the footing is the *design area*. The bottom of the structure is open to the soil but is not included in the design area.

The area required is based on the average of two percolation tests, one at the level of the bottom of the pit and one at mid-depth. If a change in soil color or texture (relative proportion of sand, silt, and clay) is visible, forming more than one soil layer, percolation tests are made at the mid-depth of each layer and the average percolation rate, weighted according to the depth of each layer, is used for design.

If the water table or evidence of a previous level of the water table is found while excavating a seepage pit, the excavation is backfilled to the required height above high water table with the soil that was removed. Its capacity must then be redetermined according to its actual depth. Backfilling with the same soil justifies use of the original percolation rate to determine the revised capacity. The same procedure may be followed if impervious material is found, although a deeper pit

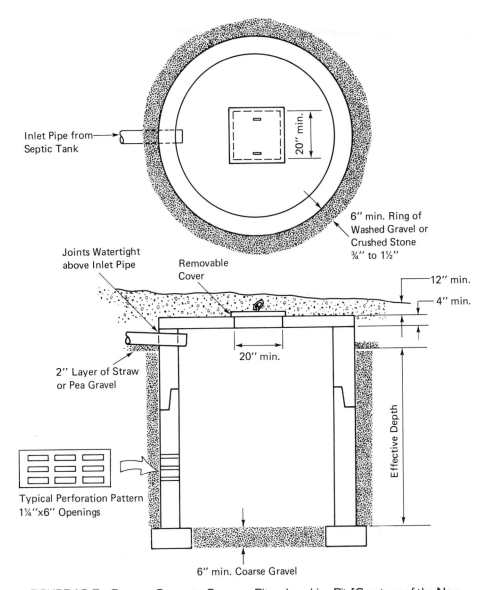

Inlet Pipe from Septic Tank

20" min.

6" min. Ring of Washed Gravel or Crushed Stone ¾" to 1½"

Joints Watertight above Inlet Pipe

Removable Cover

12" min.

4" min.

20" min.

2" Layer of Straw or Pea Gravel

Effective Depth

Typical Perforation Pattern 1¼"x6" Openings

6" min. Coarse Gravel

FIGURE 10.7 Precast Concrete Seepage Pit or Leaching Pit [Courtesy of the New York State Department of Health].

through the impervious stratum to a more permeable soil may be a better solution.

If more than one pit is needed, all must have the same capacity based on design surface and percolation rate. Sewage must be distrib-

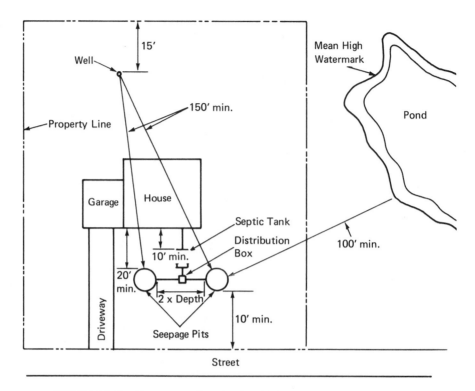

FIGURE 10.8   Clearances Required to Safeguard Public Health [Courtesy of the New York State Department of Health].

uted to them equally through the use of a distribution box. Typical design calculations are included in Appendix D.

The liners are sometimes required by regulations to be connected at the lower ends by level pipes to transfer sewage from pits with slower disposal rates to those with faster rates. Even though all pits are designed to dispose of sewage at the same rate, there will be some difference in their actual operation. The tops of the liners must be fitted with watertight covers to prevent entrance of surface water and must be provided with inspection holes also having watertight covers.

The space between structure and soil must be filled with crushed stone or washed gravel to spread the sewage and permit air to enter. The best way to prevent the migration of soil into the aggregate is to line the pit and also cover the top of the aggregate with geotextile fabric of a size that will hold back the soil. If the excavation is larger than required, it is often best to fill the excess space with the same aggregate. Clean sand might be used if it can be kept separated from the aggregate by geotextile fabric. The top of the aggregate may be covered with un-treated building paper or straw to prevent soil from migrating down-ward. Nothing should be used that prevents the aeration of the soil. Stone or gravel is also spread over the bottom to prevent scouring at the bottom and splattering of the sides.

All the principles discussed under "General Construction" apply to seepage pit construction. In addition, excavations must be braced or even completely sheeted for worker protection.

Structural stability of the liner is important. Curved-block liners are stronger than straight-block liners and precast reinforced concrete liners are the strongest.

Built-up Systems

A *built-up system* or *system in fill* is a disposal system similar to an absorption field but raised above the general ground level because of either or both of two conditions—a high water table or a poor percola-tion rate. The system is substantially more expensive than absorption trenches or seepage pits and may be unsatisfactory because of its ap-pearance.

Where the water table is too high for conventional absorption trenches but the soil percolation rate is satisfactory, the fill is built high enough to raise trench bottoms to a satisfactory height above the water table. Trenches and distributor pipes are constructed in the fill the same way as in natural ground. The fill must extend on all sides well beyond the trenches to avoid seepage of sewage that follows the original ground surface and emerges outside the fill.

Trench bottom area is based on the lower of the percolation rates of the underlying natural soil or of the fill after it has been in place over a winter or rainy season so that it is stabilized. It cannot be artificially compacted. Percolation rate of the fill is determined in place before removing it to construct the fill to approximate its in-place rate.

A built-up system may also be installed where the percolation rate of the natural soil is unsuitable whether the water table is deep enough or not. At least a foot of natural soil must be available over bedrock or hardpan. In this case, the system is designed to dispose of all sewage by evaporation and transpiration with no allowance for percolation. Although the basis for designing the trench area is different, the two systems are built exactly the same. However, the system based on evaporation and transpiration is generally much larger to dispose of the same quantity of sewage. The size comparison depends on percolation rate in the first case and climate in the second case.

Subsurface Sand Filters

A *subsurface sand filter* consists of distribution pipes that apply sewage effluent to a layer of sand, where it is filtered as it percolates through to be collected by other pipes and carried to a body of water for final disposal. Both distributor and collector pipes may be solid, short-length pipes installed with open joints or they may be perforated pipe, in which case both distributor and collector pipes are installed with perforations at the bottom. These systems are often the most expensive to build of all the facilities discussed. However, they are more reliable than built-up systems and may be the best solution when the percolation rate of the natural soil is poor and a body of water is nearby.

See Figure 10.9 for construction details. The overall view shows two filters being dosed alternately. Smaller systems are built in one unit and dosed all at once. Those small enough not to be dosed have each distributor connected to a distribution box of the kind used for absorption trenches. Dosing is discussed later in this chapter.

Sand filters may be built underground or raised above the ground to avoid ground water or bedrock. The reviewing agency might require that collectors be separated from natural soil by a watertight polyvinyl liner. Required size is based on a maximum allowable disposal rate of 1.15 gallons per day per square foot of filter area. Type, size, and length of pipe are as discussed under "Absorption Fields."

The construction practices discussed under "General Construction" apply to subsurface sand filters. However, care need not be taken to avoid smearing the sides or bottom of the excavation because effluent is collected and piped away. Aeration, evaporation, transpiration, and surface water removal are as important as they are for any other system because these affect the hydraulic load on the sand filter. Before distributor pipes are placed, the filter sand should be settled by flooding.

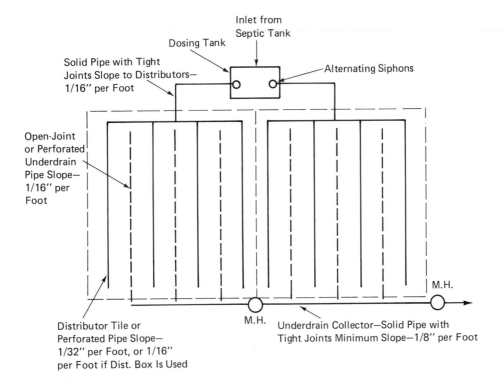

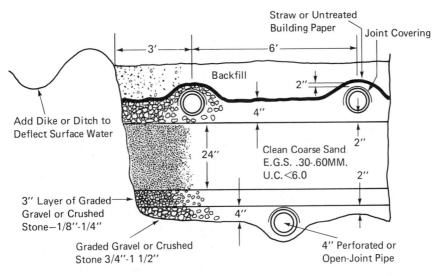

FIGURE 10.9 Subsurface Sand Filter (Courtesy of the New York State Department of Health).

Chlorination

Chlorination of the filtered effluent may be required before it is discharged to a body of water. *Chlorination* consists of adding small amounts of chlorine to the effluent, mixing them together, and allowing the two to remain together in a concrete tank called a *chlorine contact tank* for a specified time, usually 15 or 20 minutes. Tanks are of cast-in-place or precast concrete or of concrete block.

The purpose of chlorination is *disinfection* or the killing of all disease-causing microorganisms (pathogenic microbes or pathogens). Although the filtered effluent contains no visible particles and is sparkling clear, it might contain many pathogens.

Mixing is required because the chlorine must contact each microbe to kill it. The contact time needed for this is very short and the required contact time is actually to allow for thorough mixing, which is accomplished by baffles that may direct the liquid up and down or from side to side.

Chlorine is an active chemical and reacts with many substances in the effluent. It could, therefore, be depleted before completing disinfection. Residual chlorine remaining in the contact tank effluent after the contact time is proof that disinfection has been accomplished. A means must be provided to take a sample of the effluent to test for residual chlorine.

A residual of 0.5 to 1.0 part per million of chlorine to sewage by weight (ppm) is considered proof that disinfection is complete. A dose of 6 ppm is usually sufficient to provide the required residual in sand filter effluent.

The method of applying chlorine must be simple and inexpensive because not much time or money can be justified for the operation of such a small system. Chlorine is very corrosive to most materials. However, glass, rubber, and plastic are not harmed by chlorine.

One application method is to store a chlorine solution in a container of about one-gallon size and drip it into the effluent by means of a flexible hose siphon extending over the edge of the container with one end in the solution and the other at a lower elevation to feed chlorine solution to the effluent before it reaches the contact tank. The apparatus can be housed in a manhole and the solution fed into an open channel passing through the manhole. An adjustable clamp on the hose allows the chlorine feed to be set to produce a satisfactory residual at the highest rate of effluent flow. During lower rates of flow, an excess of chlorine is added because it drips at a constant rate.

The solution is prepared from sodium hypochlorite or calcium hypochlorite. Sodium hypochlorite can be purchased in solution containing 1 to 15 percent available chlorine. It may be reduced further by adding water to obtain the correct chlorine dosage at a particular rate of dripping.

High-test calcium hypochlorite can be purchased in powder form or solid pills and has approximately 70 percent available chlorine. It is dissolved in water to provide a solution that together with the drip rate produces the required residual at the highest rate of flow. The rate of chlorine feed is adjusted on the basis of actual operation to provide a satisfactory residual.

Doughnut-shaped calcium hypochlorite pills are available to be used for chlorination. They are stacked in an open channel section of the pipe on vertical plastic rods solvent-welded to the invert of plastic pipe or attached with epoxy to other types of pipe. Chlorine feed is proportional to the rate of flow of sewage because higher levels and greater velocities of sewage dissolve more of the hypochlorite. The rate of feed is also controlled by the number of stacks. As lower doughnuts are dissolved, they are replaced by the others in the stack.

Dosing

The operation of subsurface disposal systems is improved by the practice of *dosing,* which involves storing septic tank effluent until enough is stored for a dose, then discharging it rapidly to the subsurface disposal site. The advantages of dosing are that all the soil is open to aeration for a time between doses, and distribution is more uniform throughout the system because one dose nearly fills the pipes.

Without dosing, frequent, small quantities of effluent often keep the downstream end of the soil saturated most of the time by flowing in a shallow stream that does not become deep enough to reach the perforations until it backs up at the end of the line, reducing aeration there and also overloading that part of the soil. If solid pipe with open joints is used, the same difficulty occurs at the forward end of the line.

Dosing is required by many health departments when the total length of absorption trenches exceeds 500 feet and may be required for all subsurface sand filters.

The dosing tank may be a separate tank or precast as part of the septic tank. It must be separated hydraulically from the septic tank because the dosing tank receives only settled sewage. The storage capacity of the dosing tank and, therefore, the volume of one dose must be enough to fill at least 60 percent of the volume of all pipes dosed and preferably at least 75 percent. The dose is discharged from the tank to the pipes by a siphon or pump, usually a siphon.

The dosing device must be able to remove sewage from the tank as fast as it enters at the peak rate of flow or the tank could become flooded. The peak rate of sewage flow can be estimated by the fixture unit method. However, this method gives a rough approximation for a one-family house or small apartment building and a dosing rate as great as twice the estimated peak rate of inflow is often used.

Siphons operate automatically without power and have no moving parts to wear out. Therefore, they provide a long period of free service once the installation is paid for. A siphon is shown in Figure 10.10. A drop in water level is shown from the septic tank discharge to the si-

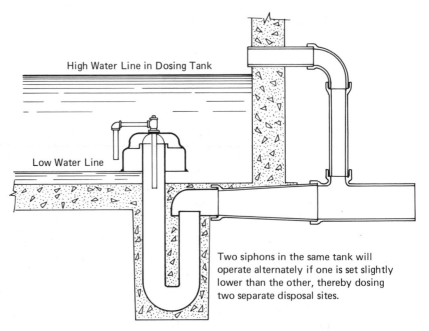

High Water Line in Dosing Tank

Low Water Line

Two siphons in the same tank will operate alternately if one is set slightly lower than the other, thereby dosing two separate disposal sites.

FIGURE 10.10   Dosing Siphon [Courtesy of Envirex, a Division of Rexnord].

phon discharge. This vertical drop or *head loss* through the siphon is about 2 feet for a residence or small apartment building, in addition to the vertical drop through the filter from distributor pipes to collector pipes. An additional vertical drop must be available to allow gravity flow from the collectors to a body of water. Unless the ground can be graded to slope away from the house, the required drop is not available and a siphon cannot be used.

For extensive disposal sites, alternate dosing is required. One septic tank and one dosing tank provide settling and dosing for two fields of equal size which are dosed alternately by separate siphons installed in the dosing tank. The dosing tank is the size of one dose for one of the fields. The siphons automatically deliver equal doses alternating between the two fields provided one siphon is set a fraction of an inch lower than the other.

Figure 10.9 shows a sand filter with alternate dosing. Note that no distribution box is used. The discharge line from each dosing siphon is connected with a tee fitting to a header and the header distributes the effluent equally to the distributors.

REVIEW QUESTIONS

10.1. Describe the three means by which sewage liquid is disposed of in soil.

10.2. Describe completely the major way in which sewage solids are disposed of in soil.

10.3. What are the differences between aerobic and anaerobic microbes?

10.4. What volume septic tank is required for a three-bedroom house, 75 gallons per person per day, and 44-hour detention time?

10.5. What is the percolation rate based on these percolation times? 11 min, 14 min, 16 min, 16 min.

10.6. Discuss the practices that assure uniform distribution of effluent to the bottom area of absorption trenches.

10.7. Discuss the practices that assist evaporation, transpiration, and percolation and those that prevent the addition of natural water to the subsurface sewage disposal system.

10.8. Batter boards are 15 feet apart. What is their elevation difference if the string line is to slope $\frac{1}{16}$ inch per foot? If a rod reading of 1.37 is read on the upstream batter board, what reading is needed on the downstream one?

10.9. With a percolation rate of 26 minutes, what length of absorption trench is needed for a five-bedroom house? Draw a sketch of the entire sewage system if trenches cannot be longer than 60 feet.

10.10. Seepage pits are to be built with an effective depth of 6 feet. How many of them, 6 feet in diameter, are needed for a four-bedroom house if percolation rate is 18 minutes?

10.11. What is the allowable loading rate for a 7-foot depth if a 2-foot layer of soil has a percolation rate of 7 minutes and a 5-foot layer has a rate of 19 minutes?

10.12. Select a sand filter size and arrangement of distributor and collector pipes for a sand filter for an apartment building with six apartments with three bedrooms each.

10.13. Absorption trenches contain 580 feet of 4-inch pipe. What is the preferred minimum size of a dose? A sand filter has three distributor lines, each 46 feet long. What is the minimum volume of a dose?

10.14. Define *disinfection* and explain why it is needed for sand filter effluent and not for other subsurface system effluent.

CHAPTER 11

Street Pavement

The municipality usually has extensive design and construction standards for street pavement. A typical cross-section is shown in Figure 11.1. The cross-slopes of pavement surface and nearby surfaces are designed primarily to remove storm water runoff. Underdrains may be necessary to remove ground water from certain areas. No surface water should enter underdrains.

The thickness of the pavement is specified to provide sufficient strength to support the expected traffic load. Pavement width, intersections, and horizontal and vertical alinement are based on requirements for safe and convenient travel for vehicles including bicycles and for pedestrians.

There are two types of street pavement. *Flexible pavement* includes asphalt concrete as the top course and *rigid pavement* includes portland cement concrete as the top course. Only flexible pavement is discussed in detail because it is far more common in subdivisions than rigid pavement. Flexible pavement includes a granular base and two courses of asphalt concrete, a binder course, and a finish course. Sometimes, a sub-base course under the base is included.

Although other asphalt mixtures are used, asphalt-concrete is the highest type and probably the most commonly used in subdivisions. It is designed of several gradations of aggregate and asphalt-cement, hot-mixed in an asphalt plant, and placed at temperatures ranging from 250°F to 300°F. It is compacted while still hot to form the upper surface of pavement that can be designed to carry the heaviest traffic.

Structural Design Principles

The rigid pavement slab spreads the wheel load as it passes from top to bottom so that it acts over a large area of the soil. The effect is to reduce the stress on the soil. The bending strength of the concrete slab is of great importance and the soil strength is of little importance. The concrete is designed thick enough and strong enough to distribute the load over a large enough area so that the soil is not overstressed. An aggregate base is usually not needed structurally but is sometimes included for drainage and protection from frost.

Asphalt-concrete has no bending strength and a greater total depth of pavement is needed to reduce stress on the soil. The required depth depends on the strength of the underlying soil. The combination

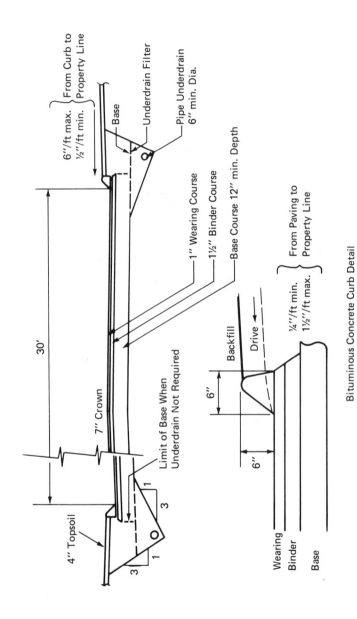

FIGURE 11.1 Municipal Design Standards—Typical Pavement and Side Slopes.

190

of a shallow depth of asphalt-concrete and a much greater depth of base and sometimes sub-base has been found to be most economical.

All pavement includes subgrade (either in-place soil or fill soil) that is improved by compaction and by removal of unsatisfactory material and replacement with better material. A base course of graded aggregate is placed and compacted on top of the soil if asphalt pavement is being constructed and the concrete is placed directly on the soil if portland cement concrete pavement is being constructed. In either case, this course is the load-bearing course that gives the pavement most of its strength.

Two courses of asphalt concrete are placed over the aggregate base. The lower one spreads the concentrated wheel load over a larger area of the base and binds the base at the top so that the aggregate is not pushed aside by the wheel load. The upper course prevents rain and surface water from penetrating and provides a smooth riding surface.

In northern climates, portland cement concrete is likely to be protected from the deterioration caused by ice removal salts by one or two courses of asphalt concrete.

Base courses perform additional functions that depend on removal of fine-grained soil from the vicinity of the concrete and replacing it with coarse-grained aggregate having larger spaces between particles. The individual soil grains in saturated soil are partially supported by the water surrounding them so that they do not bear fully on one another and cannot support as great a load as when the soil is not saturated. Base material has such large voids that water flows out by gravity and cannot saturate the base.

Shrinkage and swelling of a fine-grained subgrade is absorbed in the large voids of aggregate base material and does not damage the surface of the pavement. Damaging frost heaves depend on a supply of water moving upward by capillarity to replace soil water as it freezes. The voids in base material are too large for capillarity and, therefore, prevent frost damage.

Alinement Principles

Pavement alinement is based primarily on subdivision regulations which are based primarily on safety. Alinement requirements are contained in Appendix B. A key factor in safety is sight distance.

Sight distance is the distance at which a driver is able to see a small object in the street ahead. *Stopping sight distance* is the distance traveled from the instant the driver sees an object in the street until the driver is able to stop the vehicle to avoid hitting the object. It includes distance traveled during the time it takes to start applying the brakes plus distance traveled while braking, known as *brake reaction distance* and *braking distance.* Sight distance must be equal to or greater than the stopping sight distance for safe driving. Stopping sight distance is 200 feet at 30 mph, which is a common speed limit for subdivision streets.

Stopping sight distance is greater for greater speeds. Sight distance must, therefore, be greater for major and collector streets than for minor streets because of their higher speed limits.

Sight distance is reduced by horizontal curves with obstructions to the line of sight on the inside of the curve. A horizontal curve must be quite sharp and the obstruction close to the pavement to cause any difficulty at subdivision street speeds. A minimum radius is specified for curves. Because a smaller radius results in a sharper curve, a minimum allowable radius limits the degree of curvature or sharpness of the curve and, therefore, puts a lower limit on the available sight distance. In Appendix B, Article IV, Section 3, Paragraph J lists minimum radii for subdivision streets. Visibility can be measured by laying a scale from the center of the inside traffic lane (location of driver's eye) tangent to the R.O.W. line (limit of area that cannot be obstructed by property owner's landscaping) to the inside edge of the pavement ahead (location for an obstruction to have the shortest possible sight distance).

Curves at intersections are much sharper and speeds are slower. The line of sight crosses private property which must be clear of obstructions to provide an adequate sight distance. In Appendix B, Article IV, Section 3, Paragraph H has provisions for a clear line of sight at intersections.

Sight distances are more likely to be critical at a change of slope. A slope change from positive to negative (uphill to downhill) results in a *crest* and a slope change from negative to positive (downhill to uphill) results in a *sag.* Changes in slope from steep to flat or flat to steep while remaining either positive or negative also produce crests and sags.

In order to be able to compute sight distances over crests and across sags when designing pavement, the American Association of State Highway and Transportation Officials (AASHTO) uses a height of eye of 3.5 feet and a height of object of 0.5 foot. Safe design requires that vertical curves connect the straight slopes so that the object can be seen far enough ahead so that a vehicle can be stopped before hitting it.

The horizontal length required for a vertical curve to provide adequate sight distance depends on design speed and change in slope and also on whether the curve is at a crest or a sag. Both high speed and a large change in slope require greater lowering of a crest to permit adequate sight distance over it and, therefore, a greater horizontal length.

Vertical curves are not needed at sags for daytime visibility but are needed in darkness when visibility is limited to whatever is illuminated by the headlights. Headlights shining downward into the pavement, as they do across a sag when the car approaches it, provide only a short sight distance. Raising the grade over the sag causes the beams to shine more nearly horizontal and, therefore, farther. A greater fill across the sag requires a greater horizontal length. AASHTO standards for visibility at sags are based on a 2-foot headlight height and a 1 percent divergence of the light beam from the longitudinal axis of the vehicle.

In addition to increasing sight distance, vertical curves also provide a safe, comfortable transition from one straight slope to another. Without a connecting curve, the abrupt change in direction would be uncomfortable at the least and might possibly cause the driver to lose control of the vehicle. Generally, any curve that provides an adequate sight distance also provides safe and comfortable riding.

Required horizontal length of vertical curves at a crest for a speed of 30 mph using the AASHTO method varies from 100 feet for a 2 percent change in slope to 500 feet for a 16 percent change in slope. For vertical curves at sags, the lengths for comparable conditions are 100 feet and 650 feet.

Subgrade Construction

Rough grading to pavement subgrade is completed as one of the first steps in construction before pipe laying. A possible exception is that an embankment may be placed over pipelines after the pipelines are in place to avoid the expense of trenching through the embankment. Soft soil should be noticed under the weight of heavy equipment during pipeline construction, and should be removed and replaced with suitable fill before pavement construction is started.

At least 12 inches of soil should be compacted below subgrade. With most soils and compaction equipment, no more than a 6-inch depth can be compacted at a time. This applies in cuts, also, where it may be necessary to remove the upper 6 inches of soil, compact 6 inches of the remaining soil, and replace and compact the upper 6 inches.

The builder is guided in the construction of street pavement by plan and profile drawings and the drawing of the typical cross-section (see Figures 11.1 and 11.2). Construction stakes are set on one or both sides at offsets of 2 to 5 feet from the edge and marked with cuts or fills to the finished pavement center line if there is no curb and to the top of curb if there are curbs. Stakes are commonly set 50 feet apart except on vertical or horizontal curves where they are set 25 feet apart.

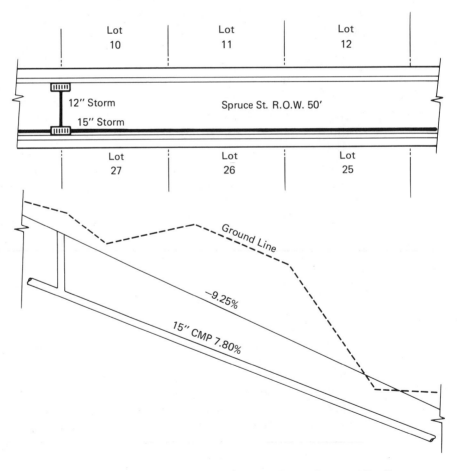

FIGURE 11.2   Construction Drawings of Street Plan and Profile.

It is difficult to build smooth looking curves with stakes farther apart than 25 feet.

The natural soil (subgrade) is graded and compacted to a surface parallel longitudinally and in cross-section with the proposed finished surface and the correct distance below it according to the pavement depth shown on the cross-section drawing. Additional construction stakes at center line and edges, driven so that the tops are at finished subgrade, are helpful for good control.

Soil that quakes or sinks because of being too wet or soft when heavy construction equipment passes over it should be removed and replaced with sand, gravel, or soil that compacts readily. A *proof roller,* which is a very heavy, rubber-tired roller with two to four wheels per axle, may be run over the entire roadbed and observed as a check for additional soft spots. The proof roller is sometimes also used for additional compaction.

If rough grading is within a few inches of subgrade, construction traffic might compact the subsoil sufficiently before pavement construction starts, especially if the municipality does not have strict compaction requirements. Fill sections must be compacted in lifts that are thin enough to achieve proper compaction. It is often difficult to do this with lifts greater than 6 inches unless the soil is granular and can be compacted by vibration.

Fine grading might require only a motor grader and a little help from dump trucks if rough grading has been accurately done. However, a grader can move only small amounts of soil over short distances. Often, additional equipment such as a bulldozer, front-end loader, and dump trucks are needed. Scrapers usually are not used. They are efficient for moving large volumes fairly long distances and cannot economically be brought back to the site for final grading. A grader is shown in Figure 11.3.

The soil is graded and compacted to an accurate crowned cross-section using construction stakes for control. (See Chapter 4 for a discussion of compaction.) Compaction accomplishes two things—it strengthens the soil and causes settlement to take place before the pavement is built. Soil settlement under the pavement caused by traffic would reduce the support and cause damage to the pavement.

Compacting of subgrade soil is done with sheepsfoot rollers, steel-wheeled rollers, static or vibratory, and pneumatic-tired rollers. The subgrade surface must be finished to a smooth surface so a sheepsfoot roller cannot be used for the final touches.

The amount of compaction obtained depends on type of soil,

FIGURE 11.3   Motor Grader (Courtesy of Champion Road Machinery).

compactive effort, and soil moisture content. Samples of the soil with various moisture contents are compacted in the laboratory using standard test procedures. Results of the tests are a *maximum compaction* (indicated by maximum density in pounds per cubic foot) obtainable with that soil and that compactive effort and *optimum moisture content,* the moisture content at which greatest compaction is achieved using the compactive effort of that standard test. The two most commonly used tests are the standard AASHTO and modified AASHTO tests of the American Association of State Highway and Transportation Officials. The modified test results in substantially greater compaction.

Construction standards require that density of the compacted soil equal or exceed a percentage of the maximum density achieved by one of the standard test methods. Criteria recommended by the Asphalt Institute are 95 to 100 percent of modified AASHTO compaction for the upper 12 inches just below finished subgrade and 90 to 95 percent for the rest of all fills. Most municipalities' requirements are not that strict. The percentage and the standard test must be specified because different densities are obtained with different test methods.

The developer uses appropriate types and sizes of compacting equipment to achieve the required compaction, which will be achieved with the fewest passes when soil is at the optimum moisture content. This optimum is usually not the same as the one determined in the lab but is close to it. It is established by making adjustments after starting with the moisture content from the lab.

The compaction actually achieved is determined by carefully excavating a cylindrical hole about 4 inches in diameter through the entire compacted soil layer, weighing every bit of soil from the hole, determining the volume of the hole, and using the weight and volume to determine the density of the compacted soil.

The volume of the hole is determined by filling it with a substance of known unit weight and converting the total weight of the substance to the volume of the hole. Substances used include dry standard sand, water inside a thin rubber membrane lining the hole, and oil of such a viscosity that it does not seep into the soil during the test.

Density of oven-dry soil is calculated by quickly determining the moisture content of a small part of the soil from the hole and using the moisture content to calculate the sample's oven dry weight from its wet weight. The moisture content is useful to indicate how close to optimum moisture content the soil is. It may be sprinkled with water or loosened by plowing to dry in the air at the borrow pit or work site as needed.

Densities and moisture content are also determined in the field with nuclear devices. Gamma rays are emitted into the soil and reflected according to the density of the soil. High-velocity neutrons are also emitted from the same device. These travel slower at increasing moisture contents. Intensity of reflected gamma rays and speed of the neutrons are measured by a separate device and then converted into density and moisture content.

It is important that the finished subgrade be at or slightly below its correct grade when finished. If it is above grade, the total depth of pavement from finished surface to subgrade will be insufficient. If subgrade is substantially below correct grade, excess base material is needed to build the pavement up to grade. In this case, the work is not economical but the pavement is stronger than intended.

All castings (manhole, storm water inlet, and valve) should be adjusted to their finished grade before base construction is started.

Pavement Construction

Some municipalities require that a layer of geotextile be placed between subgrade and base. *Geotextiles* are rolls of nondecomposing fabric consisting of plastic fibers either woven, knitted, or bonded by other means. They act as filters, letting water drain from the soil to flow through and along the plane of the geotextile or in the base without carrying soil particles. They prevent mixing of the soil and base which often happens under traffic loads. When soil and aggregate mix, the mixture has less strength than the aggregate and may become as weak as the soil. The effect is the same as reducing the thickness of the aggregate base. The fabric also distributes traffic loads over a larger area than the base alone would. The fabric is unrolled, overlapped according to the manufacturer's instructions, and the base material is built up over it.

Base courses are constructed in the same way as a fill. The usual way to place each lift is to spread the aggregate from a moving dump truck with the bed raised. The truck speed and rate at which the bed is elevated are such that a lift of approximately the desired height is formed. The lifts are usually a maximum of 6 inches deep after compaction.

Grading is required at least for the final lift and this can best be done with a motor grader. The upper surface of the base must be finished smooth and parallel with the proposed finished asphalt surface or the finished surface will not be satisfactory. It is usually compacted with a vibratory compactor. If the base surface becomes rough or uneven due to heavy rains or any other cause, a thin leveling course of asphalt concrete should be placed and compacted before the required courses are installed.

The base surface is primed before asphalt-concrete is placed on it. The purpose of the prime coat is to penetrate into the base and plug the holes, stiffening the upper surface of the base and adhering to the overlying asphalt-concrete. It is a low viscosity liquid asphalt, usually medium curing. The prime coat should be completely absorbed leaving no pools on the surface. Any excess liquid should be blotted by spreading sand on it. It should be completely cured before asphalt-concrete is placed over it.

The prime coat is applied at a rate of 0.2 to 0.5 gallon per square yard by an asphalt distributor which is a tank truck equipped with a heater and transverse spray bar. Aggregate with open gradation and warmer weather require more prime coat. The speed of travel, rate of pumping liquid to the distributor bar, and the adjustable bar length must be coordinated to achieve the desired application rate over the desired width of pavement. Areas that cannot be covered by the distributor are sprayed with a hand sprayer attached to the distributor by a hose.

All vertical surfaces that will be in contact with asphalt-concrete are coated with asphalt emulsion by spraying or painting to obtain watertight joints. Castings for manholes, storm water inlets, and valves and curb or curb and gutter are all coated. Care should be taken not to coat any part of the curb or curb and gutter where the coating will show. Storm water grates are covered so that no primer enters and remain covered during asphalt placement so that no asphalt-concrete enters.

Hot, plant-mixed asphalt is applied by specialized machines called *paving machines* or *pavers* that are operated by crews that specialize in asphalt paving only. A paver is shown in Figure 11.4.

The asphalt mix is hauled from a mixing plant to the job site in dump trucks. The mix must have a suitable temperature (200°F to 350°F) when used or it will not adhere to the base, will not have a smooth surface, and cannot be compacted sufficiently.

The truck backs over the unsurfaced base to the paver until it bears against the *truck rollers* at the front of the paver. The truck bed is raised so that the mix starts to flow into the receiving *hopper* of the paver and the truck is taken out of gear. The truck is pushed by the paver and the bed is raised as needed to feed the hopper. When the truck is empty it pulls away and the next truck backs in.

The paver consists of a tractor and a screed. The *tractor,* mounted

FIGURE 11.4   Asphalt Paver [Courtesy of Barber-Greene Company].

on wheels or tracks, provides the motive power for the paver and the unloading truck. It includes the hopper, a heater to maintain the mix at the specified temperature, bar conveyors to push the mix back to the screed, and controls to adjust the flow of mix to the screed.

The screed is pulled by two *screed arms* that are pin-connected to the tractor. The *screed* includes a *screed plate* that pushes the mix forward ahead of it, letting the desired thickness of mix pass under it. Excess mix is maintained ahead of the screed. Thickness controls are also included. The screed also includes a mechanism that compacts the mix left behind by the screed plate.

Screed controls are manual or automatic. Manual controls require the operator to match a follower that projects out to the side from the screed arm to a string or wire line. Automatic controls are more common and have a sensor that follows a guide line of string or wire and controls the screed so that the paved surface is parallel with the string or wire. The guide line is put in place at finished grade or at a set distance above grade and is set at the pavement edge or offset a small distance. In either case, the controls can be adjusted for any offset and cut.

The screed can be set for various widths up to 14 feet and can be sloped transversely to shape the crown. Usually, the screed is set for half the pavement width and two strips are laid side by side. The second strip is controlled to grade by a shoe that rides on the surface of the previous strip.

Traffic should not cross the edge of the first strip until both strips are in place if at all possible. The joint between strips is the weakest part of the pavement and is best constructed by paving the second strip against a vertical face. Compaction leaves a vertical face but it can be broken down by wheels crossing the edge.

The second strip or any subsequent strips should overlap the previous strip by at least 1 or 2 inches to provide a satisfactory longitudinal joint. The longitudinal joint of the surface course should be offset at least 6 inches from the longitudinal joint of the binder course to lessen the chance of a weak joint. Paving widths must be planned to provide the offset.

Uniformity of operation is important. The mix should all be at approximately the same temperature as it enters the hopper. The paver should proceed at a constant speed so that the pavement is placed at a fairly constant temperature. A uniform compaction operation will then produce a uniform product. Plant capacity, truck transportation, paving rate, and compaction capacity should all be matched to accomplish this.

Special care should be taken that the mix does not remain in the hopper too long. It cools rapidly there, especially at the edges where it will stick to the hopper if not removed.

If the delivery trucks cannot supply mix as fast as the paver can place it, the paver should be operated at a slower speed to avoid any waiting periods. It is possible that the paving crew might deliberately operate the paver at a fast rate so that they can rest while waiting for the next truck. This should not be allowed. Flow of mix through the paver should be kept at a constant depth to provide pavement that is uniform in gradation, thickness, and temperature.

The tried and true method of compacting requires that edges and longitudinal joint be rolled immediately behind the paver with steel-wheeled rollers. An edge should be rolled with the wheel extending a few inches beyond the edge. A joint should be rolled with only 3 to 6 inches of the roller on the newly laid mix.

Breakdown rolling for compaction follows, beginning on the gutter side and working toward the crown with a steel-wheeled roller. Intermediate rolling is preferably done with a pneumatic-tired roller because the kneading action rearranges aggregate particles to achieve greater stability and greater watertightness than can be obtained with steel-wheeled rollers. The finish rolling is preferably done with a steel-wheeled roller to obtain as smooth a surface as possible.

Vibratory steel-wheeled rollers are sometimes used instead for all phases. They are used with vibration for edge, joint, and breakdown rolling and without vibration for intermediate and finish rolling.

Rollers produce better compaction at very slow speeds and are generally not permitted to travel faster than 3 miles per hour. Compaction must be completed while the mix is hot. If this is not being accomplished, rolling faster is no remedy because it accomplishes less compaction in the same time and increases the amount of displaced surface caused by changing directions. Either the asphalt mix must be placed slower or more rollers must be used. There should be at least two rollers used on even the smallest job.

Curbs and Sidewalks

Asphalt-concrete pavement is constructed with or without curbs. If there are no curbs, ditches on both sides of the pavement carry storm water and a culvert is required under each driveway. Ditches should be shallow and wide with gently sloping sides for traffic safety, easy maintenance, and to prevent erosion of the sides. They should be sodded or seeded to help prevent erosion and for a satisfactory appearance. Ditches are in the public right of way but appear to be part of the property owners' front lawns and are likely to be maintained by them when they are built for easy maintenance.

Curbs of asphalt-concrete are built on top of the pavement after the pavement is completed. Stone curbs and integral portland cement concrete curb and gutter are constructed first and the base and surface courses are built using them as guides. Portland cement concrete curbs are usually built before pavement but can be built on top of pavement.

When pavement is built first, construction stakes are marked with cut or fill to the finished pavement center line and offset to the back or near side of curb. The edge of the pavement is constructed to extend an inch or so beyond the back of the curb for additional support to the curb. When curb or curb and gutter are built first, cut or fill is to the top of the curb and offset is to the *face* of the curb (side toward pavement).

Backfill, including the required depth of topsoil, should be placed and compacted behind curbs as soon as it can conveniently be done. The curbs and curb and gutter need this support. Those placed before pavement especially need support because compaction of the pavement right to the edge of the curb exerts a thrust against them. Asphalt-concrete curbs are often broken by traffic in everyday use and are much better able to resist breaking if supported by backfill.

Asphalt-concrete curbs are built with a curb machine. The machine rides on the pavement surface. Hot mix is fed into its hopper from where it is extruded by a worm gear through a template of the desired shape, forming the finished curb as the machine is forced forward as a reaction to the extrusion. No forms are needed. The machine is guided along a chalk line offset the correct distance from surveyors' construction stakes. No grade control is needed because the curb is simply added to the pavement. Unless the pavement surface is still tacky and free of dust, a light tack coat of liquid asphalt should be sprayed on the pavement before curbs are built.

Portland cement concrete curbs are precast, formed and cast in place on the job, or made by slip forming with a curb machine. The integral curb and gutter are formed and cast in place or placed by slip forming. In addition, concrete curb may be extruded by machine on top of pavement in much the same way as asphalt-concrete curbs. String lines are used for all but the extruded curb. Stakes are set at 50-

or 25-foot intervals but may be set as close together as 10 feet on vertical and horizontal curves. String line supports are the same distance apart as the stakes. Curb and gutter being placed by a slipform paver is shown in Figure 11.5.

If forms are used or if precast sections are used, the string line is set to line and grade for the back form or back of curb and they are built right to the line. Although the string line is a series of straight lines around a horizontal curve, flexible steel forms are available to set a smooth curve based on the string line. Curved precast curb is also available. If a curb or curb and gutter machine is used, the string line is offset a small amount such as a half foot and may be at grade or elevated a constant height above grade. The curb machines follow a string line automatically the same way an asphalt paver does.

A sand-cement grout consisting of equal parts of sand and cement is sometimes required for the exposed surface of concrete curb or curb and gutter to resist de-icing salt attack. Curb cut from natural stone is available in straight and curved lengths with top and one side surfaced for appearance's sake. The curved pieces are used for short-

FIGURE 11.5 Curb and Gutter by Slip Form Paver (Courtesy of Puckett Brothers Manufacturing Company, Inc.).

radius curves at intersections. Flatter curves are approximated with straight pieces.

Precast or stone curb may be set on a sand or gravel base or on a concrete footing. Each piece of curb is set in place by pushing a slight excess of aggregate under it and working it down into alinement. If a concrete footing is to be used, each piece is shimmed into alinement using stones, bits of wood, or similar material and concrete is poured under and partly up the sides of the curb. Aggregate base must be compacted and concrete must be vibrated or puddled to remove air bubbles.

Storm water inlets are in place before curbs are built. The curb can be built with the curb hoods already in place. When a curb machine is used, it may be more efficient to build a continuous curb and saw openings for curb hoods. Tops of inlets must be covered to prevent material from falling into the inlets.

Public sidewalks are sometimes required and must be built within the public right of way. Asphalt-concrete and portland cement concrete are used. Other types of asphalt paving may also be permitted. Walks are from 3 to 6 feet wide and should slope toward the pavement at a slope of ¼ inch per foot. They need not follow the profile of the curb if it is more economical to follow the finished grades of the front lawns. If at all possible, they should be above the curb.

Both asphalt and portland cement concrete are placed 4 inches thick. The thickness is increased to 6 inches or more at driveways. Asphalt is placed with or without forms by hand or without forms by a small paver and is placed in two courses similar to street pavement but on a base of sand or similar fine material about 1 inch thick over compacted subgrade. Walks are often compacted with small rollers but full-size rollers are better.

Portland cement concrete is placed 4 inches thick directly on a subgrade of compacted soil or with a leveling course of sand over the compacted soil to raise the subgrade surface to conserve concrete. Forms are necessary and are commercially available in the same style as for street pavement. Two-by-four lumber is often used even though it is only 3½ inches deep. Transverse joints are usually placed the same distance apart as the width of the walk so that squares are formed.

The joints can be made by placing concrete in alternate squares with joint forms in place and a day or more later removing the forms and placing the other squares with a strip of building paper or fiberboard separating squares or with no separation. This limits random cracking but will not prevent cracking caused by tree roots growing under the walk or by some comparable disturbance. If cracking occurs, each broken square can be removed and replaced with little expense, leaving the rest of the walk and joints intact.

The walk may be placed in one long strip and control joints built in by troweling deep grooves so that shrinkage cracking takes place through the weakened sections at the joints and does not show. Most other cracks that occur for any reason will also occur at the joints.

Concrete, General

Usually, ready-mixed portland cement concrete is delivered to the job site in satisfactory condition. It must be placed before it begins to set (harden) so that it can be made to fill the forms without air pockets and so it can be given a satisfactory finish. It must be vibrated with a mechanical vibrator or sliced with a shovel or similar tool, especially near the forms, to fill the forms completely with no air pockets. Curb machines automatically vibrate concrete as they place it.

After placing and finishing, evaporation must be prevented so that *hydration* (the chemical union of cement and water that gives concrete its strength) can take place. Any surface exposed to the atmosphere should be covered with a watertight cover immediately after the surface is finished to prevent evaporation of water from the concrete. Too much evaporation reduces the water available for hydration and could reduce strength and cause surface cracking. Plastic sheets or a colored spray that seals the concrete from the air are commonly used.

If the mixer truck is kept waiting, the concrete can begin the hydration process sufficiently to set up in the mixer. Therefore, the site must be ready when the mixer truck arrives. The subgrade must be thoroughly wet with no standing water so that no water will be drawn from the concrete by dry soil and none added from puddles. Water and cement are correctly proportioned at the batching plant and the proportions should not be changed by adding water to make the concrete easier to work with. Concrete should be deposited where needed by moving the truck and the chute and should then be leveled with a minimum of movement. It should not be deposited in a pile and pushed into place.

APPENDIX A

Excerpts from a Typical Zoning Law (Land Use Ordinance)

The following excerpts include only a small portion of an actual land use ordinance. They are intended merely to acquaint the reader with the more common methods of controlling the use of land. The zoning law of any municipality may be consulted for further information.

Purposes

This Ordinance regulates the location, construction, alteration, occupancy, and use of buildings and structures and the use of land in the Town and for said purposes divides the Town into land use districts or zones.

This Ordinance is enacted to protect and promote public health, safety, comfort, convenience, economy, aesthetics, and general welfare and for the following additional purposes:

1. To promote and effectuate the orderly physical development of the Town in accordance with the Town Master Plan.
2. To encourage the most appropriate use of land in the community in order to conserve and enhance the value of property.
3. To eliminate the spread of strip business developments and provide for more adequate and suitably located commercial facilities.
4. To create a suitable system of open spaces and to protect and enhance existing wooded areas, scenic areas, and waterways.
5. To regulate building densities in order to assure access of light and circulation of air, in order to facilitate the prevention and fighting of fires, in order to prevent undue concentration of population, and in order to lessen congestion on streets and highways and to facilitate the adequate provision of water and sewerage.
6. To improve transportation facilities and traffic circulation, and to provide adequate off-street parking and loading facilities.
7. To realize a development plan properly designed to conserve the use of land and the cost of municipal services.
8. To assure privacy for residences and freedom from nuisances and things harmful to the senses.
9. To protect the community against unsightly, obtrusive, and noisome land uses and operations.
10. To enhance the aesthetic aspects throughout the entire community and maintain its present character and natural beauty.
11. To encourage the continuation of commercial agricultural activity within the Town.

Land Use Districts

The Town hereby establishes and divides the Town into the following land use districts:

R   Residential District
RA   Residential/Agricultural District
RR1   Rural Residential 1 District
RR2   Rural Residential 2 District
CLI   Commercial/Light Industrial District
PD   Planned Development District

The location and boundaries of said Districts are shown on the "LAND USE DISTRICT MAP."

Except as hereinafter otherwise provided:

1. No building, structure, or land shall hereafter be used or occupied, and no building or structure or part thereof shall hereafter be erected, moved, altered, reconstructed, or enlarged except in conformance with the use and area and bulk regulations herein specified for the district in which it is located.
2. No part of a yard or other open space required in connection with any building or use shall be included as part of a yard or other open space similarly required for another building.
3. No yard or lot existing at the time of passage of this Ordinance shall be reduced in size or area below the minimum requirements set forth herein. Yards or lots created after the effective date of this Ordinance shall meet the minimum requirements established by this Ordinance.
4. No off-street parking or loading space required for one building or use shall be included as meeting, in whole or part, the off-street parking or loading space required for another building or use except as otherwise provided for by this Ordinance.
5. No off-street parking or loading space shall be so reduced in area that it does not meet the requirements of this Ordinance.
6. Within each district, the Use and Area and Bulk regulations set forth by this Ordinance shall be considered minimum regulations and shall apply uniformly to each kind of building, structure, or land.

The general use regulations in each land use district or zone are set forth in the attached "DISTRICT SCHEDULE OF USE REGULATIONS." This Schedule is supplemented, as appropriate, by other provisions of this Ordinance. Any use which is not listed specifically, or through a similar use, as a permitted, special permit, or accessory use in the attached Schedule shall be considered a prohibited use in all land use districts under this Ordinance.

DISTRICT SCHEDULE OF USE REGULATIONS

Structure/Land Use	Land Use Districts				
	R	RA	RR1	RR2	CLI
Residential Uses					
One-family dwelling	P	P	P	P	
Two-family dwelling	SP	P	P	P	
Multi-family dwelling			SP	SP	
Mobile home				SP	
Boarding and rooming house	SP	SP	SP	SP	
Community residence	SP	SP	SP	SP	
General Uses					
Agriculture	P	P	P	P	P
Keeping of fowl and livestock on non-farm parcels	SP	P	SP	P	SP
Noncommercial stable for horses	SP	P	SP	P	
Vacation resort, day camp, camp for public use			SP	SP	
Church or other place of worship	SP		SP	SP	
Private academic, technical, or nursery school	SP	SP	SP	SP	
Hospital, nursing home, or medical clinic	SP		SP	SP	
Cultural facilities (library, art gallery, museum, etc.), institutions and philanthropic uses	SP	SP	SP	SP	
Nonprofit membership club	SP	SP	SP	SP	
Nonprofit recreational or athletic facility	SP		SP	SP	
Cemetery or crematory	SP		SP	SP	
Public utility or transportation use					
excluding garage or maintenance facilities	SP	SP	P	P	P
including garage or maintenance facilities					SP

(cont.)

DISTRICT SCHEDULE OF USE REGULATIONS (*continued*)

Structure/Land Use	Land Use Districts				
	R	RA	RR1	RR2	CLI
Golf course or country club	SP		SP	SP	
Accessory use or structure customarily incidental to and of the uses mentioned herein, and on the same lot	P	P	P	P	P
Class I home occupation, occurring within the dwelling	P	P	P	P	P
Class II home occupation, occurring within a customary accessory structure		SP	SP	SP	SP
Roadside stand	SP	P	SP	SP	
Commercial Uses					
Riding academy		SP		SP	
General office			SP	SP	P
Professional office			SP	SP	P
Retail business or service, not otherwise mentioned herein			SP	P	P
Personal service (beauty shop, barber shop, etc.)				SP	P
Restaurant	SP	SP	SP	SP	P
Tavern, bar, or nightclub			SP	SP	SP
Commercial recreation or amusement facility					P
Gasoline station				SP	SP
Recreational vehicle campgrounds				SP	
Boarding or breeding kennel		SP		SP	
Veterinarian's office or animal hospital		P		P	
Light Industrial Uses					
Research laboratories					SP
Warehousing, light manufacturing, or light processing					SP
Auto or equipment rental or sales					SP

Key: P = Permitted principal use
      SP = Special permit required

Area and Bulk Regulations

The general area and bulk requirements in each land use district are set forth in the attached "DISTRICT SCHEDULE OF AREA AND BULK REGULATIONS."

Height Exceptions

The height restrictions set forth in the "District Schedule of Area and Bulk Regulations" shall not be applicable to the following:

1. Flagpoles, radio or television antennae, transmission towers or cables, agricultural silos, and similar features, any of which shall be restricted to a maximum height of one hundred (100) feet above average finished grade at its base.
2. A spire, belfry, chimney, skylight, water or cooling tower, parapet or railing, elevator, stair bulkhead, solar collector, air conditioning unit, or similar structure which in their aggregate coverage occupy no more than ten percent (10%) of the roof area of the building of which they are a part. Such features shall be erected only to such minimum height as is necessary to accomplish the purpose for which they are intended.

No structure, or other exception, shall be used as a place for habitation or for advertising not otherwise authorized by this Ordinance.

Corner Lots

1. *Required Front Yards.* On a corner lot, each street frontage shall be deemed a front street line, and the required yard along each such lot line shall be a required front yard. The Building Inspector in consultation with the owner shall decide which of the remaining yards shall be the required side yard and the required rear yard.
2. *Obstructions at Street Intersections.* At all street intersections, no obstructions to vision, such as a fence, wall, hedge, structure, or planting over three (3) feet in height shall be erected on any lot within the triangle formed by the intersecting street lines, or their projections where corners are rounded, and a straight line joining

said street lines at points which are fifty (50) feet distant from their point of intersection measured along said street lines and/or projections.

Architectural Features and Accessory Structures Permitted in Required Yards

1. The following architectural features of a building may extend into a required yard subject to the limitations provided herein:

   a. Ordinary projections of window sills, belt courses, cornices, eaves, and other architectural features, provided, however, that such features shall not project more than three (3) feet into any required yard.

   b. Chimneys or pilasters.

   c. Open arbor or trellis.

   d. Unroofed steps, patio or terrace not less than twenty (20) feet from the highway right-of-way nor less than ten (10) feet from any side or rear lot line provided that the building complies with the yard requirements of this Ordinance.

   e. Awning or movable canopy not to exceed twelve (12) feet in height, nor projecting more than six (6) feet into any required yard.

   f. Retaining wall, fence or masonry wall.

   g. Open fire escape on the side or rear of a building and extending not more than six (6) feet into any required side or rear yard.

2. The following accessory structures may be located in any side or rear yard, subject to the limitations stated herein:

   a. Private in-ground or above-ground swimming pool not less than twenty (20) feet from the side or rear lot line, which swimming pool shall be fenced to a minimum height of four (4) feet and provided with a locking gate to prevent accidental entry or unauthorized use.

   b. Permitted accessory structure provided:

      (1) no such structure shall exceed twenty (20) feet in height in any residence district;

      (2) no such structure shall be set back less than twenty (20)

feet from any lot line nor less than ten (10) feet from the principal building;

(3) all such structures in the aggregate shall not occupy more than thirty percent (30%) of any required yard; and

(4) no such structure shall be closer to the fronting street than the principal building on the lot, or a distance of fifty (50) feet, whichever shall be less.

Residential Cluster Development

The Planning Board is authorized simultaneously with the approval of a plat or plats to modify applicable provisions of this Ordinance subject to the requirements set forth below:

1. The average residential density throughout the plat shall not exceed the maximum density permitted for the land use district in which the plat is located, with such calculation of maximum density based solely upon those portions of the site considered by the Planning Board to be suitable for building development based upon analysis of the site's topographic and hydrological characteristics.

2. Central water supply and common sewage disposal facilities shall be provided in accordance with the requirements of the Town and the County Health Departments.

3. While either attached, semi-detached, or detached dwelling units are permissible, no individual structure shall contain more than six (6) attached units. Minimum required side yards shall be provided at the ends of said structure.

4. Maximum height shall be restricted to thirty-five (35) feet, as otherwise applicable within all land use districts within the Town.

5. Common open space totalling not less than twenty-five percent (25%) of the total development site shall be provided in perpetuity.

6. A homeowner's association, or similar mechanism, for the long-term ownership and maintenance of common open space shall be provided subject to approval of the Town Planning Board. Provision, satisfactory to the Town, shall also be made for the long-term ownership and maintenance of roadways, drainageways, and other features.

DISTRICT SCHEDULE OF AREA AND BULK REGULATIONS

Land Use District		Minimum Lot Area	Maximum Residential Density (1 D.U. per)	Minimum Lot Width at Front Setback	Maximum Building Coverage	Minimum Open Space	Minimum Yard Dimensions			Maximum Height
							Front Setback	Side Setback (ea.)	Rear Setback	
R	Residential	1 acre	1 acre	150 ft	10%	60%	50 ft	25 ft	50 ft	35 ft
RA	Residential/Agricultural	2 acres	1 acre	200 ft	10%	75%	50 ft	25 ft	50 ft	35 ft
RR1	Rural Residential 1	2 acres	1 acre	200 ft	10%	75%	50 ft	25 ft	50 ft	35 ft
RR2	Rural Residential 2	2 acres	1 acre	200 ft	10%	75%	50 ft	25 ft	50 ft	35 ft
CLI	Commericial/Light Industrial	2 acres	NA	200 ft	20%	40%	100 ft	50 ft	100 ft	35 ft

APPENDIX B

Excerpts from Typical Subdivision Regulations, Design Standards, and Construction Standards

The following excerpts include most of the Subdivision Regulations of a typical town, which include procedural rules in detail, responsibility and authority, and land planning and design principles to be followed.

Also included are brief examples from Design Standards and Construction Standards of a typical town. Standards specify the details of design and construction so that the municipality is not asked to take over poorly designed or poorly built facilities and also so that the new facilities are compatible with the town's existing facilities. They are written much the same as construction specifications.

Article I Declaration of Policy

It is declared to be the policy of the Planning Board to consider land Subdivision Plats as part of a plan for the orderly, efficient, and economical development of the Town. This means, among other things, that land to be subdivided shall be of such character that it can be used safely for building purposes without danger to health, or peril from fire, flood or other menace; that proper provision shall be made for drainage, water supply, sewerage, and other needed improvements; that all proposed lots shall be so laid out and of such size as to be in harmony with the development pattern of the neighboring properties; that the proposed streets shall compose a convenient system conforming to the Official Map and the Master Plan, if such exist, and shall be of such width, grade, and location as to accommodate the prospective traffic, to facilitate fire protection, and to provide access of fire-fighting equipment to buildings; and that proper provision shall be made for open spaces for parks and playgrounds.

Article II Definitions

For the purpose of these regulations, certain words and terms used herein are defined as follows:

Subdivision means the division of any parcel of land into three or more lots, blocks, or sites, with or without streets or highways and includes re-subdivision in whole or in part of any plat which is entirely or partially undeveloped. Any division of land containing a new street shall be considered a subdivision.

Minor Subdivision means any subdivision containing not more than four lots fronting on an existing street, not involving any new street or road or the extension of municipal facilities, and not adversely affecting the development of the remainder of the parcel or adjoining property and not in conflict with any provision or portion of these regulations.

Major Subdivision means any subdivision not classified as a Minor Subdivision, including, but not limited to, subdivisions of five or more lots, or any size subdivision requiring any new street or extension of municipal facilities.

Sketch Plan means a sketch of a proposed subdivision showing a general layout of the proposed development, including its relationship to physical features, adjacent streets and highways, and developed areas.

Preliminary Plat means a drawing or drawings clearly marked "Preliminary Plat" showing the layout of a proposed subdivision, as specified in Article V, Section 3 of these regulations, submitted to the Planning Board for approval prior to submission of the Plat in final form and of sufficient detail to apprise the Planning Board of the layout of the proposed subdivision.

Subdivision Plat or Final Plat means a drawing, in final form, showing a proposed subdivision containing all information or detail required by law and by these regulations to be presented to the Planning Board for approval, and which if approved, may be duly filed or recorded by the applicant in the office of the County Clerk.

Street means and includes streets, roads, avenues, lanes, or other traffic ways, between right-of-way lines:

Major Street means a street which serves or is designed to serve heavy flows of traffic and which is used primarily as a route for traffic between communities and/or other heavy traffic-generating areas.

Minor Street means a street intended to serve primarily as an access to abutting properties.

Collector Street means a street which serves or is designed to serve as a traffic way for a neighborhood or as a feeder to a major street.

Dead-End Street or Cul-de-Sac means a street or a portion of a street with only one vehicular traffic outlet.

Street Pavement means the wearing or exposed surface of roadway used by vehicular traffic.

Street Width means the width of right-of-way, measured at right angles to the center line of the street.

Master or Comprehensive Plan means a comprehensive plan, prepared by the Planning Board, which indicates the general locations recommended for various functional classes of public works, places, and structures and for general physical development of the Town and includes any unit or part of such plan separately prepared and any amendment to such plan or parts therein.

Official Map means the map established by the Town Board, showing streets, highways, and parks and drainage, both existing and proposed.

Article III Procedure in Filing Subdivision Applications

Whenever any subdivision of land is proposed to be made, and before any contract for the sale of, or any offer to sell any lots in such subdivision or part thereof is made, and before any permit for the erection of a structure in such proposed subdivision shall be granted, the subdivider or a duly authorized agent shall apply in writing for approval of such proposed subdivision in accordance with the following procedures.

Section 1. Sketch Plan

A. Submission of Sketch Plan. Any owner of land shall, prior to subdividing or re-subdividing land, submit to the Secretary of the Planning Board at least ten days prior to the regular meeting of the Board two copies of a Sketch Plan of the proposed subdivision, which shall comply with the requirements of Article V, Section 1, for the purposes of classification and preliminary discussion.

B. Discussion of Requirements and Classification. The subdivider, or his duly authorized representative, shall attend the meeting of the Planning Board to discuss the requirements of these regulations for street improvements, drainage, sewerage, water supply, fire protection, and similar aspects, as well as the availability of existing services and other pertinent information.

Classification of the Sketch Plan is to be made at this time by the Planning Board as to whether it is a Minor or Major Subdivision as defined in these regulations. The Board may require, however, when it deems it necessary for protection of the public health, safety and welfare, that a Minor Subdivision comply with all or some of the requirements specified for Major Subdivisions. If the Sketch Plan is classified as a Minor Subdivision, the subdivider shall then comply with the procedure outlined in Article III, Section 2 of these regulations. If it is classified as a Major Subdivision, the subdivider shall then comply with the procedures outlined in Article III, Section 3, Section 4, and Section 5.

C. Study of Sketch Plan. The Planning Board shall determine whether the Sketch Plan meets the purposes of these regulations and shall, where it deems it necessary, make specific recommendations in writing to be incorporated by the applicant in the next submission to the Planning Board.

Section 2. Approval of Minor Subdivision

A. Application and Fee. Within six months after classification of the Sketch Plan as a Minor Subdivision by the Planning Board, the subdivider shall submit an application for approval of a Subdivision Plat. Failure to do so shall require re-submission of the Sketch Plan to the Planning Board for re-classification. The Plat shall conform to the layout shown on the Sketch Plan plus any recommendations made by the Planning Board. Said application shall also conform to the requirements listed in Article V, Section 2-A.

All applications for Plat approval for Minor Subdivisions shall be accompanied by a fee of $10.00 plus $2.00 per lot in the proposed subdivision.

B. Number of Copies. Five copies of the Subdivision Plat shall be presented to the Clerk of the Planning Board at the time of submission of the Subdivision Plat.

C. Subdivider to Attend Planning Board Meeting. The subdivider, or a duly authorized representative, shall attend the meeting of the Planning Board to discuss the Subdivision Plat.

D. When Officially Submitted. The time of submission of the Subdivision Plat shall be considered to be the date on which the application for Plat approval, complete and accompanied by the required fee and all data required by Article V, Section 2 of these regulations, has been filed with the Clerk of the Planning Board.

E. Public Hearing. A public hearing shall be held by the Planning Board within forty-five (45) days from the time of submission of the Subdivision Plat for approval. Said hearing shall be advertised in a newspaper of general circulation in the town at least five (5) days before such hearing.

F. Water and sewage facility proposals contained in the Subdivision Plat shall be properly endorsed and approved by the County Department of Health. Applications for approval of plans for sewage or water facilities will be filed by the Subdivider with all necessary Town, County, and State agencies. Endorsement and approval by the County Department of Health shall be secured by the subdivider before official submission of Subdivision Plat. Approval shall be secured for intersection design and construction within state rights of way from the State Department of Transportation.

G. Action on Subdivision Plat. The Planning Board shall, within forty-five (45) days from the date of the public hearing, act to conditionally approve, conditionally approve with modification, disapprove, or grant final approval and authorize the signing of the Subdivision Plat. This time may be extended by mutual consent of the Subdivider and the Planning Board. Failure of the Planning Board to act within such time shall constitute approval of the Plat.

Upon granting conditional approval with or without modification to the Plat, the Planning Board shall empower a duly authorized officer to sign the Plat upon compliance with such conditions and requirements as may be stated in its resolution of conditional approval. Within five (5) days of the resolution granting conditional approval, the Plat shall be certified by the Clerk of the Planning Board as conditionally approved, and a copy filed, and a certified copy mailed to the Subdivider. The copy mailed to the Subdivider shall include a certified statement of such requirements which, when completed, will authorize the signing of the conditionally approved Plat. Upon completion of such requirements, the Plat shall be signed by the duly designated officer of the Planning Board. Conditional approval of a Plat shall expire one hundred eighty (180) days after the date of the resolution granting such approval unless the requirements have been certified as completed within that time. The Planning Board may, however, extend the time within which a conditionally approved Plat may be submitted for signature, if in its opinion such extension is warranted in the circumstances, for not to exceed two additional periods of ninety (90) days each.

Section 3.   Preliminary Plat for Major Subdivision

A. Application and Fee. Prior to the filing of an application for the approval of a Major Subdivision Plat, the Subdivider shall file an application for the approval of a Preliminary Plat of the proposed subdivision. Such Preliminary Plat shall be clearly marked "Preliminary Plat" and shall be in the form described in Article V, Section 3, hereof.

The application for approval of the Preliminary Plat shall be accompanied by a fee of twenty ($20.00) dollars, plus two ($2.00) dollars per lot for each lot in the proposed subdivision.

B. Number of Copies. Five copies of the Preliminary Plat shall be presented to the Clerk of the Planning Board at the time of submission of the Preliminary Plat.

C. Subdivider to Attend Planning Board Meeting. The subdivider, or duly authorized representative, shall attend the meeting of the Planning Board to discuss the Preliminary Plat.

D. Study of Preliminary Plat. The Planning Board shall study the practicability of the Preliminary Plat, taking into consideration the requirements of the community and the best use of the land being subdivided. Particular attention shall be given to the arrangement, location, and width of streets, their relation to the topography of the land, water supply, sewage disposal, drainage, lot sizes and arrangement, the future development of adjoining lands as yet unsubdivided, and the requirements of the Master Plan, the Official Map, and Zoning Regulations, if such exist.

E. When Officially Submitted. The time of submission of the Preliminary Plat shall be considered to be the date on which the application for approval of the Preliminary Plat, complete and accompanied by the required fee and all data required by Article V, Section 3 of these regulations, has been filed with the Clerk of the Planning Board.

F. Approval of the Preliminary Plat. Within forty-five (45) days after the receipt of such Preliminary Plat by the Clerk of the Planning Board, the Planning Board shall hold a public hearing, which hearing shall be advertised at least once in a newspaper of general circulation in the Town at least five (5) days before such hearing. The Planning Board may provide that the hearing be further advertised in such manner as it deems most appropriate for full public consideration of such Preliminary Plat. Within forty-five (45) days after the date of such hearing, the Planning Board shall approve with or without modification or disapprove such Preliminary Plat, and the ground of a modification, if any, or the ground for disapproval shall be stated upon the records of the Planning Board. The time in which the Planning Board must take action on such Plat may be extended by mutual consent of the Subdivider and the Planning Board. When so approving a Preliminary Plat, the Planning Board shall state in writing modifications, if any, that it deems necessary for submission of the Plat in final form. Within five (5) days of the approval of such Preliminary Plat it shall be certified by the Clerk of the Planning Board as granted preliminary approval and a copy filed, a certified copy mailed to the owner, and a copy forwarded to the Town Board. Failure of the Planning Board to act within such forty-five (45) day period shall constitute approval of the Preliminary Plat.

When granting approval to a Preliminary Plat, the Planning Board shall state the terms of such approval, if any, with respect to

(1) the modifications to the Preliminary Plat,
(2) the character and extent of the required improvements for which waivers may have been requested and which in its opinion may be waived without jeopardy to the public health, safety, morals, and general welfare,
(3) the amount of improvement or the amount of all bonds therefor which it will require as prerequisite to the approval of the Subdivision Plat.

Section 4.   Plat for Major Subdivision

A. Application for Approval and Fee. The Subdivider shall, within six (6) months after the approval of the Preliminary Plat, file with the Planning Board an application for approval of the Subdivision Plat in final form, using the approved application blank available from the Clerk of the Planning Board. All applications for Plat approval for Major Subdivisions shall be accompanied by a fee of twenty-five ($25.00) dollars plus two ($2.00) dollars per lot. If the final Plat is not submitted within six (6) months after the approval of the Preliminary Plat, the Planning Board may refuse to approve the final Plat and require re-submission of the Preliminary Plat.

B. Number of Copies. A Subdivider intending to submit a proposed Subdivision Plat for the approval of the Planning Board shall provide the Clerk of the Board with a copy of the Application and three copies (one copy in ink on linen or an acceptable equal) of the Plat, the original and one true copy of all offers of cession, covenants, and agreements and two prints of all construction drawings.

C. When Officially Submitted. The time of submission of the Subdivision Plat shall be considered to be the date on which the application for approval of the Subdivision Plat, complete and accompanied by the required fee and all data required by Article V, Section 4 of these regulations, has been filed with the Clerk of the Planning Board.

In addition, if the applicant elects to construct any or all required improvements (as specified in Article III, Section 5-A 2), the Town Engineer must file a certificate with the Planning Board stating that these improvements have been satisfactorily installed before the Subdivision Plat shall be considered officially submitted.

D. Endorsement of State and County Agencies. Water and sewage facility proposals contained in the Subdivision Plat shall be properly endorsed and approved by the County Department of Health. Applications for approval of plans for sewage or water facilities will be filed by the Subdivider with all necessary Town, County, and State agencies. Endorsement and approval by the County Department of Health shall be secured by the Subdivider before official submission of Subdivision Plat.

E. Public Hearing. Within forty-five (45) days of the submission of a Plat in final form for approval, a hearing shall be held by the Planning Board. This hearing shall be advertised at least once in a newspaper of general circulation in the town at least five (5) days before such hearing, provided however, that when the Planning Board deems the final Plat to be in substantial agreement with a Preliminary Plat approved under Section 3 of this article, and modified in accordance with requirements of such approval if such Preliminary Plat has been approved with modification, the Planning Board may waive the requirement for such public hearing.

F. Action on Proposed Subdivision Plat. The Planning Board shall by resolution conditionally approve with or without modification, disapprove, or grant final approval and authorize the signing of such Plat, within forty-five (45) days of its receipt by the Clerk of the Planning Board if no hearing is held, or in the event a hearing is held, within forty-five (45) days after the date of such hearing. This time may be extended by mutual consent of the Subdivider and the Planning Board. Failure to take action on a final Plat within the time prescribed therefor shall be deemed approval of the Plat.

Upon resolution of conditional approval of such final Plat the Planning Board shall empower a duly authorized officer to sign the Plat upon completion of such requirements as may be stated in the resolution. Within five (5) days of such resolution the Plat shall be certified by the Clerk of the Planning Board as conditionally approved and a copy filed in the Clerk's Office and a certified copy mailed to the Subdivider. The copy mailed to the Subdivider shall include a certified statement of such requirements which, when completed, will authorize the signing of the conditionally approved final Plat. Upon completion of such requirements the Plat shall be signed by said duly authorized officer of the Planning Board. Conditional approval of a final Plat shall expire one hundred eighty (180) days after the date of the resolution granting such approval unless the requirements have been certified as completed within that time. The Planning Board may, however, extend the time within which a conditionally approved Plat may be submitted for signature, if in its opinion such extension is warranted in the circumstances, for not to exceed two additional periods of ninety (90) days each.

Section 5.   Required Improvements

A. Improvements and Performance Bond. Before the Planning Board grants final approval of the Subdivision Plat, the Subdivider shall follow the procedure set forth in either sub-paragraph (1) or sub-paragraph (2) below:

(1) In an amount set by the Planning Board, either the Subdivider shall file with the Town Clerk a certified check to cover the full cost of the required improvements; or the Subdivider shall file with the Town Clerk a performance bond to cover the full cost of the required improvements. Any such bond must be satisfactory to the Town Board and the Town Engineer as to form, sufficiency, manner of execution, and surety. A period of one year (or such other period as the Planning Board may determine appropriate,

not to exceed three years) shall be set forth in the bond within which required improvements must be completed.

(2) The Subdivider shall complete all required improvements to the satisfaction of the Town Engineer, who shall file with the Planning Board a letter signifying the satisfactory completion of all improvements required by the Board. For any required improvements not so completed, the Subdivider shall file with the Town Clerk a bond or certified check covering the cost of such improvements and the cost of satisfactorily installing any improvement not approved by the Town Engineer. Any such bond shall be satisfactory to the Town Board and the Town Engineer as to form, sufficiency, manner of execution, and surety.

B. Modification of Design of Improvements. If at any time before or during the construction of the required improvements it is demonstrated to the satisfaction of the Town Engineer that unforeseen conditions make it necessary or preferable to modify the location or design of such required improvements, the Town Engineer may, upon approval by a previously delegated member of the Planning Board, authorize modifications provided these modifications are within the spirit and intent of the Planning Board's approval and do not extend to the waiver or substantial alteration of the function of any improvements required by the Board. The Town Engineer shall issue any authorization under this Section in writing and shall transmit a copy of such authorization to the Planning Board at their next regular meeting.

C. Inspection of Improvements. At least five (5) days prior to commencing construction of required improvements the Subdivider shall pay to the Town Clerk the inspection fee required by the Town Board and shall notify the Town Board in writing of the time when he proposes to commence construction of such improvements so that the Town Board may cause inspection to be made to assure that all Town specifications and requirements shall be met during the construction of required improvements, and to assure the satisfactory completion of improvements and utilities required by the Planning Board.

D. Proper Installation of Improvements. If the Town Engineer shall find, upon inspection of the improvements performed before the expiration date of the performance bond, that any of the required improvements have not been constructed in accordance with plans and specifications filed by the Subdivider, he shall so report to the Town

Board, Building Inspector, and Planning Board. The Town Board then shall notify the Subdivider and, if necessary, the bonding company, and take all necessary steps to preserve the Town's rights under the bond. No Plat shall be approved by the Planning Board as long as the Subdivider is in default on a previously approved Plat.

Section 6. Filing of Approved Subdivision Plat

A. Final Approval and Filing. Upon completion of the requirements in Sections 4 and 5 above and notation to that effect upon the Subdivision Plat, it shall be deemed to have final approval and shall be properly signed by the duly designated officer of the Planning Board and may be filed by the applicant in the Office of the County Clerk after which lots may be sold. Any Subdivision Plat not so filed or recorded within thirty (30) days of the date upon which such Plat is approved or considered approved by reason of the failure of the Planning Board to act, shall become null and void.

B. Plat Void if Revised after Approval. No changes, erasures, modifications, or revisions shall be made in any Subdivision Plat after approval has been given by the Planning Board and endorsed in writing on the Plat, unless the said Plat is first resubmitted to the Planning Board and such Board approves any modifications. In the event that any such Subdivision Plat is recorded without complying with this requirement, the same shall be considered null and void, and the Board shall institute proceedings to have the Plat stricken from the records of the County Clerk.

Section 7. Public Streets, Recreation Areas

A. Public Acceptance of Streets. The approval by the Planning Board of a Subdivision Plat shall not be deemed to constitute or be evidence of any acceptance by the Town of any street, easement, or other open space shown on such Subdivision Plat.

B. Ownership and Maintenance of Recreation Areas. When a park, playground, or other recreation area shall have been shown on a Plat, the approval of said Plat shall not constitute an acceptance by the Town of such area. The Planning Board shall require the Plat to be endorsed with appropriate notes to this effect. The Planning Board may also require the filing of a written agreement between the applicant and the Town Board covering future deed and title, dedication, and provision for the cost of grading, development, equipment, and maintenance of any such recreation area.

Article IV   General Requirements and Design Standards

In considering applications for subdivision of land, the Planning Board shall be guided by the standards set forth hereinafter.

Section 1.   General

A. Character of Land. Land to be subdivided shall be of such character that it can be used safely for building purposes without danger to health or peril from fire, flood, or other menace.

B. Conformity to Official Map and Master Plan. Subdivisions shall conform to the Official Map of the Town and shall be in harmony with the Master Plan, when such exists.

C. Specifications for Required Improvements. All required improvements shall be constructed or installed to conform to the Town Design and Construction Standards.

Section 2.   Street Layout

A. Width, Location, and Construction. Streets shall be of sufficient width, suitably located, and adequately constructed to conform with the Town Master Plan, to accommodate the prospective traffic and afford access for fire fighting, snow removal, and other road maintenance equipment. The arrangement of streets shall be such as to cause no undue hardship to adjoining properties and shall be coordinated so as to compose a convenient system.

B. Arrangement. The arrangement of streets in the subdivision shall provide for the continuation of principal streets of adjoining subdivisions, and for proper projection of principal streets into adjoining properties which are not yet subdivided, in order to make possible necessary fire protection, movement of traffic and the construction or extension, presently or when later required, of needed utilities and public services such as sewers, water and drainage facilities. Where, in the opinion of the Planning Board, topographic or other conditions make such continuance undesirable or impracticable, the above conditions may be modified.

C. Minor Streets. Minor streets shall be so laid out that their use by through traffic will be discouraged.

D. Special Treatment Along Major Arterial Streets. When a subdivision abuts or contains an existing or proposed major arterial street, the Board may require marginal access streets, reverse frontage with screen planting contained in a non-access reservation along the rear property line, deep lots with rear service alleys, or such other treatment as may be necessary for adequate protection of residential properties and to afford separation of through and local traffic. In no case shall a subdivision provide for direct driveway access to any state or county road. All intersections with state or county roads shall at least meet standards for a minor street even if access serves only one lot.

E. Provision for Future Resubdivision. Where a tract is subdivided into large lots or acreage substantially larger than the minimum size required in the zoning district in which a subdivision is located, the Board may require that streets and lots be laid out so as to permit future re-subdivision in accordance with the requirements contained in these regulations.

F. Dead-End Streets. The creation of dead-end or loop residential streets will be encouraged wherever the Board finds that such type of development will not interfere with normal traffic circulation in the area. In the case of dead-end streets, where needed or desirable, the Board may require the reservation of a 20-foot-wide easement to provide for continuation of pedestrian traffic and utilities to the next street. Subdivisions containing twenty (20) lots or more shall have at least two street connections with existing public streets, or streets shown on the Official Map, when such exists, or streets on an approved Subdivision Plat for which a bond has been filed.

G. Block Size. Blocks generally shall not be less than 400 feet nor more than 1200 feet in length. In general, no block width shall be less than twice the normal lot depth. In blocks exceeding 800 feet in length, the Planning Board may require the reservation of a 20-foot-wide easement through the block to provide for the crossing of underground utilities and pedestrian traffic where needed or desirable and may further specify, at its discretion, that a 4-foot-wide paved foot path be included.

H. Intersections with Collector or Major Arterial Roads. Minor or secondary street openings into such roads shall, in general, be at least 500 feet apart.

I. Street Jogs. Street jogs with center line offsets of less than 150 feet shall be avoided.

J. Angle of Intersection. In general, all streets shall join each other so that for a distance of at least 100 feet the street is approximately at right angles to the street it joins.

Section 3.   Street Design

A. Widths of Rights of Way. Streets shall have the following widths. (When not indicated on the Master Plan or Official Map, if such exists, the classification of streets shall be determined by the Board):

	Minimum Right of Way	Minimum Pavement
Major Streets	66 feet	38 feet
Collector Streets	60 feet	30 feet
Local Streets	50 feet	20 feet

B. Improvements. Streets shall be graded and improved to Town specifications, including storm drainage facilities, street lights and signs, and street trees. Water mains, sewers, and fire hydrants shall be installed where connections are available. The Planning Board may waive, subject to appropriate conditions, such improvements as it considers may be omitted without jeopardy to the public health, safety, and general welfare. Pedestrian easements shall be improved as required by the Town Engineer. Such grading and improvements shall be approved as to design and specifications by the Town Engineer.

C. Utilities in Streets. The Planning Board shall, wherever possible, require that underground utilities be placed in the street right of way between the paved roadway and street line to simplify location and repair of lines when they require attention. The subdivider shall install underground service connections to the property line of each lot within the subdivision for such required utilities before the street is paved.

D. Utility Easements. Where topography is such as to make impractical the inclusion of utilities within the street rights of way, perpetual unobstructed easements at least 20 feet in width shall be otherwise provided with satisfactory access to the street. Wherever possible, easements shall be continuous from block to block and shall present as few irregularities as possible. Such easements shall be cleared and graded where required.

E. Grades. Grades of all streets shall conform in general to the terrain, and shall not be less than one-half (½) nor more than 6 percent for major or collector streets, or 10 percent for minor streets in residential zones, but in no case more than 3 percent within 50 feet of any intersection.

F. Changes in Grade. All changes in grade shall be connected by vertical curves of such length as meet with the approval of the Town Engineer so that clear visibility shall be provided for a safe distance.

G. Curve Radii at Street Intersections. All street right-of-way lines at intersections shall be rounded by curves of at least 20 feet radius and curbs shall be adjusted accordingly.

H. Steep Grades and Curves; Visibility at Intersections. A combination of steep grades and curves shall be avoided. In order to provide visibility for traffic safety, that portion of any corner lot lying within a triangle formed by the two street lines and the same lines extended and a line connecting a point on each street line 40 feet from the point of intersection of the two street lines (whether at an intersection entirely within the subdivision or of a new street with an existing street) shall be cleared of all growth (except isolated trees) and obstructions above the level three feet higher than the center line of the street. If directed, ground shall be excavated to achieve visibility.

I. Dead-End Streets (Cul-de-Sacs). Where dead-end streets are designed to be so permanently, they should, in general, not exceed 500 feet in length, and shall terminate in a circular turn-around having a minimum right-of-way radius of 60 feet and pavement radius of 50 feet. At the end of temporary dead-end streets a temporary turn-around with a pavement radius of 50 feet shall be provided, unless the Planning Board approves an alternative arrangement.

J. Curve Radii. In general, street lines within a block, deflecting from each other at any one point by more than 10 degrees, shall be connected with a curve, the radius of which for the center line of street shall not be less than 400 feet on major streets, 200 feet on collector streets, and 100 feet on minor streets.

Section 4. Street Names

A. Type of Name. All street names shown on a Preliminary Plat or Subdivision Plat shall be approved by the Planning Board. In general, streets shall have names and not numbers or letters.

B. Names to Be Substantially Different. Proposed street names shall be substantially different so as not to be confused in sound or spelling with present names except that streets that join or are in alinement with streets of an abutting or neighboring property shall bear the same name. Generally, no street should change direction by more than 90 degrees without a change in street name.

Section 5. Lots

A. Lots to be Buildable. The lot arrangement shall be such that in constructing a building in compliance with the Zoning Ordinance, if any, there will be no foreseeable difficulties for reasons of topography or other natural conditions. Lots should not be of such depth as to encourage the later creation of a second building lot at the front or rear.

Lot sizes shall conform with County Health Department requirements, based on the particular soil conditions of the proposed lots; however, each lot will have a minimum area of 20,000 square feet and a minimum lot frontage of 125 feet.

B. Side Lines. All side lines of lots shall be at right angles to straight street lines and radial to curved street lines, unless a variance from this rule will give a better street or lot plan.

C. Corner Lots. In general, corner lots should be larger than interior lots to provide for proper building setback from each street and provide a desirable building site.

D. Monuments and Lot Corner Markers. Permanent monuments meeting specifications approved by the Town Engineer as to size, type, and installation shall be set at such block corners, angle points, points of curves in streets and other points as the Town Engineer may require, and their location shall be shown on the Subdivision Plat.

Section 6. Drainage Improvements

A. Removal of Spring and Surface Water. The subdivider may be required by the Planning Board to carry away by pipe or open ditch any spring or surface water that may exist either previous to, or as a result of, the subdivision. Such drainage facilities shall be located in the street right of way where feasible, or in perpetual unobstructed easements of appropriate width.

B. Drainage Structure to Accommodate Potential Development Upstream. A culvert or other drainage facility shall, in each case, be large enough to accommodate potential run-off from its entire drainage area above, whether inside or outside the subdivision. The Town Engineer shall approve the design and size of facility based on anticipated run-off from a "ten-year" storm under conditions of total potential development in the watershed.

C. Responsibility for Drainage Downstream. The subdivider's engineer shall also study the effect of each subdivision on the existing drainage facilities downstream and outside the area of the subdivision; and this study shall be reviewed by the Town Engineer. Where it is anticipated that the additional run-off incident to the development of the subdivision will overload an existing downstream drainage facility during a five-year storm, the Planning Board shall notify the Town Board of such potential condition. In such case, the Planning Board shall not approve the subdivision until provision has been made for the improvement of said condition.

D. Land Subject to Flooding. Land subject to flooding or land deemed by the Planning Board to be uninhabitable shall not be platted for residential occupancy, nor for such other uses as may increase danger to health, life or property, or aggravate the flood hazard, but such land within the plat shall be set aside for such uses as shall not be endangered by periodic or occasional inundation or improved in a manner satisfactory to the Planning Board to remedy said hazardous conditions.

Section 7.   Parks, Open Spaces, and Natural Features

A. Recreation Areas Shown on Town Plan. Where a proposed park, playground or open space shown on the Town Plan is located in whole or in part in a subdivision, the Board shall require that such area or areas be shown on the Plat in accordance with the requirements specified in paragraph (B) of this section. Such area or areas may be dedicated to the Town or County by the subdivider if the Town Board approves such dedication.

B. Parks and Playgrounds Not Shown on Town Plan. The Planning Board may require that the Plat show sites of a character, extent, and location suitable for the development of a park, playground, or other recreation purpose. The Planning Board may require that the developer satisfactorily grade any such recreation areas shown on the Plat.

The Board may require that not less than three acres of recreation space be provided per 100 dwelling units shown on the Plat. However, in no case need the amount be more than 10 percent of the total area of the subdivision. Such area or areas may be dedicated to the Town or County by the subdivider if the Town Board approves such dedication.

C. Reserve Strips Prohibited. Reserve strips of land, which might be used to control access from the proposed subdivision to any neighboring property, or to any land within the subdivision itself, shall be prohibited.

Article V   Documents to Be Submitted

Section 1.   Major Subdivision Preliminary Plat and Accompanying Data

The following documents shall be submitted for Conditional Approval:

A. Five copies of the Preliminary Plat prepared at a scale of not more than one hundred (100) but preferably not less than fifty (50) feet to the inch, showing:

(1) Proposed Subdivision name, name of Town and County in which it is located, date, true north direction, scale, name and address of record owner, subdivider and engineer or surveyor, including license number and seal.

(2) The name of all subdivisions immediately adjacent and the name of the owners of record of all adjacent property.

(3) Zoning District, if any, including exact boundary lines of district, if more than one district, and any proposed changes in the zoning district lines and/or the zoning ordinance text applicable to the area to be subdivided.

(4) All parcels of land proposed to be dedicated to public use and the conditions of such dedication.

(5) Location of existing property lines, easements, buildings, water courses, marshes, rock outcrops, wooded areas, single trees with a diameter of 8 inches or more as measured 3 feet above the base of the trunk, and other significant features for the proposed subdivision and adjacent property.

(6) Location of existing sewers, water mains, culverts, and drains on the property, with pipe sizes, grades, and direction of flow.

(7) Contours with intervals of 5 feet or less as required by the Board, including elevations on existing roads. Approximate grading plan if natural contours are to be changed more than 2 feet.

(8) The width and location of any streets or public ways or places shown on the Official Map or the Master Plan, when such exist, within the area to be subdivided, and the width, location, grades and street profiles of all streets or public ways proposed by the developer.

(9) The approximate location and size of all proposed water lines, valves, hydrants and sewer lines, and fire alarm boxes. Connection to existing lines or alternate means of water supply or sewage disposal and treatment as provided in the Public Health Law. Profiles of all proposed water and sewer lines.

(10) Storm drainage plan indicating the approximate location and size of proposed lines and their profiles. Connection to existing lines or alternate means of disposal.

(11) Preliminary designs of any bridges or culverts which may be required.

(12) The proposed lot lines with approximate dimensions and area of each lot.

(13) Where the topography is such as to make difficult the inclusion of any of the required facilities within the public areas as laid out, the Preliminary Plat shall show the boundaries of proposed permanent easements over or under private property, which permanent easements shall not be less than 20 feet in width and which shall provide satisfactory access to an existing public highway or public open space shown on the subdivision plat or the official map.

(14) An actual field survey of the boundary lines of the tract, giving complete descriptive data by bearings and distances, made and certified to by a licensed land surveyor. The corners of tract shall also be located on the ground and marked by substantial monuments of such size and type as approved by the Town Engineer, and shall be referenced and shown on the Plat.

B. If the application covers only a part of the Subdivider's entire holding, a map of the entire tract, drawn at a scale of not less than 400 feet to the inch showing an outline of the platted area with its proposed streets and indication of the probable future street system with its grades and drainage in the remaining portion of the tract and the probable future drainage layout of the entire tract shall be submitted. The part of the Subdivider's entire holding submitted shall be considered in the light of the entire holdings.

C. A copy of such covenants or deed restrictions as are intended to cover all or part of the tract.

Section 2.   Major Subdivision Plat and Accompanying Data

The following documents shall be submitted for Plat approval:

A. The Plat to be filed with the County Clerk shall be printed upon linen, or be clearly drawn in India ink upon tracing cloth. The size of the sheets shall be 20 inches by 32 inches, including a margin for binding of two inches, outside of the border, along the left side and a margin of one inch outside of the border along the remaining sides. The Plat shall be drawn at a scale of no more than 100 feet to the inch and oriented with the north point at the top of the map. When more than one sheet is required, an additional index sheet of the same size shall be filed showing to scale the entire subdivision with lot and block numbers clearly legible.

The Plat shall show:

(1) Proposed subdivision name or identifying title and the name of the Town and County in which the subdivision is located, the name and address of record owner and Subdivider, name, license number and seal of the licensed land surveyor.

(2) Street lines, pedestrian ways, lots, reservations, easements, and areas to be dedicated to public use.

(3) Sufficient data acceptable to the Town Engineer to determine readily the location, bearing, and length of every street line, lot line, boundary line, and to reproduce such lines upon the ground. Where applicable, these should be referenced to monuments included in the State system of plane coordinates, and in any event should be tied to reference points previously established by a public authority.

(4) The length and bearing of all straight lines, and radii, length and central angles of all curves shall be given for each street. All dimensions and angles of the lines of each lot shall also be given. All dimensions shall be shown in feet and decimals of a foot. The Plat shall show the boundaries of the property, location, graphic scale, and true north direction.

(5) The Plat shall also show by proper designation thereon all public open spaces for which deeds are included and those spaces title to which is reserved by the developer. For any of the latter, there shall be submitted with the Subdivision Plat copies of agreements or other documents showing the manner in which such areas are to be maintained and the provisions made therefor.

(6) All offers of cession and covenants governing the maintenance of unceded open space shall bear the certificate of approval of the Town Attorney as to their legal sufficiency.

(7) Lots and blocks within a Subdivision shall be numbered and

lettered in alphabetical order in accordance with the prevailing Town practice.

(8) Permanent reference monuments shall be shown, and shall be constructed in accordance with Town specifications. When referenced to the State system of plane coordinates, they shall also conform to the requirements of the State Department of Public Works. They shall be placed as required by the Town Engineer and their location noted and referenced upon the Plat.

(9) All lot corner markers shall be permanently located satisfactorily to the Town Engineer, at least three-quarter (¾) inches (if metal) in diameter and at least 24 inches in length, and located in the ground to existing grade.

(10) Monuments of a type approved by the Town Engineer shall be set at all corners and angle points of the boundaries of the original tract to be subdivided; and at all street intersections, angle points in street lines, points of curve, and such intermediate points as shall be required by the Town Engineer.

(11) A map shall be submitted to the satisfaction of the Planning Board, indicating the location of monuments marking all underground utilities as actually installed. If the subdivider completes all required improvements according to Article III, Section 5(2), then said map shall be submitted prior to final approval of the Subdivision Plat. However, if the subdivider elects to provide a bond or certified check for all required improvements as specified in Article III, Section 5(1), such bond shall not be released until such a map is submitted in a form satisfactory to the Planning Board.

Design Standards

3. Storm Drainage

3.0. General

In designing for storm drainage, the Water Pollution Control Federation's *Manual of Practice on Design and Construction of Sanitary and Storm Sewers* (MOP-9) shall be used as a guide. The procedures of the

Manual are not binding and other good engineering practices may be accepted by the Town.

3.1. Design Criteria

All components shall be designed for runoff from the entire contributing watershed taking future development into account. In addition, the design shall be considered as part of a larger storm drainage system and shall provide drains to the limits of the subdivision.

The following criteria shall be used in designing for storm drainage:

1. Rational method shall be used for all drainage areas smaller than 100 acres. An approved method shall be used for larger areas.
2. Runoff coefficient of not less than 0.35.
3. Inlet time not greater than 20 minutes from the farthest point to the first inlet.
4. Rainfall-intensity-duration-frequency curves of the U.S. Weather Bureau shall be used.
   a. Five-year storm for local and collector streets and residential districts.
   b. 25-year storm for arterial highways, potentially highly developed commercial or industrial districts, and culverts carrying major streams.
5. Surface flow on streets shall be limited to a maximum of 350 feet and discharge shall be carried to a stream with bed and banks.
6. Gutter profiles may be required at intersections which involve steep grades.

3.2. Pipe

Required pipe sizes shall be determined by use of the Manning formula. Full pipe velocities shall not be less than 3 feet per second. Full pipe velocities greater than 10 feet per second shall be avoided whenever possible. If such velocities are unavoidable, measures shall be taken to protect pipe from scour. The minimum size of pipe to be used shall be 12 inches. All pipe shall be installed with a minimum of 3 feet of cover. Pipe shall be designed for the overburden and live loads it will be subject to. Type and class of pipe and bedding conditions shall be specified. All pipe junctions shall be in manholes or catch basins. Storm drainage shall be designed to the limits of the Subdivision and the upper end shall terminate at a catch basin or manhole.

3.3. Catch Basins and Manholes

Catch basins, manholes, frames, covers, and grates shall conform to Town standards.

Storm inlets shall be located to intercept runoff before it enters an intersection and at all low points. Catch basins on storm mains shall be provided with sumps where required by the Board.

3.4. Trash Racks

Trash racks may be required where the intake of branches or debris to the storm system may clog the line. The design of the trash rack shall be based on conditions and requirements of each particular case.

3.5. Grading

Lots shall be graded so that runoff from roofs, drives, and other impervious surfaces flows toward a street except that such runoff may flow to the rear where a watercourse abuts the rear of the lot. If it is not practicable to direct runoff to the street, a grading plan for the area may be required by the Board. Such grading plan shall show that grading is designed to prevent ponding and to direct water away from all buildings.

Lots having driveways sloping away from streets shall have driveways paved so as to provide a "high-point" at or near the R.O.W. It is intended that this high point prevent street runoff from entering the lot.

6. Pipeline Construction

6.0. General

All labor, materials, equipment, tools, and services required for the furnishing and installation of any type of pipe shall conform to the following specifications.

6.1. Pipe

All pipe shall be installed in the sizes and to the lines and grades shown on the approved subdivision drawings. The type and specifications of pipe to be furnished and installed in each location shall be as designated on the subdivision drawings. Pipe shall be new number one pipe and shall be rejected if found not to meet the minimum requirements set by the Town.

All pipelines and appurtenances of whatever type or description shall be constructed in an approved manner to the complete satisfaction of the Town.

Where lift holes are provided in concrete pipe, they shall be filled with a stiff mortar mix after the pipe is installed in the trench.

The Developer, at all times during the progress of the work, shall keep the trenches and excavations free from water. Water from trenches and excavations shall be disposed of in such a manner as will neither cause injury to the public health, nor to the surface of streets, nor cause any interference with the use of public rights of way. Water shall not be allowed to flow away through newly laid sewers.

All pipe shall be installed to the limits of the approved subdivision section and shall terminate in a manhole, catch basin, hydrant, or blowoff as appropriate. Stubs shall be installed in manholes and catch basins to provide for future extension of pipe lines.

6.2 Excavation—General

Necessary arrangements shall be made by the Developer with all persons, firms, or corporations owning or using any poles, pipes, tracks, or conduits, etc., affected by construction to maintain and protect such facilities during construction. In the event any existing gas pipes, water pipes, conduits, sewers, tile drains, or poles are blocked or interfered with by the excavation required on this project, the Developer shall maintain them in continuous operation and restore them to the same condition as they were prior to the start of construction.

Sidewalks and pavements must be in no case blocked or obstructed by excavated material except with the approval of the Town and then only when adequate provisions have been made for a satisfactory temporary passage of pedestrians and vehicles. Adequate bridging and planked crossings must be provided and maintained across all open trenches for pedestrians and vehicles when so ordered by the Town. Barriers, lights, flares, and watchmen shall be provided and maintained by the Developer at all trenches, excavations, and embankments as required by the Town.

The excavation of the trench shall not advance more than 200 feet ahead of the completed masonry or pipe work except where it is necessary to drain wet ground. The width of trenches in which pipe is to be installed shall be such as to provide adequate space for workmen to place and joint the pipe properly and shall be in accordance with the following:

MAXIMUM TRENCH WIDTH
ONE (1) FOOT ABOVE TOP OF PIPE

Pipe Size	Trench Width
8″ to 12″	30″
15″ to 18″	O.D. + 16″
21″ to 27″	O.D. + 18″
30″ to 36″	O.D. + 24″

Note: O.D. is outside diameter of pipe barrel.

The Developer shall furnish, put in place, and maintain such sheeting and bracing as may be required to support properly the sides and ends of excavations, and to prevent injury to the structure built or to persons or property.

If at any time the Town so orders, the Developer shall install such additional sheeting and bracing as may be required by the State Department of Labor, by adverse soil conditions, or by the Town; but compliance with such orders or failure on the part of the Town to exercise its right to give such order shall in no way release the Developer from liability for damage caused by weak or insufficient sheeting nor from responsibility to protect the work and adjacent property. Voids appearing outside the sheeting shall be immediately and compactly filled with suitable material and to the satisfaction of the Town.

All sheeting and bracing shall be in accordance with the Industrial Code Rule No. 23 of the State Department of Labor, Board of Standards and Appeals.

Trench bottoms shall be excavated to conform to the type of bedding specified for the project.

Where excavations are opened and, in the opinion of the Town, the materials in place are not adequate for structural stability of the completed work, the Town may order the Developer to carry the excavation to an additional depth, furnish and place concrete cradles, sand or gravel refill, and/or timber and piling foundations.

6.3. Rock Excavation

Excavation and trenches in rock shall be carried to a depth of one-fourth the diameter of the pipe but in no case less than 6 inches below the pipe bottom, and shall be made by any acceptable method, including use of explosives.

Where blasting is necessary, it shall be done by workers experienced in such work. All blasts shall be well covered, and provisions made to protect pipes, conduits, sewers, structures, persons, and property adjacent to the site of the work. Prior to blast, all persons in the vicinity shall be given ample warning. Blasting will not be permitted between the hours of 6:30 p.m. and 6:30 a.m., except with special permission, nor within twenty-five (25) feet of the completed work.

All handling and use of explosives shall be in accordance with Industrial Code Rules No. 23 and 39 of the State Department of Labor, Board of Standards and Appeals and Article 16 of the State Labor Law.

The Developer shall secure all permits required by law for blasting operations and any additional hazard insurance required.

6.4. Lines and Grades

Line and grade shall be controlled by the use of construction laser.

6.5. Bedding

The class of bedding to be used shall be as specified in the final submission drawings. There shall be excavation for bells and flanges in all classes of bedding. Beddings for pipe shall conform to one or more of the following:

a. First Class Bedding. First Class Bedding is that method of laying pipe in which the pipe is carefully bedded in compacted granular materials placed on a flat trench bottom. The granular material shall be crushed stone, pea gravel, or sand and maximum particle size shall be ¾ inch. The depth of the granular bedding below the bottom of the pipe shall be one-fourth the outside pipe diameter or 4 inches, whichever is greater, and shall extend to a point 4 inches over the top of the pipe. If mechanically tamped, material may be placed in 6-inch layers; 3-inch layers if tamped by hand. If a clean, dry, free-flowing sand is used, no compaction will be required. All materials up to 12 inches over the top of the pipe shall be placed by hand.

b. Concrete Cradle Bedding. Concrete Cradle Bedding is that method of bedding pipe in which the lower part of the pipe exterior is bedded in plain or reinforced concrete of 2,500 psi or greater, having a minimum thickness under the pipe of one-fourth the nominal inside diameter and extending up the sides of the pipe for a height equal to one-fourth of the outside diameter.

The cradle shall have a width at least equal to the outside diameter of the barrel of the pipe plus 8 inches and it shall be constructed monolithically without horizontal construction joints. The remainder of the bedding to a point four (4) inches over the top of the pipe shall conform to "First Class Bedding."

c. Concrete Encasement. Concrete Encasement is that method of bedding pipe in which the entire pipe is jacketed by plain or reinforced concrete having a compressive strength of 2,500 psi or greater. The encasement width and height shall be at least equal to the outside diameter of the barrel of the pipe plus 8 inches, or as shown on the approved subdivision drawings. Normally, stronger pipe should be used, with concrete cradle or encasement being permitted only in unusual cases.

6.6.   Pipe Laying

Pipe shall be protected during handling against impact shocks and free fall. Pipe shall be kept clean at all times.

The laying of pipe in prepared trenches shall be commenced at the lowest point with the spigot ends pointing in the direction of flow.

All pipe shall be laid with ends abutting and true to line and grade. They shall be carefully centered, so that when laid they will form a uniform invert.

Preparatory to making pipe joints, all surfaces of the portions of the pipe to be jointed or of the factory-made jointing material shall be clean and dry. Lubricants, primers, adhesives, etc., shall be used as recommended by the pipe or joint manufacturer. The jointing materials or factory-fabricated joints shall then be placed, fitted, joined, and adjusted in such a workmanlike manner as to obtain the degree of watertightness required.

Trenches shall be kept water-free and as dry as possible during bedding, laying and jointing, and for as long a period as required. As soon as possible after the joint is made, sufficient backfill material shall be placed along each side of the pipe to offset conditions that might tend to move the pipe off line and grade.

All ends of pipe runs shall be capped with standard stoppers or with a fitting provided with an approved joint. If stoppers are used they must be wedged in place with boulders or masonry blocks. Large items may be bricked off at the ends or otherwise sealed in a manner approved by the Engineer.

6.7. Backfilling

All backfilling to a point four (4) inches over the top of the newly laid pipe shall be as specified under "Bedding." To a point 18 inches over the top of the pipe there shall be no stones larger than two (2) inches.

No frozen material shall be used for backfill.

When backfilling in open-cut across or within the right of way limits of any street, road, highway or railroad, the remainder of the backfill shall be select granular material. Compaction for the entire depth shall be as directed under paragraph 6.5 "Bedding" or with water if satisfactory drainage is provided for free water.

When backfilling in unpaved areas outside the right of way, the excavated material may be used to complete the backfilling, provided all deleterious contents, if any, are removed as directed by the Town. The backfill shall be rounded off over the trench not higher than eight (8) inches. Material shall be compacted in layers not more than two (2) feet thick by hand or by machine.

No pipe shall be covered before permission is given by the Town.

Under no circumstances shall water be permitted to rise in trenches before they are backfilled.

Backfilling shall be completed to a point two (2) feet above the top of all pipe laid each day. Operations shall be scheduled so that the trench is completely backfilled to within two hundred (200) feet of the end of the completed, installed sewer at the end of each day.

Whenever timber sheeting is driven to a depth below the elevation of the top of the pipe, that portion of the sheeting below the elevation of the top of the pipe shall not be disturbed or removed. Whenever timber sheeting is driven for the protection of trench walls in water-bearing soil, no portion of such sheeting below a level four (4) feet over the top of the pipe shall be removed.

6.8. Tunnels

Methods of excavation support and backfill in tunnels made beneath existing structures, railroads, pavements, and sidewalks for the installation of pipe or conduits shall be subject to approval of the Town before work is begun.

6.9. Jacking and Boring

Methods of jacking or boring to install pipe shall be approved by the Town before such work is started.

6.10. Manholes and Catch Basins

Materials shall be approved by the Town. Concrete block masonry shall be constructed in horizontal courses with vertical joints staggered.

Brick masonry shall be constructed in horizontal courses, with a header course every seventh course.

Concrete block and brick sidewalls shall be laid in a full bed of mortar. Joints on interior walls shall be struck smooth. All joints in block and brick shall be completely filled.

Concrete block and brick manholes shall be plastered with a mortar coat one-half (½) inch thick on the outside.

Precast concrete rings shall be laid with full mortar joints.

Mortar shall consist of one part portland cement and two parts clean torpedo sand with 10 percent hydrated lime added.

Pipe placed through manhole or catch basin sidewalls, and stubs for future extensions, shall be installed in rubber gaskets.

Frame castings shall be set in full mortar beds on top of masonry.

The top four (4) to twelve (12) inches of the manhole directly under the casting shall be constructed of brick to provide for adjustment to grade and future construction. Field cutting of precast manhole sections shall not be allowed for grade adjustment.

6.11. Connections

Connections of new lines to existing lines when encountered in construction and not shown on the subdivision drawings shall be made where ordered by the Town. Such connections shall be made within a manhole or catch basin in the case of sewers or storm drains except for house sewer and drain connections.

Junctions for future sewer connections indicated on the final sub-division drawings shall be sealed as specified in paragraph 6.6 Pipe Laying.

APPENDIX C

Recommended Standards for Sewage Works

Chapter 20 of *Recommended Standards for Sewage Works,* Great Lakes–Upper Mississippi River, Board of State Sanitary Engineers.

21. APPROVAL OF SEWERS

In general, the appropriate reviewing agency will approve plans for new systems, extensions to new areas or replacement sanitary sewers only when designed upon the separate plan, in which rain water from roofs, streets, and other areas, and groundwater from foundation drains are excluded.

22. DESIGN CAPACITY

In general, sewer capacities should be designed for the estimated ultimate tributary population, except in considering parts of the systems that can be readily increased in capacity. Similarly, consideration should be given to the maximum anticipated capacity of institutions, industrial parks, etc. Where future relief sewers are programmed, economic analysis of alternatives should accompany initial permit applications.

In determining the required capacities of sanitary sewers the following factors should be considered:

a. Maximum hourly domestic sewage flow;

b. Additional maximum sewage or waste flow from industrial plants;

c. Inflow and groundwater infiltration;

d. Topography of area;

e. Location of sewage treatment plant;

f. Depth of excavation; and

g. Pumping requirements.

The basis of design for all sewer projects shall accompany the plan documents. More detailed computations may be required by the appropriate reviewing agency for critical projects.

23. DESIGN FLOW

23.1 Per Capita Flow

New sewer systems shall be designed on the basis of an average daily per capita flow of sewage of not less than 100 gallons per day ($.38\ m^3/day$). This figure is assumed to cover normal infiltration; but an additional allowance should be made where conditions are unfavorable.

For existing sewer systems an additional per capita allowance shall be made where the average annual flow exceeds this value and immediate remedial measures are not proposed.

23.2 Peak Design Flow

Sanitary sewers shall be designed on a peak design flow basis using one of the following methods:

a. The ratio of peak to average daily flow as determined from Figure 1; or

b. Values established from an infiltration/inflow study acceptable to the approving agency.

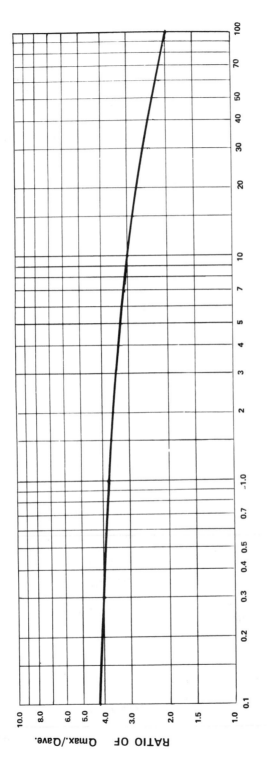

FIGURE 1.
RATIO OF EXTREME FLOW TO DAILY AVERAGE FLOW

POPULATION IN THOUSANDS

Qmax: Maximum Rate of Sewage Flow (Peak Hourly Flow)

Qave: Average Daily Sewage Flow

Source: $Qmax./Qave. = \dfrac{18 + \sqrt{P}}{4 + \sqrt{P}}$ – – –   (P = population in thousands)

Fair, G.M. and Geyer, J.C. "Water Supply and Waste-Water Disposal"
1st Ed., John Wiley & Sons, Inc., New York (1954), p. 136

Use of other values for peak design flow will be considered if justified on the basis of extensive documentation.

23.3 Combined Sewer Interceptors

In addition to the above requirements, interceptor sewers that will receive combined sewage, shall have sufficient additional capacity to insure attainment of the appropriate state and federal water quality standards.

24. DETAILS OF DESIGN AND CONSTRUCTION

24.1 Minimum Size

No gravity sewer conveying raw sewage shall be less than 8 inches (*20 cm*) in diameter.

24.2 Depth

In general, sewers should be sufficiently deep to receive sewage from basements and to prevent freezing. Insulation shall be provided for sewers that cannot be placed at a depth sufficient to prevent freezing.

24.3 Slope

24.31 All sewers shall be designed and constructed to give mean velocities, when flowing full, of not less than 2.0 feet per second (*0.61 m/s*), based on Kutter's formula using an "n" value of 0.013. The following are the minimum slopes which should be provided; however, slopes greater than these are desirable:

Sewer Size	Minimum Slope in Feet Per 100 Feet (m/100 m)
8 inch (*20 cm*)	0.40
9 inch (*23 cm*)	0.33
10 inch (*25 cm*)	0.28
12 inch (*30 cm*)	0.22
14 inch (*36 cm*)	0.17
15 inch (*38 cm*)	0.15
16 inch (*41 cm*)	0.14
18 inch (*46 cm*)	0.12
21 inch (*53 cm*)	0.10
24 inch (*61 cm*)	0.08
27 inch (*69 cm*)	0.067
30 inch (*76 cm*)	0.058
36 inch (*91 cm*)	0.046

24.32 Slopes slightly less than those required for the 2.0 feet per second (*0.61 m/s*) velocity, when flowing full, may be permitted. Such decreased slopes will only be considered where the depth of flow will be 0.3 of the diameter or greater for design average flow. Whenever such decreased slopes are selected, the design engineer must furnish with his report his computations of the anticipated flow velocities of average and daily or weekly peak flow rates. The pipe diameter and slope shall be selected to obtain the greatest practical velocities to minimize settling problems. The operating authority of the sewer system will give written assurance to the appropriate reviewing agency that any additional sewer maintenance required by reduced slopes will be provided.

24.33 Sewers shall be laid with uniform slope between manholes.

24.34 Where velocities greater than 15 feet per second (*4.6 m/s*) are attained, special provision shall be made to protect against displacement by erosion and shock.

24.35 Sewers on 20 percent slopes or greater shall be anchored securely with concrete anchors or equal, spaced as follows:

a. Not over 36 feet (*11 m*) center to center on grades 20 percent and up to 35 percent;

b. Not over 24 feet (*7.3 m*) center to center on grades 35 percent and up to 50 percent; and

c. Not over 16 feet (*4.9 m*) center to center on grades 50 percent and over.

24.4 Alignment

Sewers 24 inches (*61 cm*) or less shall be laid with straight alignment between manholes. The alignment shall be checked by either using a laser beam or lamping.

24.5 Changes in Pipe Size

When a smaller sewer joins a large one, the invert of the larger sewer should be lowered sufficiently to maintain the same energy gradient. An approximate method for securing these results is to place the 0.8 depth point of both sewers at the same elevation.

Sewer extensions should be designed for projected flows even when the diameter of the receiving sewer is less than the diameter of the proposed extension. The appropriate reviewing agency may require a schedule for future downstream sewer relief.

24.6 Materials

Any generally accepted material for sewers will be given consideration, but the material selected should be adapted to local conditions, such as: character of industrial wastes, possibility of septicity, soil characteristics, exceptionally heavy external loadings, abrasion and similar problems.

All sewers shall be designed to prevent damage from superimposed loads. Proper allowance for loads on the sewer shall be made because of the width and depth of trench. Where necessary to withstand extraordinary superimposed loading, special bedding, concrete cradle or special construction may be used.

24.7 Installation

24.71 Standards

Installation specifications shall contain appropriate requirements based on the criteria, standards and requirements established by industry in its technical publications. Requirements shall be set forth in the specifications for the pipe and methods of bedding and backfilling thereof so as not to damage the pipe or its joints, impede cleaning operations and future tapping, nor create excessive side fill pressures or ovalation of the pipe, nor seriously impair flow capacity.

24.72 Trenching

a. The width of the trench shall be ample to allow the pipe to be laid and jointed properly and to allow the backfill to be placed and compacted as needed. The trench sides shall be kept as nearly vertical as possible. When wider trenches are dug, appropriate bedding class and pipe strength shall be used.

b. Ledge rock, boulders, and large stones shall be removed to provide a minimum clearance of 4 inches (*10 cm*) below and on each side of all pipe(s).

24.73 Bedding

a. Bedding classes A, B, or C, as described in ASTM C12-74 (ANSI A106.2) or WPCF MOP No. 9 (ASCE MOP No. 37) shall be used for all rigid pipe provided the proper strength pipe is used with the specified bedding to support the anticipated load.

b. Bedding classes I, II, or III, as described in ASTM D2321-74 (ANSI K65.171) shall be used for all flexible pipe provided the proper strength pipe is used with the specified bedding to support the anticipated load.

24.74 Backfill

a. Backfill shall be of a suitable material removed from excavation except where other material is specified. Debris, frozen material, large clods or stones, organic matter, or other unstable materials shall not be used for backfill within 2 feet (*0.61 m*) of the top of the pipe.

b. Backfill shall be placed in such a manner as not to disturb the alignment of the pipe.

24.75 Deflection Test

a. Deflection tests shall be performed on all flexible pipe. The test shall be conducted after the final backfill has been in place at least 30 days.

b. No pipe shall exceed a deflection of 5%.

c. If the deflection test is to be run using a rigid ball or mandrel, it shall have a diameter equal to 95% of the inside diameter of the pipe. The test shall be performed without mechanical pulling devices.

24.8 Joints and Infiltration

24.81 Joints

The installation of joints and the materials used shall be included in the specifications. Sewer joints shall be designed to minimize infiltration and to prevent the entrance of roots throughout the life of the system.

24.82 Leakage Tests

Leakage tests shall be specified. This may include appropriate water or low pressure air testing. The leakage outward or inward (exfiltration or infiltration) shall not exceed 200 gallons per inch of pipe diameter per mile per day ($0.19\ m^3/cm\ of\ pipe\ dia./km/day$) for any section of the system. An exfiltration or infiltration test shall be performed with a minimum positive head of 2 feet ($0.61\ m$). The air test, if used, shall, as a minimum, conform to the test procedure described in ASTM C-828-76T, entitled "Tentative Recommended Practice for Low-Pressure Air Test of Vitrified Clay Pipe Lines." The testing methods selected should take into consideration the range in groundwater elevations projected and the situation during the test.

24.83 Inspection

The specifications shall include a requirement for inspection of manholes for water-tightness prior to placing into service.

25. MANHOLES

25.1 Location

Manholes shall be installed: at the end of each line; at all changes in grade, size, or alignment; at all intersections; and at distances not greater than 400 feet ($120\ m$) for sewers 15 inches ($38\ cm$) or less, and 500 feet ($150\ m$) for sewers 18 inches ($46\ cm$) to 30 inches ($76\ cm$), except that distances up to 600 feet ($180\ m$) may be approved in cases where adequate modern cleaning equipment for such spacing is provided. Greater spacing may be permitted in larger sewers. Cleanouts may be used only for special conditions and shall not be substituted for manholes nor installed at the end of laterals greater than 150 feet ($46\ m$) in length.

25.2 Drop Type

A drop pipe should be provided for a sewer entering a manhole at an elevation of 24 inches ($61\ cm$) or more above the manhole invert. Where the difference in elevation between the incoming sewer and the manhole invert is less than 24 inches ($61\ cm$), the invert should be filleted to prevent solids deposition.

Drop manholes should be constructed with an outside drop connection. Inside drop connections (when necessary) shall be secured to the interior wall of the manhole and provide access for cleaning.

Due to the unequal earth pressures that would result from the backfilling operation in the vicinity of the manhole, the entire outside drop connection shall be encased in concrete.

25.3 Diameter

The minimum diameter of manholes shall be 48 inches ($1.22\ m$); larger diameters are preferable for large diameter sewers. A minimum access diameter of 22 inches ($56\ cm$) shall be provided.

25.4 Flow Channel

The flow channel through manholes should be made to conform in shape and slope to that of the sewers.

258

25.5 Watertightness

Manholes shall be of the pre-cast concrete or poured-in-place concrete type. Manholes shall be waterproofed on the exterior.

Inlet and outlet pipes shall be joined to the manhole with a gasketed flexible watertight connection or any watertight connection arrangement that allows differential settlement of the pipe and manhole wall to take place.

Watertight manhole covers are to be used wherever the manhole tops may be flooded by street runoff or high water. Locked manhole covers may be desirable in isolated easement locations or where vandalism may be a problem.

25.6 Electrical

Electrical equipment installed or used in manholes shall conform to paragraph 32.35.

26. INVERTED SIPHONS

Inverted siphons should have not less than 2 barrels, with a minimum pipe size of 6 inches (*15 cm*) and shall be provided with necessary appurtenances for convenient flushing and maintenance. The manholes shall have adequate clearances for rodding; and in general, sufficient head shall be provided and pipe sizes selected to secure velocities of at least 3.0 feet per second (*0.92 m/s*) for average flows. The inlet and outlet details shall be so arranged that the normal flow is diverted to 1 barrel, and that either barrel may be cut out of service for cleaning. The vertical alignment should permit cleaning and maintenance.

27. SEWERS IN RELATION TO STREAMS

27.1 Location of Sewers on Streams

27.11 Cover Depth

The top of all sewers entering or crossing streams shall be at a sufficient depth below the natural bottom of the stream bed to protect the sewer line. In general the following cover requirements must be met:

a.   One foot (*0.3 m*) of cover is required where the sewer is located in rock;

b.   Three feet (*0.9 m*) of cover is required in other material. In major streams, more than three feet (*0.9 m*) of cover may be required; and

c.   In paved stream channels, the top of the sewer line should be placed below the bottom of the channel pavement.

Less cover will be approved only if the proposed sewer crossing will not interfere with the future improvements to the stream channel. Reasons for requesting less cover should be given in the project proposal.

27.12 Horizontal Location

Sewers located along streams shall be located outside of the stream bed and sufficiently removed therefrom to provide for future possible stream widening and to prevent pollution by siltation during construction.

27.13 Structures

The sewer outfalls, headwalls, manholes, gate boxes, or other structures shall be located so they do not interfere with the free discharge of flood flows of the stream.

27.14 Alignment

Sewers crossing streams should be designed to cross the stream as nearly perpendicular to the stream flow as possible and shall be free from change in grade. Sewer systems shall be designed to minimize the number of stream crossings.

27.2 Construction

27.21 Materials

Sewers entering or crossing streams shall be constructed of cast or ductile iron pipe with mechanical joints; otherwise they shall be constructed so they will remain watertight and free from changes in alignment or grade. Material used to backfill the trench shall be stone, coarse aggregate, washed gravel, or other materials which will not cause siltation.

27.22 Siltation and Erosion

Construction methods that will minimize siltation and erosion shall be employed. The design engineer shall include in the project specifications the method(s) to be employed in the construction of sewers in or near streams to provide adequate control of siltation and erosion. Specifications shall require that cleanup, grading, seeding, and planting or restoration of all work areas shall begin immediately. Exposed areas shall not remain unprotected for more than seven days.

28. AERIAL CROSSINGS

Support shall be provided for all joints in pipes utilized for aerial crossings. The supports shall be designed to prevent frost heave, overturning and settlement.

Precautions against freezing, such as insulation and increased slope, shall be provided. Expansion jointing shall be provided between above-ground and below-ground sewers.

For aerial stream crossings the impact of flood waters and debris shall be considered. The bottom of the pipe should be placed no lower than the elevation of the fifty (50) year flood.

29. PROTECTION OF WATER SUPPLIES (refer also to Recommended Standards for Water Works)

29.1 Water Supply Interconnections

There shall be no physical connections between a public or private potable water supply system and a sewer, or appurtenance thereto which would permit the passage of any sewage or polluted water into the potable supply. No water pipe shall pass through or come in contact with any part of a sewer manhole.

29.2 Relation to Water Works Structures

While no general statement can be made to cover all conditions, it is generally recognized that sewers shall meet the requirements of the appropriate reviewing agency with respect to minimum distances from public water supply wells or other water supply sources and structures.

29.3 Relation to Water Mains

29.31 Horizontal Separation

Sewers shall be laid at least 10 feet (*3.0 m*) horizontally from any existing or proposed water main. The distance shall be measured edge to edge. In cases where it is not practical to maintain a ten foot separation, the appropriate reviewing agency may allow deviation on a case-by-case basis, if supported by data from the design engineer. Such deviation may allow installation of the sewer closer to a water main, provided that the water main is in a separate trench or on an undisturbed earth shelf located on one side of the sewer and at an elevation so the bottom of the water main is at least 18 inches (*46 cm*) above the top of the sewer.

29.32 Crossings

Sewers crossing water mains shall be laid to provide a minimum vertical distance of 18 inches (*46 cm*) between the outside of the water main and the outside of the sewer. This shall be the case where the water main is either above or below the sewer. The crossing shall be arranged so that the sewer joints will be equidistant and as far as possible from the water main joints. Where a water main crosses under a sewer, adequate structural support shall be provided for the sewer to prevent damage to the water main.

29.33 Special Conditions

When it is impossible to obtain proper horizontal and vertical separation as stipulated above, the sewer shall be designed and constructed equal to water pipe, and shall be pressure tested to assure watertightness prior to backfilling.

APPENDIX D

Typical Subsurface Sewage Disposal Calculations

Typical Absorption Field Design

An absorption field in soil with a percolation rate of 23 minutes is needed for a three-bedroom house. The sewage flow rate is 450 gal/day and the maximum allowable application rate is 0.6 gal/day sq ft.

Total trench bottom area needed is 450/0.6 = 750 sq ft.

Total trench length needed is 750 sq ft/2 ft width = 375 ft.

If lines are to be no longer than 60 ft the number of lines needed is 375/60 = 6+. Use 7.

Use 7 lines @ 54 ft = 378 ft total length.

Typical Seepage Pit Design

Test pits show that throughout the area the soil is uniform, the water table at its highest is approximately 13 feet below the ground surface and bedrock is generally 14.5 feet below the ground surface. Assume the bottom of the footing is required to be 2 feet above the water table and 4 feet above bedrock or other impervious material. Percolation test results range from 25 to 35 minutes. A time of 35 minutes will be used for preliminary design.

Although the top of the footing is the lower limit of the design area, some sewage seeps into the soil at the bottom and through the footing. Therefore, the bottom must be built clear of the water table and impervious material (see Figure 10.7 for details).

Ground water clearance requires the bottom of the footing to be 13 − 2 = 11 feet below the surface and clearance above impermeable material requires the bottom to be 14.5 − 4 = 10.5 feet below the surface. The 10.5-foot depth controls. This is approximate and must be checked at the time of construction. Deducting the height of a 6-inch footing leaves a 10-foot design depth.

The level of the bottom of the inlet pipe to the pit, based on a slope of 1/8 inch per foot from the septic tank outlet, is 0.8 feet below ground level. (This is an assumption for this problem.) If more than one pit is needed, the pipe will be somewhat longer and deeper because of branching off from a distribution box. Therefore, the inlet pipe may be set a little lower than calculated. Say the bottom of pipe (not invert) is 1.0 feet below ground. Usable height is 10.0 − 1.0 = 9 feet.

If a four-bedroom house is to be built the load on the disposal system is 600 gal/day from Figure 10.2. The allowable application rate from Figure 10.2 is 0.50 gal/day/sq ft for a percolation rate of 35 minutes.

600 gal/day ÷ 0.50 gal/day/sq ft = 1200 sq ft required
Try 6 ft diameter pit

area = $9 \times \pi \times 6^2/4$ = 254 sq ft
1200/254 = 4+ (5 pits needed)

$\pi \times 6^2/4$ = 28.3 sq ft per ft of depth
total depth needed = 1200/28.3 = 42.4 ft
42.4/5 = 8.5
say 5 pits at 8.5 ft usable depth

If 3 pits are desired try 8 ft diameter
area = $9 \times \pi \times 8^2/4$ = 452 sq ft
1200/452 = 2+ (3 pits needed)
$\pi \times 8^2/4$ = 50.3 sq ft per ft of depth
total depth needed = 1200/50.3 = 23.8 ft
23.8/3 = 7.9

Use 3 pits at 8 ft usable depth.

Suppose that, when excavating from the first seepage pit a change in soil is observed at a depth of 5 ft below the surface and a percolation test indicates the lower soil has a rate of 10 minutes. Therefore the upper 3.5 ft of usable depth has a percolation rate of 35 min and the lower 5.5 ft of usable depth has a percolation rate of 10 min.

$$\frac{\begin{array}{r}3.5 \times 35 = 122.5 \\ 5.5 \times 10 = 55\end{array}}{9.0} = \frac{}{177.5}$$

177.5/9.0 = 19.7 weighted average percolation rate

Allowable application rate is 0.70 gal/day/sq ft
600 gal/day ÷ 0.70 gal/day/sq ft = 857 sq ft required
Try 8 ft diameter pit
857/452 = 1+ (2 pits needed)
total depth needed = 857/50.3 = 17.0
17.0/2 = 8.5
Use 2 pits at 9.0 ft usable depth.

If they are made with 8.5 feet of usable depth the weighted average percolation rate is less than calculated for 9 feet because the lower half foot of soil with good percolation is not included. The pits would, therefore, be underdesigned.

Typical Subsurface Sand Filter Design

A subsurface sand filter is needed for a five-bedroom house. The sewage flow rate is 750 gal/day and the maximum allowable application rate is 1.15 gal/day/sq ft. The application rate is based on the characteristics of the sand and not on a percolation test.

Total filter area needed is 750/1.15 = 653 sq ft

The filter consists of a six ft strip for each distributor (see Fig. 10–8).

The total length of six ft strip needed is 653/6 = 109 ft

Use 2 strips 55 ft long

Use 2 distributors @ 55−6 = 49 ft and one collector @ 49 ft

The filter is 2 × 6 = 12 ft wide and 55 ft long

If dosing is required, the dosing tank capacity for a dose equal to 75 percent of the distributor volume is 0.75 × 98 ft × π × $0.33^2/4$ = 6.3 cu ft

The chlorine contact tank must be large enough to hold the maximum rate of effluent flow for the length of time required by regulations (say 20 minutes). Effluent rate of flow at the chlorine contact tank is somewhat slower than the rate at which it leaves the dosing tank because the quantity of one dose takes a longer time to pass through the filter. The rate of discharge through the siphon is published by the manufacturer. If the contact tank is designed for a rate of flow of 6 gal/min, the required size is 6 × 20 min = 120 gal.

Index